Street by Stre

BOURNEMOUTH
CHRISTCHURCH, POOLE,
WIMBORNE MINSTER

Bransgore, Brockenhurst, Corfe Mullen, Ferndown, Lymington, Lyndhurst, Milford on Sea, New Milton, Ringwood, Verwood, West Moors

3rd edition July 2007
© Automobile Association Developments Limited 2007

Original edition printed May 2001

 This product includes map data licensed from Ordnance Survey® with the permission of the Controller of Her Majesty's Stationery Office. © Crown copyright 2007. All rights reserved. Licence number 100021153.

The copyright in all PAF is owned by Royal Mail Group plc.

Published by AA Publishing (a trading name of Automobile Association Developments Limited, whose registered office is Fanum House, Basing View, Basingstoke, Hampshire RG21 4EA. Registered number 1878835).

Produced by the Mapping Services Department of The Automobile Association. (A02669)

A CIP Catalogue record for this book is available from the British Library.

Printed by Oriental Press in Dubai

Ref: ML002y

Key to map pages	ii-iii
Key to map symbols	iv-1
Enlarged map pages	2-3
Main map pages	4-87
Index – towns & villages	88
Index – streets	89-105
Index – featured places	106-108
Acknowledgements	108

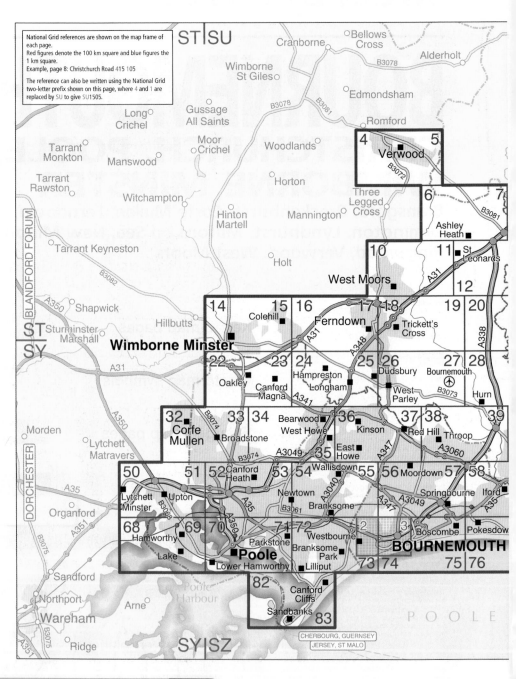

ii

National Grid references are shown on the map frame of each page.
Red figures denote the 100 km square and blue figures the 1 km square.
Example, page 8: Christchurch Road 415 105

The reference can also be written using the National Grid two-letter prefix shown on this page, where 4 and 1 are replaced by SU to give SU1505.

ST SU

Cranborne
Bellows Cross
Alderholt
B3078

Wimborne St Giles

Edmondsham

Long Crichel
Gussage All Saints
B3078
B3061
Romford

Tarrant Monkton
Moor Crichel
Woodlands
4 Verwood 5
B3072

Manswood
Horton
Three Legged Cross
6 7
B3081

Tarrant Rawston
Witchampton
Hinton Martell
Mannington
Ashley Heath

Tarrant Keyneston
B3082
Holt
10
11 St Leonards
A31
12

BLANDFORD FORUM
A350
Shapwick
Hillbutts
West Moors
14
15 Colehill
16
17 18 Ferndown
19 20
A31
A348
Trickett's Cross
A338

ST SY
Sturminster Marshall
Wimborne Minster
22
23
24 Hampreston
25
26 Dudsbury
27 28
Bournemouth
Hurn

A31
Oakley
Canford Magna
Longham
West Parley
B3073

A341
32
33
34 Bearwood
36 Kinson
37 38
39
Corfe Mullen
Broadstone
West Howe
Red Hill Throop
A3060

B3074
B3074
A3049
35 East Howe
A347
Morden
Lytchett Matravers
50
51
52 Canford Heath
53
54 Wallisdown
55
56 Moordown
57 58

DORCHESTER
A35
Newtown
A3040
Springbourne Iford
A35
Lytchett Minster
Upton
A35
Branksome
A347
A3049

Organford
A351
68 Hamworthy
69
70
71 72
2
3 Boscombe
Pokesdow
Lake
B3061
Parkstone
Westbourne
Branksome Park
BOURNEMOUTH

B3075
Poole
Lower Hamworthy
Lilliput
73 74
75 76
Sandford
Poole Harbour
82 Canford Cliffs
Northport
Arne
Sandbanks
83
POOLE
Wareham
SY SZ
CHERBOURG, GUERNSEY
JERSEY, ST MALO
Ridge
B3075

Scale of enlarged map pages 1:10,000 6.3 inches to 1 mile

0 .... 1/4 .... miles 1/2
0 ...... 1/4 ...... 1/2 .. kilometres .. 3/4 1

SALISBURY Blissford Fritham Brook M27 Cadnam A336
Stuckton Netley Totton
North Gorley A337 Bartley Marsh SOUTHAMPTON
Woodlands
A338 South Minstead Ashurst
Gorley A35
Ibsley

84 85
Emery
Down
Lyndhurst
Bank

NEW FOREST B3056

8 9
Poulner A35
Ringwood NATIONAL PARK A337

Burley
Street 86 87
Burley Brockenhurst B3055
13
21 SU
Bisterne Sandford
Thorney SZ
Hill
29 30 31 B3055
Avon Ripley Sway Boldre B3054
Bransgore B3058 Pilley Norleywood
40 41 Neacroft 43 44 45 46 47 48 49
Sopley East
Burton New Milton Hordle Lymington End
B3073 42 Ashley
59 60 A35 61 62 Highcliffe 63 64 A337 65 Everton 67
Somerford Downton
Tuckton Christchurch Barton-on-Sea B3058 66
Wick Mudeford 78 79 Milford Keyhaven
Southbourne on Sea
77 Hengistbury Head 80 81 Sconce
Point Yarmouth
Colwell
Bay
BAY Totland
Totland Freshwater
Bay
ISLE OF WIGHT

A31 A338 A337 A35 A336

4.2 inches to 1 mile **Scale of main map pages** 1:15,000

0   1/4   miles   1/2   3/4   1
0   1/4   1/2   kilometres 3/4   1   1 1/4   1 1/2

iv

Junction 9	Motorway & junction	*LC*	Level crossing
Services	Motorway service area	●—●—●—●	Tramway
	Primary road single/dual carriageway	-----------	Ferry route
Services	Primary road service area	....	Airport runway
	A road single/dual carriageway	— · — · —	County, administrative boundary
	B road single/dual carriageway	▼▼▼▼▼▼▼▼▼	Mounds
	Other road single/dual carriageway	**17**	Page continuation 1:15,000
	Minor/private road, access may be restricted	**3**	Page continuation to enlarged scale 1:10,000
← ←	One-way street		River/canal, lake, pier
	Pedestrian area		Aqueduct, lock, weir
============	Track or footpath	465 ▲ Winter Hill	Peak (with height in metres)
	Road under construction		Beach
⊏ — — — ⊐	Road tunnel		Woodland
P	Parking		Park
P+🚌	Park & Ride		Cemetery
🚌	Bus/coach station		Built-up area
	Railway & main railway station		Industrial/business building
	Railway & minor railway station		Leisure building
⊖	Underground station		Retail building
⊖	Light railway & station		Other building
++++++++++	Preserved private railway		

City wall			Castle	
Hospital with 24-hour A&E department			Historic house or building	
Post Office			National Trust property	
Public library			Museum or art gallery	
Tourist Information Centre			Roman antiquity	
Seasonal Tourist Information Centre			Ancient site, battlefield or monument	
Petrol station, 24 hour Major suppliers only			Industrial interest	
Church/chapel			Garden	
Public toilets			Garden Centre Garden Centre Association Member	
Toilet with disabled facilities			Garden Centre Wyevale Garden Centre	
Public house AA recommended			Arboretum	
Restaurant AA inspected			Farm or animal centre	
Hotel AA inspected			Zoological or wildlife collection	
Theatre or performing arts centre			Bird collection	
Cinema			Nature reserve	
Golf course			Aquarium	
Camping AA inspected			Visitor or heritage centre	
Caravan site AA inspected			Country park	
Camping & caravan site AA inspected			Cave	
Theme park			Windmill	
Abbey, cathedral or priory			Distillery, brewery or vineyard	

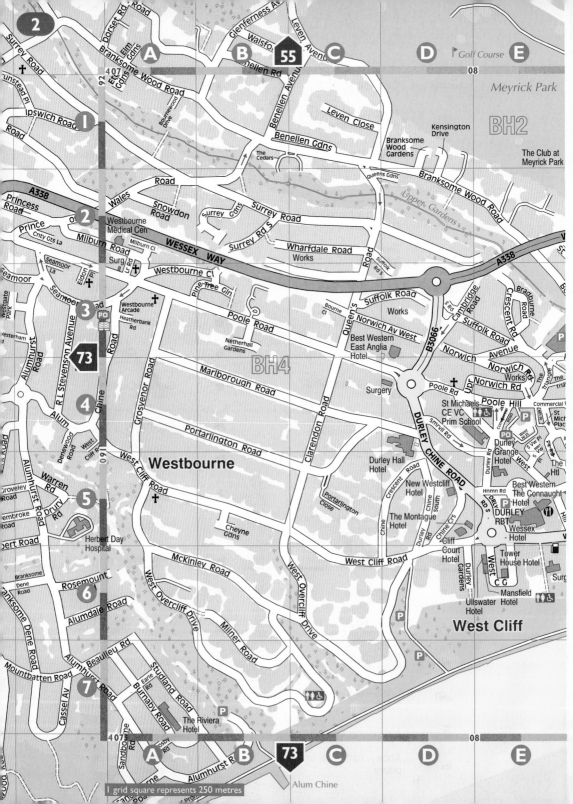

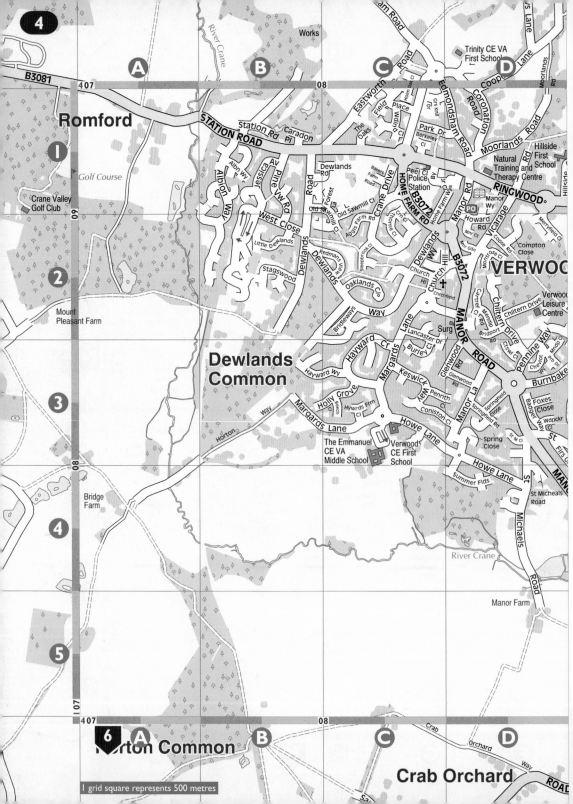

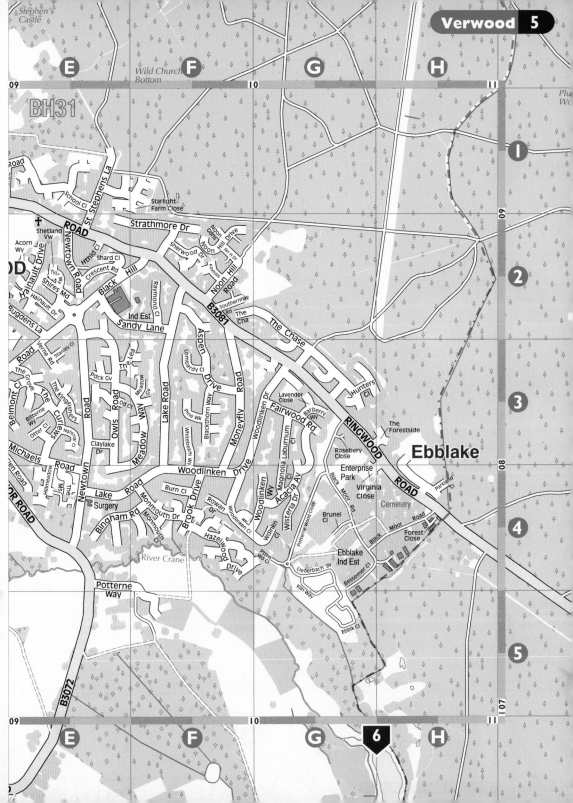

Stephen's Castle

E   F   G   H

Wild Church Bottom

09   10   11

Plu Wo

BH31

I

School Cl

St Stephens La

Starlight Farm Close

Strathmore Dr

ROAD

Shetland Vw

Newtown Road

Acorn Wy

Hainault Drive

TVl

Shires Md

Hainault Dr

Htnld

Shard Cl

Crescent Rd

Black Hill

Sherwood Dr

Noon Gdns

Noon

Hill Drive

Nn H Dr

Fomlls

Noon Hill Road

60

2

OD

Baugdens La

Ind Est

Sandy Lane

Raymond Cl

B3081

Southernhav

Rd

The Cha

The Chase

3

Road

Verne Rd

Stanley Cl

Aspen Drive

Lombardy Cl

Pdck Gv

The Lea

Meadow Gv

Od Ct

Pine Wk

Blackthorn Way

Whitebeam Wy

Moneyfly Road

Fairwood Rd

Woodlinken Dr

Lavender Close

Barberry Wy

Hunters Cl

The Grove

The Kingfishers

Belmont

Bitterne Wy

Otter Cl

Nightche

Claylake Dr

Owls Road

Lake Road

Meadow Way

Woodlinken

Wv

Magnolia

Laburnum Cl

Acacia Cl

Wisteria Dr

Barberry

The Forestside

Ebblake

08

The Curlew

St Michaels Road

Hillmeadow

Ms

The

Newtown Road

Lake Road

Surgery

Bingham Rd

Monmouth Dr

Monmouth

Brook Drive

Rowan Dr

Woodlinken Cl

Burn Cl

Walnkn

Av

Potterne Wood Close

Ptrn Wd Cl

Brunel Cl

Rosebery Close

Enterprise Park

Virginia Close

RINGWOOD ROAD

Black Moor Rd

Cemetery

Parkland

Cl

4

OR ROAD

River Crane

Hazelwood Drive

Liederbach Dr

Kiln Way

Ebblake Ind Est

Bessemer Cl

Black

Moor

Forest Close

Road

B3072

Potterne Way

09

Ebblk Cl

5

10   107   11

E   F   G   H

6

I

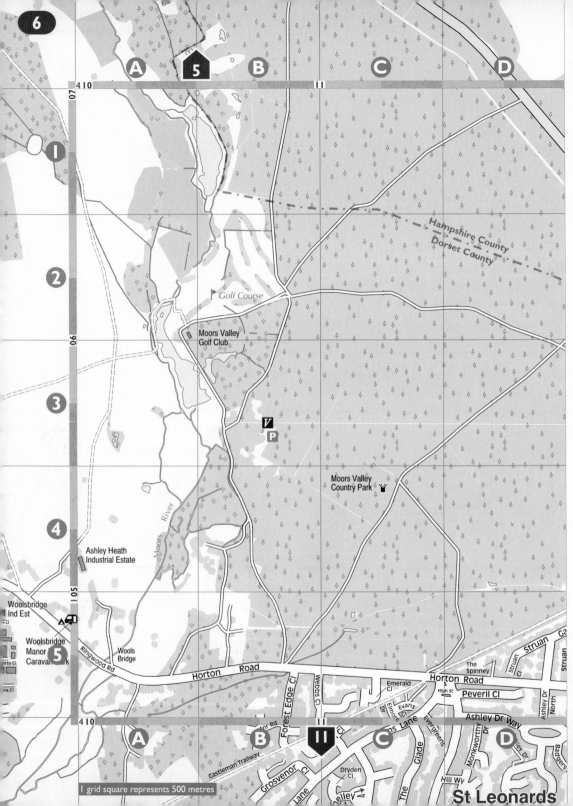

6

5

A **5** B C D

410
07

II

I

Hampshire County
Dorset County

Golf Course

2
06

Moors Valley
Golf Club

3
05

⚑
P

4

Moors Valley
Country Park Ψ

Ashley Heath
Industrial Estate

Woolsbridge
Ind Est

⛺

Woolsbridge
Manor
Caravan Park

5

Ringwood Rd

Wools
Bridge

Moors River

410

A B **II** C D

Horton Road

Forest Edge Cl

Webbs Cl

Castleman Trailway

Mnr Rd

Grosvenor
Lane

Emerald
Cl

Elmor Cl

Evans
Cl

Evans Lane

The
Spinney

Horton Road

High St

Peveril Cl

Emerald
Cl

Dryden
Cl

helley

The Glade

Evergreens

Ashley Dr Way

Monkworthy Dr

Ashley Dr
North

Struan
Dr

Struan Ga

Struan Ga

Badger Cl

Hill Wy

St Leonards

1 grid square represents 500 metres

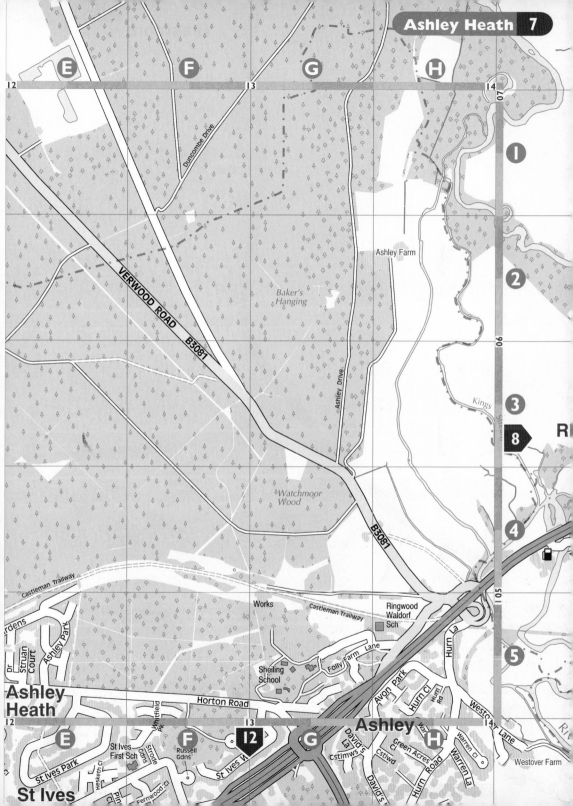

E   F   G   H

12   13   14   07

I

VERWOOD ROAD B3081

Duncombe Drive

Ashley Farm

Baker's
Hanging

Ashley Drive

Kings

R

8

Watchmoor
Wood

B3081

Castleman Trailway

Castleman Trailway

Works

Ringwood
Waldorf
Sch

Ashley Park

Struan Court
Dr

Sheiling
School

Folly Farm Lane

Avon Park

Hurn La

Hurn Cl
Hurn
Rd

Westover Lane

**Ashley
Heath**

Whitfield
Pk

Strode
Gdns

Horton Road

Ashley

David's St

Green Acres

Hurn Road

Warren La

Warren Cl

Gardens

E

St Ives Park

Heskeln Cl

F

St Ives First Sch

Russell
Gdns

Fernwood Cl

Pine

12

St Ives Vl

G

David's St

Cstimws

Cstlwd

H

Westover Farm

R

St Ives

2

06

3

4

05

5

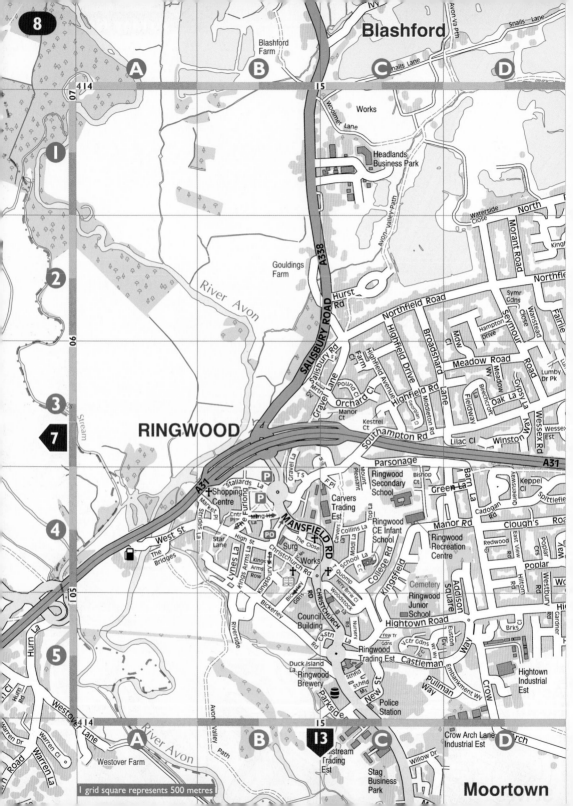

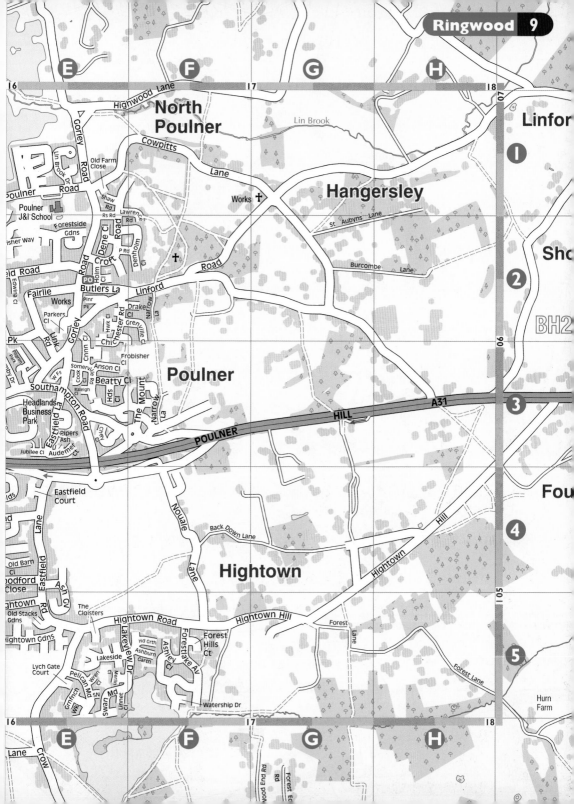

E F G H

16 17 18

07

Highwood Lane

North Poulner

Lin Brook

Linfor

1

Cowpitts

Gorley Road

Old Farm Close

Lin Brook Dr

Poulner Road

Lane

Works ✝

Hangersley

Sho

Poulner J&I School

Forestside Gdns

Shaw Rd

Lawrence Rd

Rs Rd

St Aubyns Lane

Fisher Way

Dene Cl

Denholm

Holm Cl

P Rd

Burcombe Lane

Field Road

Croft

Road

✝

Road

2

06

BH2

Edwina Cl

Butlers La

PO

Fairlie

Linford

Works

Pinr Pk

Parkers Cl

Chester Rd

Drake Cl

Narrow La

Grenville Cl

Gorley

Link Rd

Hwk Cl

Cnnn Cl

Chi

Frobisher Cl

Poulner

Pk

Somerv'lle Rd

Anson Cl

Cook

WFs

Raleigh

Beatty Cl

HDs

3

A31

Headlands Business Park

Southampton Road

The Mount

Narrow La

HILL

Eastfield Rd

Pipers Ash

Audemer Ct

CNRY

POULNER

Jubilee Cl

Eastfield Court

Lane

Novale Lane

Back Down Lane

Hightown Hill

4

05

Old Barn Cl

Woodford Close

Ash Gv

Eastfield Rd

Hightown

Forest Lane

Lane

Old Stacks Gdns

The Cloisters

Hightown Road

Hightown Hill

Forest

5

Hightown Gdns

Lakeview Dr

Ashley Cl

Ashburn Garth

Forestrake Av

Forest Hills Ct

Lych Gate Court

Lakeside

Hd Grth

Forest Lane

Pelican Md

Merlin Md

Wren

SN

Hurn Farm

Grnfnch Wk

Swan Md

Cygnet Md

Watership Dr

16 17 18

E F G H

Lane

Crow

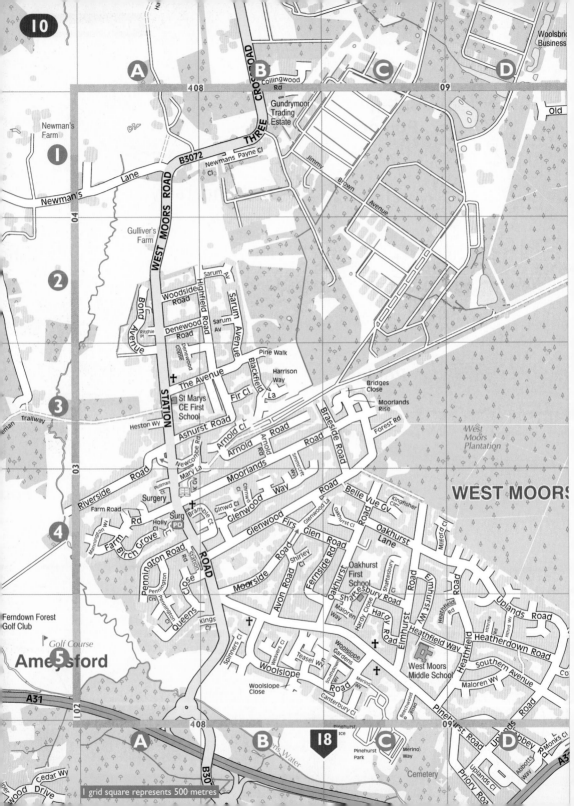

Woolsbridge
Manor Farm
Caravan Park

Liberty Cl

ge Small
Centre

Farm

Azura

Barn

Condor

E

Ringwood Rd

Wools
Bridge

Horton   Road

Webbs Cl

Forest Edge Cl

F

6

G

Emerald

High St

Evans

Lismore

H

The Spinney

Horton Road

Peveril Cl

Ashley Dr Wa

Monkworthy Dr

Struan

Castleman Trailway

Pine Mnr Rd

Burton Cl

Grosvenor Cl

Lions Lane

Shelley Cl

Dryden Cl

Lions Lane

The Glade

Bushmead Drive

Hill

Gainsborough Rd

Windsor

San

1

St Leon

Castleman Trailway

Lions

Hill

Way

St Leonards
Way

Bracken
Close

Fernlea Cl

Norris
Cl

Lions

Lane

Braeside

Laurel Close

Wisbrdg Rd

King Cl

Wonds Wy

Pine Drive

Surgery

Hobbs Park

Knoll Gdn

2

Moors River

Willow
Cl

Garth Cl

Heath

Sylvan Rd

Holly Cl

Ivy Cl

Craigm Gdns

Spinney
Cl

Conifer
Cl

Gorse
Cl

Rowan Cl

Rd

Drive

Acorn
Cl

Heather
Rd

Malmesbury

Laurel Lane

Haz

Hz

Gdn La

mere

Travelodge

3

Brocks

Pine

Oaks

Birch
Close

Cedar   Avenue

Cherry Tree
Cl

St Leona
Hotel

12

4

Oaks

Brckwd

Fir Tree Cl

Drive

RINGWOOD   ROAD

Beech Lane

03

102

Moors River

East Moors
Farm

Back of Beyond
Touring Park

RINGWOOD

Forest Edge
Touring Park

Grange
Rd

Grange

Road

ngemoor
Rd

mpton Crs

A31

St Leonards
Community Hospital

Boundary Lane

Ways

Bound

5

E

The
Sq

The Crs

F

19

G

H

Road

Works

**Grange
Estate**

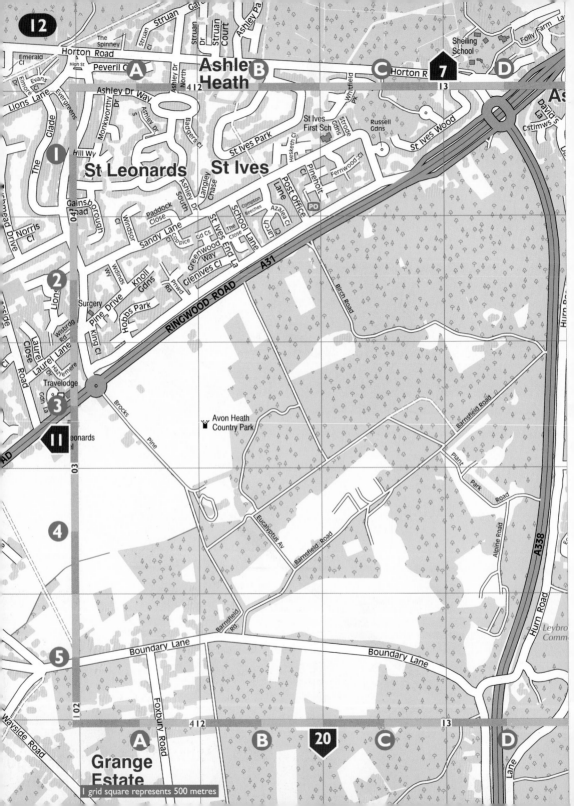

12

The Spinney

Struan
Struan Cl
Struan Dr
Struan Gate
Struan Court

Ashley Pa

Horton Road

Emerald Cl

High St

Elmore

Evans

Peveril C **A**

Ashley Dr North

Ashley Dr

Ashley Heath **B**

C Horton R **7**

Sheiling School

Folly Farm

D

13

Lions Lane

Ashley Dr Way

412

Evergreens

Whitfield

Cstlmws

A

Monkworthy Dr

Ashley dr

Badger's Cl

St Ives Park

St Ives First Sch

Strode Gdns

Russell Gdns

St Ives Wood

David's

1

Hill Wy

The Glade

Gainsborough Road

St Leonards

Ashley Dr South

Langley Chase

St Ives

Hesketh Cl

Pinehoft Cl

Fernwood Cl

2

Lions Lane

Windsor Cl

Paddock Close

Sandy Lane

Coppice

St Ives Eng La

School Lane

Greenwood Way

Compton Beeches

The Close

Azalea Cl

Christ

Cd Cs

POST OFFICE

PO

Surgery

Pine Drive

Knoll Gdns

Hobbs Park

Wclnds

pnwd

Glenives Cl

Birch Road

Travelodge

Laurel Close

Laurel Lane

Wibprog Rd

King Cl

Haxemere

Gdn La

Brocks

RINGWOOD ROAD

A31

3

II

Leonards

Pine

Avon Heath Country Park

Barnsfield Road

03

4

Eucalyptus Av

Barnsfield Road

Plant

Park

Road

Alpine Road

A338

Hurn Road

5

Boundary Lane

Barnsfield Rd

Boundary Lane

Leybro Comm

102

Wayside Road

A

Foxbury Road

412

B

20

C

13

D

Lane

Grange Estate

1 grid square represents 500 metres

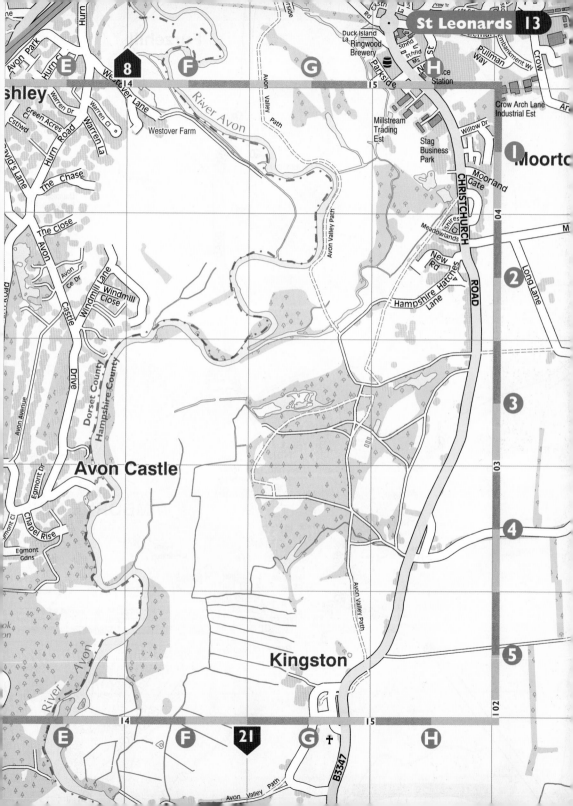

Ashley

E   **8**   F   G   H

I Moorto

Avon Park

Hurn Cl

Hurn

Westover Lane

14

River Avon

Duck Island La
Ringwood Brewery

Parkside

Police Station

Crow Arch Lane
Industrial Est

Ar

Moorto

Warren Dr

Green Acres

Hurn Road

Warren Cl

Warren La

Westover Farm

Avon Valley Path

Millstream Trading Est

Stag Business Park

Willow Dr

Moorland Gate

Crow

Pullman Way

St.hfld St.nhd

Yew Tr

Cstlwd

David's Lane

CHRISTCHURCH

M

The Chase

The Close

Meadowlands

Shires

Avon

Avon Ce Dr

Windmill Lane

Windmill Close

Avon Valley Path

Hampshire Hatches Lane

New Rd

ROAD

04

2

Long Lane

M

Castle

Dorset County
Hampshire County

Drive

3

03

Avon Avenue

Egmont Dr

Avon Castle

Egmont Cl

Chapel Rise

4

Egmont Gdns

Avon Valley Path

5

102

River Avon

Kingston

B3347

E   F   **21**   G   H

Avon Valley Path

14

Furzehill

400

PO

River Allen

Higher
Honeybrook
Farm

Council
Building

Furzel

Smugglers Lane

1

Wilksworth
Farm

Wilksworth Farm
Caravan Park

Dogdean

Dumpton
School

Grove

Deans
Grove

2

R Allen

Deans

Long

WIMBORNE ROAD

Walford
Close

Milton
Rd

Shake-
speare Rd

Tennyson Rd

Hill

Greenhill
Cl

Boundary Dr

Greenhill
Lane

Tower Cl

Burt's

Giddylake

Venator Pl

Venator
Place

River Cl

Bryon Rd

LaCy

Drive

Cherdon

Wy

Lacy Close

Onslow Gdns

Highland

3

Queen
Elizabeths
School

Broads

St
Mrgrts
Hl

The Broads

Stone Lane
Ind Est

Walford Mill
Medical Cen

CW
F

Wimbd Gdns

CW
F

knobcrook Rd

Sh Fld

Courtenay
Drive

Glendale
Cl

Marlborough
Cl

Beaufort Dr

Melverley Gdn

VW

Badbury

Highland
Rd

Melverley
Pl

Marlborough

Highland
Hill

VW

Highland Ct

STONE

Cem

Cl Pl

Culverhayes Rd

Cem

Blind La

Chpl

Allenbourn
Middle
School

Eliza
Ct

WIMBORNE MINSTER

R
H

4

Road

Cowgrove

Cemetery

Road

ST MARGARET'S HL B3082

VICTORIA ROAD

WEST BOROUGH

B3078

EAST BOROUGH

PRIORS

WK

Netherwood
Place

Wimborne
Hospital

Wimborne
Town FC

Stour Valley Way

River Stour

Redcotts Rd

Wimborne
First School

Tivoli
Theatre

School La

Three Lions Cl

Victoria
Cl

Redcotts La

Westfield

Works
The
Kings
Head Hotel

Allen
Ct

Allenview

Greenhays Rd

P

HNHM

Police
Station

Rowlands

St John's Hl

Cranfield Avenue

Wesle

Ashdene
Close

Pine Tree

Birchdale

Greenclose

Ppar

Cl

R
R

Cumbur
Gdns

B3073

Yew
Tree

Bourne
Ct

5

B3078

JULIAN'S RD

Cuthbury
Close

Cuthbury Gdns

Victoria
R

Pye Lane

P

KING ST

W ST

West
Row

HIGH ST

Church

PO

cook
Rw

EAST ST

LEIGH RD

i

Mill La

Ind
Est

Crwn Md

Cncl
Bldg

Priest's House
Mus & Garden

Park Lane

Hn La

Surg

Deans
Ct La

RODWAY

St CATHERINES

Grove
Road

Parkwood Rd

Legg La

School

St John's
Cl

Ashmore
Cl

Ingrm

Osbo

Crescent Rd

Avenue Road

Stevensons
Close

Ha Rd

Parkwood Rd

Chene
Rd

Fairfield

Retreat Rd

Grenville Rd

Leigh Gdns

D Ct

Wimborne
Minster

Grammar
School
Lane

Millstream
Close

Deans
Court

POOLE ROAD

New Borough Rd

Allen's
Rd

Eden

Works

Wimborne
Mkt

P

Et Rd

Gv

Leigh Gdns

Hardy

Crs

Riverside
Park Ind Est

Station
Road

Twmns
Rd

OAK

22

400   01

I grid square represents 500 metres

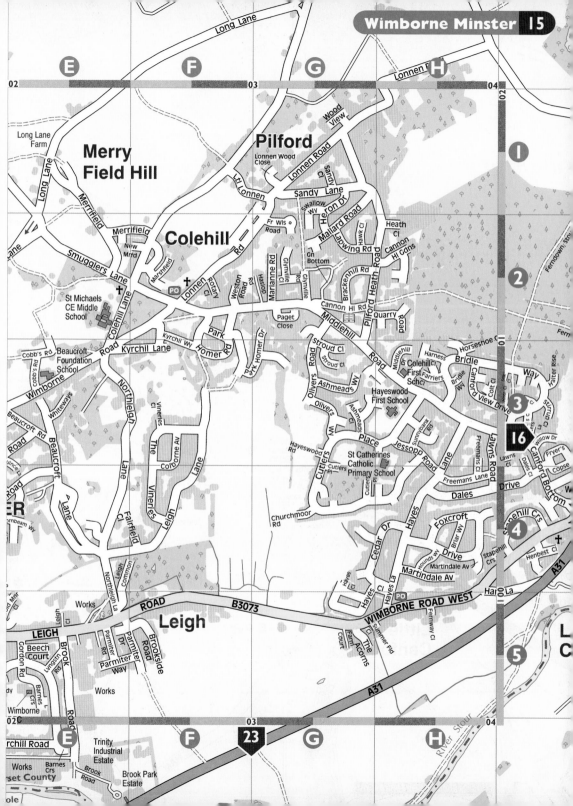

Long Lane

E F G H

02 03 04

Lonnen R

I

Long Lane Farm

Merry Field Hill

Pilford

Lonnen Wood Close

Lonnen Road

Wood View

Sandy Cl

Merrifield

Ltl Lonnen

Sandy Lane

Swallow Wy

Heron Dr

Heath Cl

2

Ferndown Stou

Merrifield

Colehill

Fr Wls Road

Marshfield Rd

Mallard Road

Lapwing Rd

Hawk Cl

Cannon Hl Gdns

Fern

Smugglers Lane

New Mrfd

Marshfield

Lonnen

PO

Rotary Cl

Weston Rd

Haslop Rd

Marianne Rd

Glynville Cl

Glynville Rd

Glynville

Gn Bottom

Brackenhill Rd

Pilford Heath Road

Cannon Hl Rd

Quarry

Heath Cl

St Michaels CE Middle School

Colehill Lane

Park Rd

Kyrchil Wy

Homer Rd

Paget Close

Middlehill

Cannon Hl Rd

Quarry Road

Horseshoe Cl

01

Beaucroft Foundation School

Cobb's Rd

Pk Sq Rd

Kyrchil Lane

Park Homer Dr

Stroud Cl

Stroud Cl

Olivers Road

Middlehill Dr

Colehill First Schl

Harness Cl

Farriers

Bridle Wy

Bridle Way

Carford View Drive

Colt Cl

Alter Rise

3

J.S.

Wimborne Road

Northleigh

Whiteways

Vineries Cl

The Coldrene Av

Ashmeads Wy

Olivers

Hayeswood First School

Ashmeads Wy

Lawns Road

Freemans Cl

Lawns Cl

Dales Ct

Willow Dr

Fryer's Cl

stirrup Dr

Carford Bottom

Copse

16

Beaucroft Rd

Beaucroft Road

Lane

Fairfield Cl

Vineries Lane

Leigh Lane

Hayeswood Rd

Cutlers Pl

Cutlers Pl

Jessopp Road

St Catherines Catholic Primary School

Sunnybank

Freemans Lane

Lane

Dales

Carford Bottom Drive

4

Stapehill Crs

Henbest Cl

Hornbeam Wy

Churchmoor Rd

Hayes Pl

Cedar Dr

Hayes

Foxcroft Drive

Hounds Wy

Briar Wy

Stapehill Crs

A31

Northleigh La

Leigh Common

Leigh

Works

Leigh

ROAD

B3073

Martindale Av

Martindale Av

Hayes La

Hayes Cl

PO

WIMBORNE ROAD WEST

Hare La

Fernway Cl

L C

LEIGH

Beech Court

Cordon Rd

Lvlngarn Rd

Parmiter Dr

Parmiter Rd

Parmiter Way

Brookside Road

Brook

Summer Fld

The Acorns

Farm Court

5

Works

Barnes Crs

Works

Wimborne

Road

Brook Road

A31

River Stour

rchill Road

E

Trinity Industrial Estate

F

23

G

H

set County

Barnes Crs

Brook Park Estate

02 03

ole

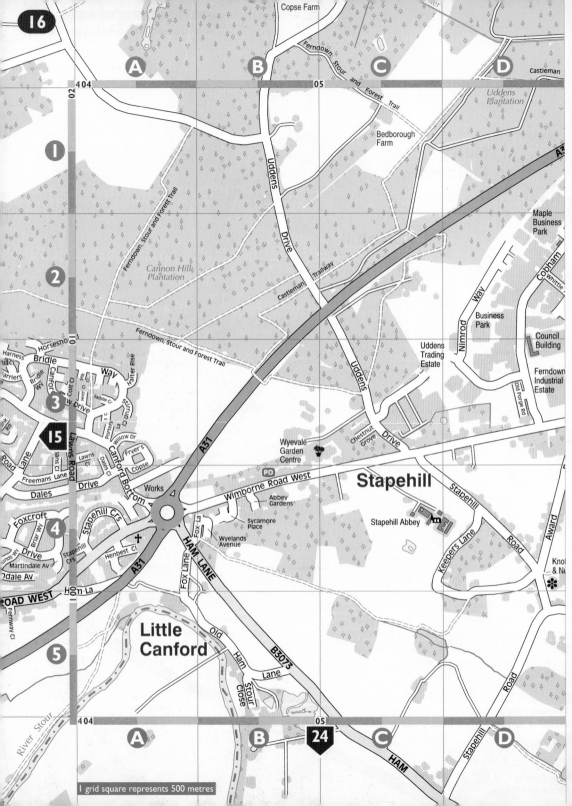

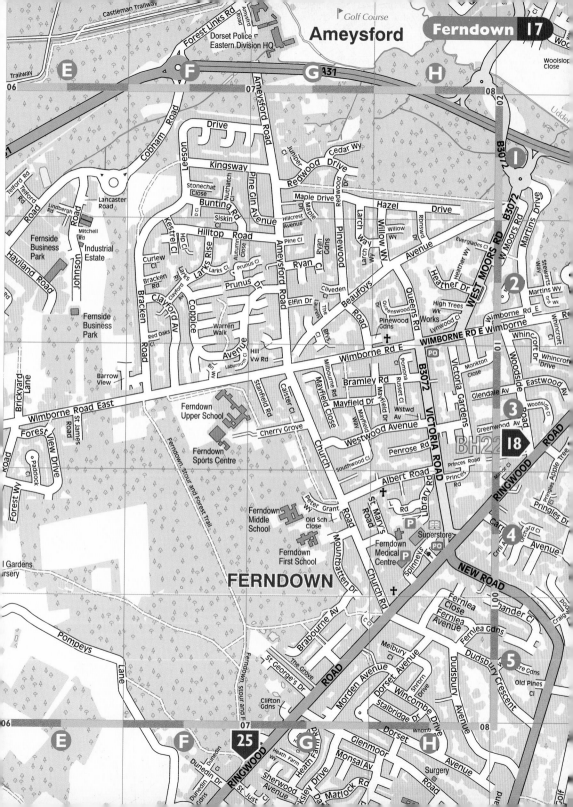

Golf Course

Ameysford

Castleman Trailway

Forest Links Rd

Dorset Police
Eastern Division HQ

Trailway

E 06   **F** 07   **G** A31   **H** 08   02   **I**

Woolslop
Close

Uddr

B3072

Cobham Road

Drive

Leeson

Kingsway

Ameysford Road

Juniper Rd

Cedar Wy

Redwood Drive

Redwood Dr

Stonechat Close

Bunting Avenue

Pine Gin Avenue

Nuthatch

Siskin Cl

Maple Drive

Maple

Hazel

Drive

Hillcrest Avenue

Larch Way

Willow Wy

Rnswd

Wk

Everglades Cl

Telford Rd

Telford Rd

Lancaster Road

Road

Lindbergh Rd

Mitchell Rd

Hilltop Road

Kestrel Cl

Hp Cl

Pine Cl

Pinewood

Ryan Gdns

Larch Dr

Willow Vw

Avenue

Heather Wy

Martins Drive

Martins Wy

Stewarts Way

WEST MOORS RD

B3072

I

Fernside Business Park

Industrial Estate

Curlew Cl

Larks Rise

Autumn Close

Prunus Cl

Ryan

Dr

Ryan

Cliveden

Heather Dr

High Trees

Wimborne Rd E

2

Martins Wy

Whincroft

Haviland Road

Johnson Road

Bracken Rd

Clayford Rd

Prunus

Elfin Dr

The Laurels

Queenswood

Pinewood Gdns

Works

Lynwood Cl

Wimborne Rd E

Wstwd
Av

Woodside Road

Whincroft Dr

Whincroft Drive

Fernside Business Park

Bracken Road

Clayford Av

Coppice

Red Oaks

Warren Walk

Hill Vw Rd

Beaufoys

Queens Rd

Queenswood

WIMBORNE RD E Wimborne

Monkton Close

Glendale Av

Eastwood Rd

Woods Cl

3

Greenwood Av

Brickyard Lane

Barrow View

Avenue

Laburnum

Wimborne Road East

Mayfield Close

Millbourne Rd

Bramley Rd

Pomona

Russet Cl

B3072

Victoria Gardens

BH22

18

RINGWOOD ROAD

Forest View Drive

St James Road

Stanfield Road

Caister Cl

Mayfield Dr

Mayfield Dr

Mayfield Way

Westwood Avenue

Penrose Rd

VICTORIA ROAD

Princes Road

Princes Rd

4

Pringles Avenue

Pringles Apple Green

Forest Wy

Paddock

Forest Wy

Ferndown, Stour and Forest Trail

Ferndown Upper School

Cherry Grove

Church Road

Southwood Cl

Albert Road

St Mary's Road

Library

Oleander Cl

Carl

Cyril Cl

Grll Cl

Craig

Ferndown Sports Centre

Peter Grant Way

Old Sch Close

St George's Dr

Ferndown Middle School

Ferndown First School

Mountbatten Dr

Ferndown Medical Centre

Spinneys

P

Superstore

P

PO

NEW ROAD

Oleander Cl

Manor Rd

Fernlea Close

Fernlea Avenue

Fernlea Gdns

Dudsbury Crescent

5

Tre Gdns

Old Pines Cl

FERNDOWN

Pompeys Lane

Ferndown, Stour and Forest Trail

Clifton Gdns

The Grove

Melbury Cl

Morden Avenue

Dorset Avenue

Wincombe Drive

Shrm

Dudsbury Avenue

Stalbridge Dr

Wncmb

RINGWOOD ROAD

Heath Farm Wy

Sherwood Avenue

Heath Farm Rd

Kingsley Drive

Glenmoor

Monsal Av

Dorset

Matlock Rd

Avenue

Surgery

St Just

E 06   **F** 07   **25** RINGWOOD   **G** 07   **H** 08

Dunedin Dr

Dunedin Gdns

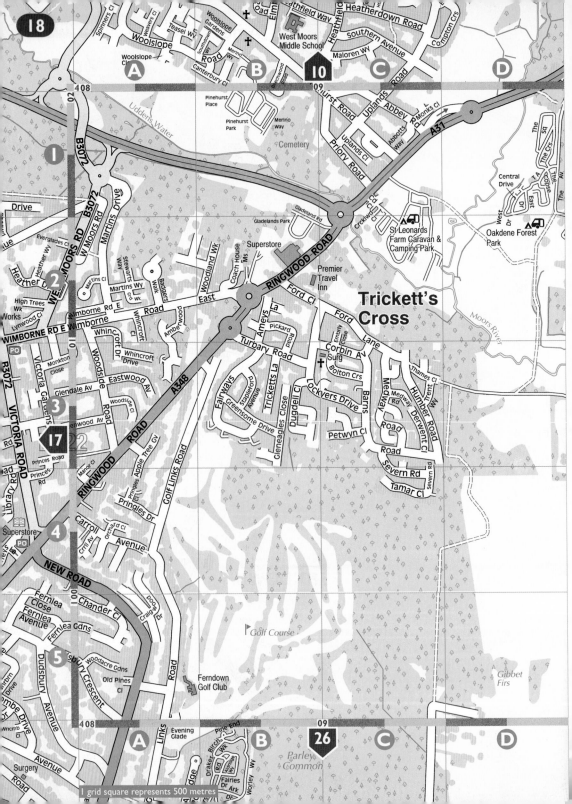

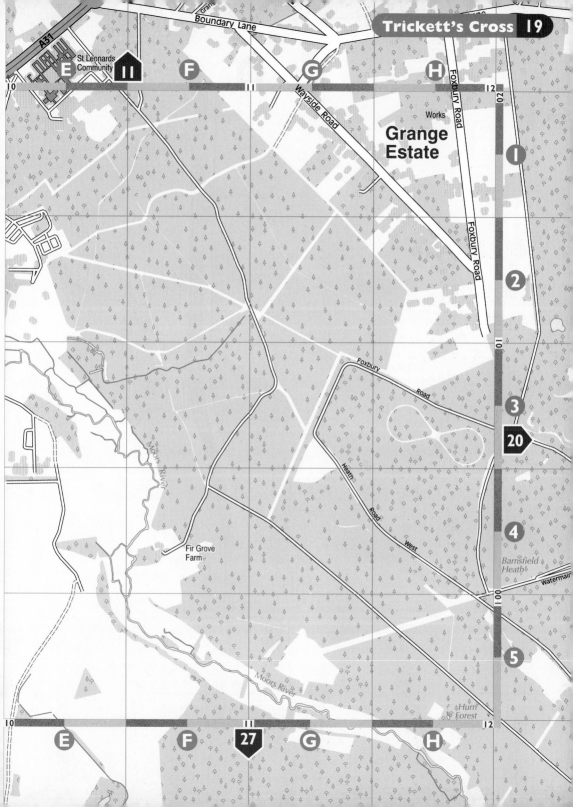

St Leonards
Community

**Grange
Estate**

Works

Boundary Lane

Wayside Road

Foxbury Road

Foxbury Road

Foxbury

Road

Heath

Road

West

Watermai

Barnsfield
Heath

Moors River

Fir Grove
Farm

Moors River

Hurn
Forest

A31

E

F

G

H

I

2

3

20

4

5

E

F

27

G

H

10

11

12

01

02

00

Kingston

E **13** F G H

14 15 16

Wilkins Farm

I

Avon Valley Path

B3347

Dragon Lane

Avon valley Path

Upper Bisterne
Farm

2

Bisterne

3

Bisterne
Manor

B3347

Lower Bisterne
Farm

4

Ripley
Wood

Avon Valley Pth

5

Anna Lane

Tyrrells
Ford Country
House Hotel

14 15 16

E F **29** G H

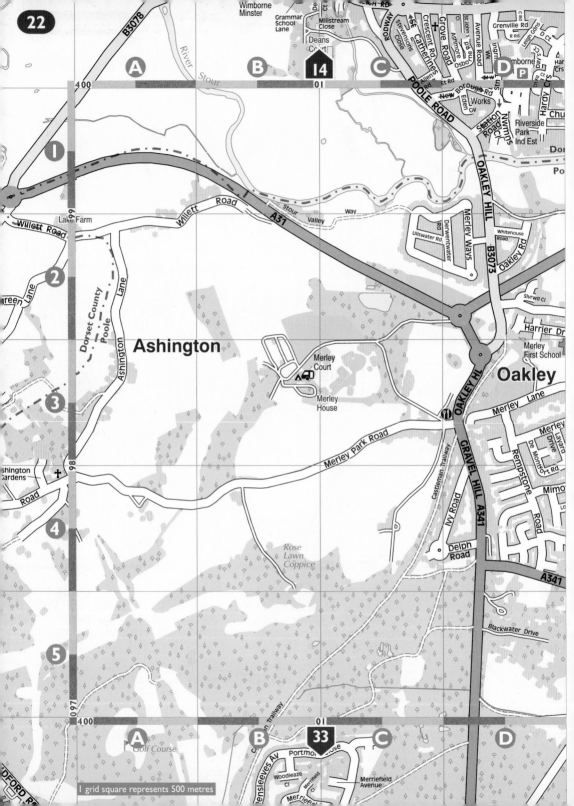

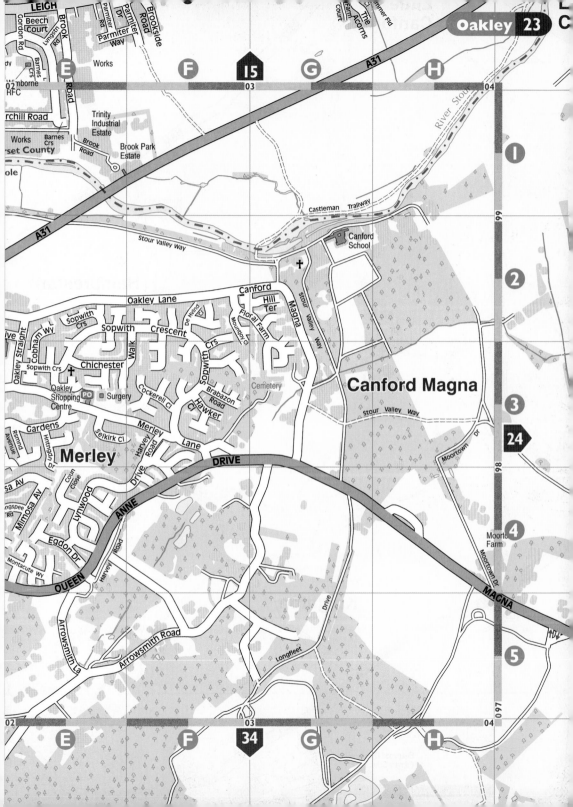

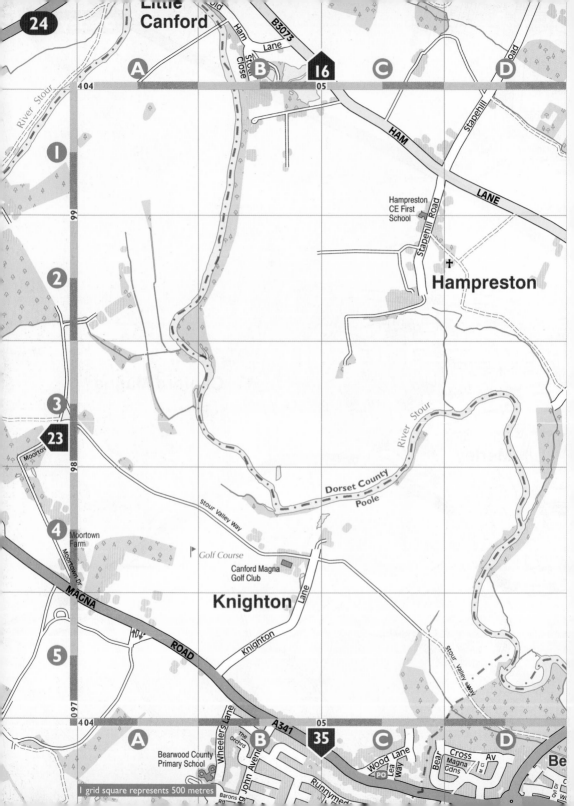

24

Little
Canford

B3073

A 404 **B** **16** **C** **D**

Old
Ham Lane
Stour Close

HAM

Stapehill Road

Oad

1 06

LANE

Hampreston
CE First
School

Stapehill Road

2 † **Hampreston**

River Stour

3

23 98

Moortow

Dorset County
Poole

Stour Valley Way

4 Moortown
Farm

Golf Course

Canford Magna
Golf Club

Knighton

MAGNA

Knighton Lane

Moortown Dr.

River Stour

Stour Valley Way

5 97

ROAD

Wheelers Lane
The Orchard

A 404 **B** A341 **35** **C** **D**

Bearwood County
Primary School

John Aven

Barons Rd.

Runnymed

Wood Lane

PO

Lea Way

Bear

Magna
Gdns

M Cl

Cross
Av

Be

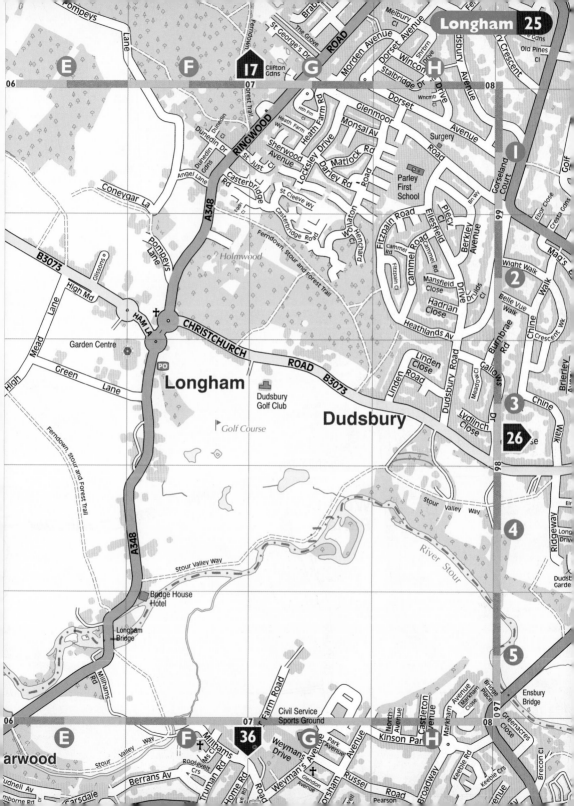

West Parley

I grid square represents 500 metres

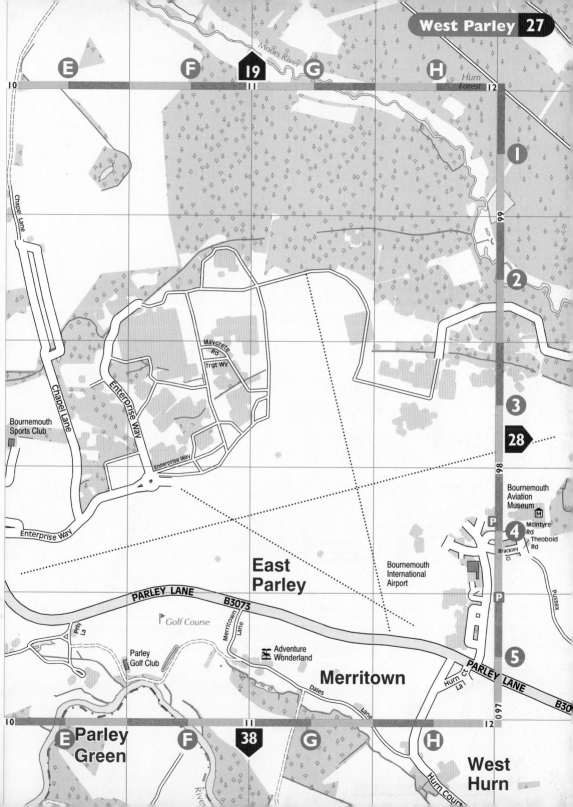

E F 19 G H Hurn Forest
10 11 12

I

99

2

3

28

Chapel Lane

Moors River

Maycrete Rd
Trgt Wy

Enterprise Way

Bournemouth Sports Club

Chapel Lane

Enterprise Way

Enterprise Way

Bournemouth Aviation Museum
M
McIntyre Rd
Theobold Rd
P
4
Brackley Cl
98

East Parley

Bournemouth International Airport

Pussex

PARLEY LANE B3073

Golf Course

Priv La

Merritown Lane

Adventure Wonderland

Parley Golf Club

Merritown

Dales Lane

Hurn Ct La

P
PARLEY LANE
5
B30

097

10 11 38 12

E **Parley Green** F G H **West Hurn**

Hurn Court

28

A   B   **20** C   D
13

I

2

3

27

4

5

A   B   **39** C   D
13

Hurn Forest

412

66

98

97

412

Plantation Road

A338

Christchurch Ski & Leisure Centre

Avon Common

Matchams Lane

Pithouse Farm

Pithouse Lane

Works

Bournemouth Aviation Museum

M

McIntyre Rd
Theobold Rd
Brackley Cl

P

P

Government Offices & Works Depot

Pussex Lane

Moors Cl

Moors River

Hurn

Sopley Common

Hurn Ct
La

HARLEY LANE

B3073

Works

PO

Hurn Bridge

Mill

West Hurn

Hurn Court

A338

1 grid square represents 500 metres

E F G H

Anna Lane

Tyrrell
Ford
House H 21

I

Avon Tyrrell
Farm

London Lane

London Lane

Avon

Avon Valley Path

B3347

2

Ri

Sopley
Primary
School

Parsonage Farm

3

30

River Avon

Court Farm

4

B3347

Avon Causeway

RINGWOOD

Avon Valley Path

Meadow
Cl

Priest Lane

5

ROAD

Sopley

E F G H

40

B3347

Avon Valley Path

Sopley Park

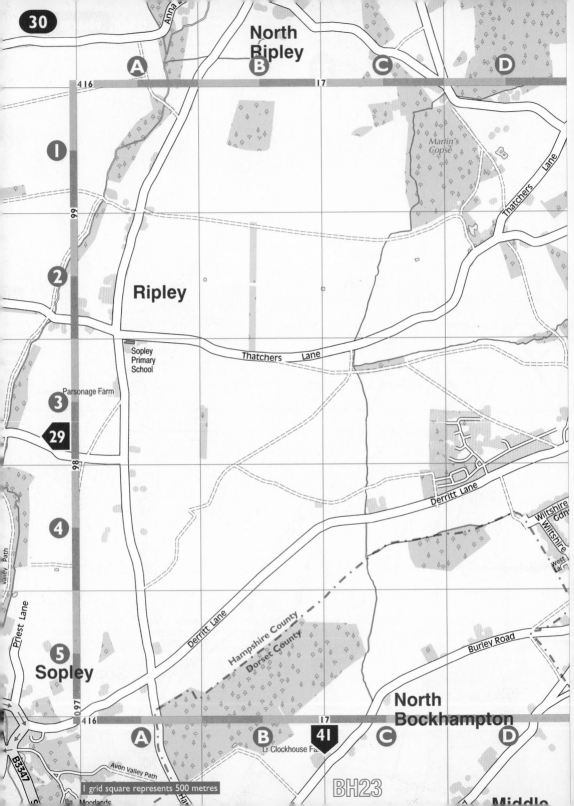

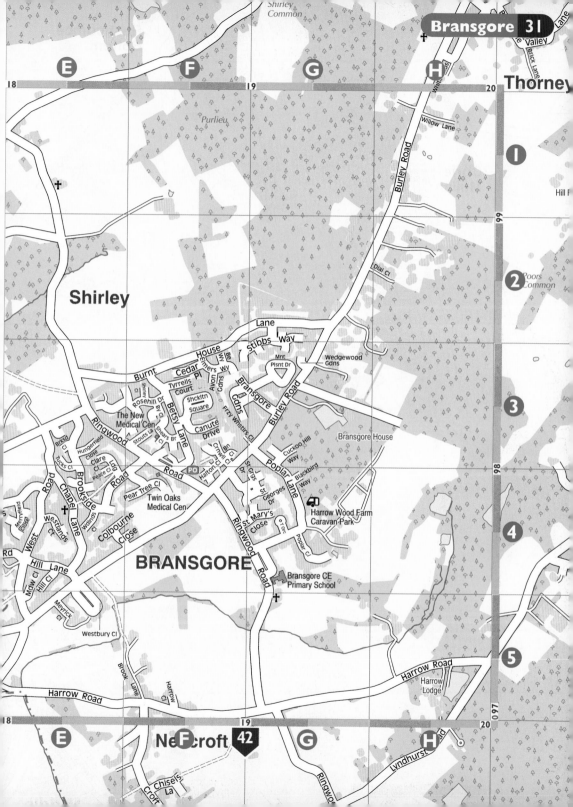

Shirley Common

Brick Lane

Valley

† Thorney

18 E **19** F G **20** H

Purlieu

Willow Lane

Burley Road

I

Hill F

96

Shirley

Dial Cl

Poors
2 Common

Lane

Stibbs Way

Burnt House Cedar Pl

Elners Wy Be

Mnt

Wedgewood
Gdns

Tyrrells
Court

Avon Gdns

Plsnt Dr

Shirley
Rosehill Dr

BV Cl

Shckltn
Square

Bransgore
Gdns

Burley Road

3

The New
Medical Cen

Ringwood

Betsy Lane

Stouts La

Spears Br

Canute
Drive

Fray Wnstrs Cl

Crnwll Cl

Bransgore House

98

Brksd
Cl

Hungerfield
Close

Clare
Cl

Peace Cl

Road

Hatton PO

St Grgs
Dr

Cuckoo Hill
Way

Tucks Cl

Cl

St
Georges
Dr

Blackbird
Way

West
Road

Chapel Lane

Brookside

Wdlnds

Colbourne
Close

Pear Tree Cl

Twin Oaks
Medical Cen

Ringwood Road

Poplar Lane

Harrow Wood Farm
Caravan Park

4

Mervnfield
Close

Westlands
Ct

St Mary's
Close

Poplar
Cl

Rd

West Hill Lane

Mdw Cl

Hill Cl

BRANSGORE

Bransgore CE
Primary School †

Meyrick
Cl

Brook Lane

Harrow
Cl

Harrow Road

Harrow
Lodge

5

Westbury Cl

Harrow Road

97

18 E **19** F G **20** H

New Milton F **42**

Chisels
La

Croft

Ringwo

Lyndhurst Rd

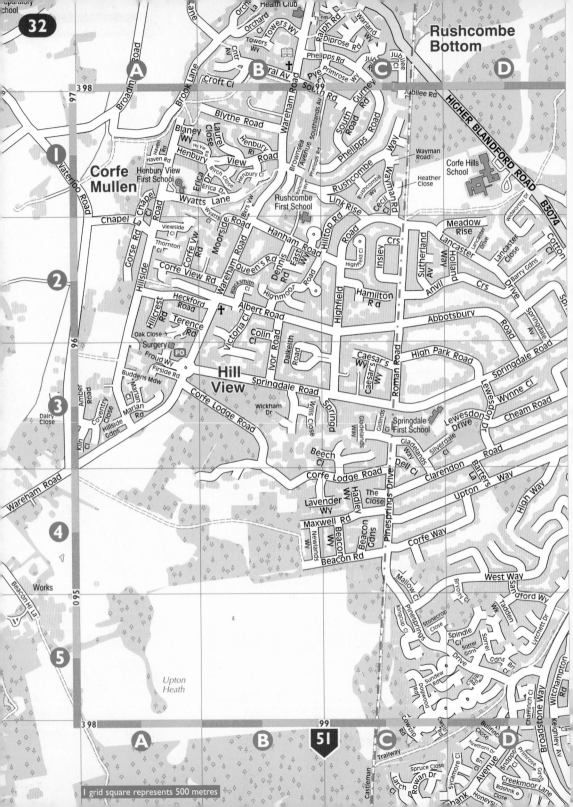

1 grid square represents 500 metres

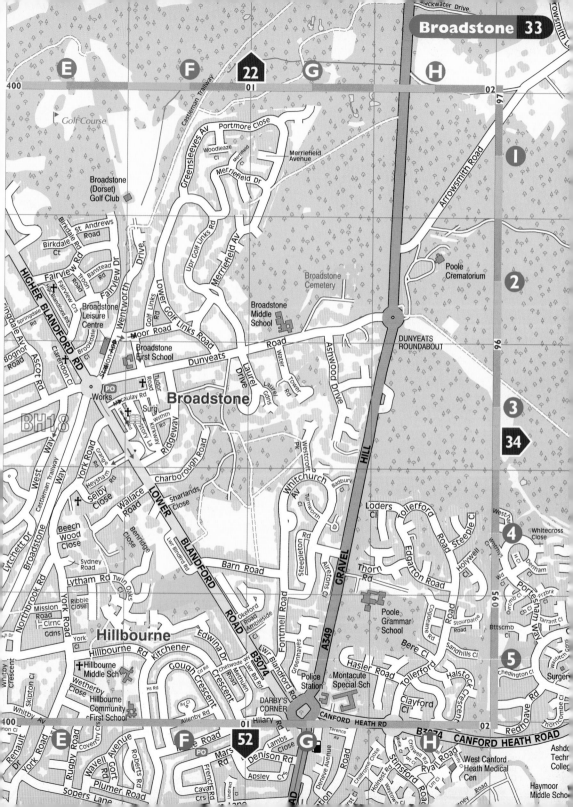

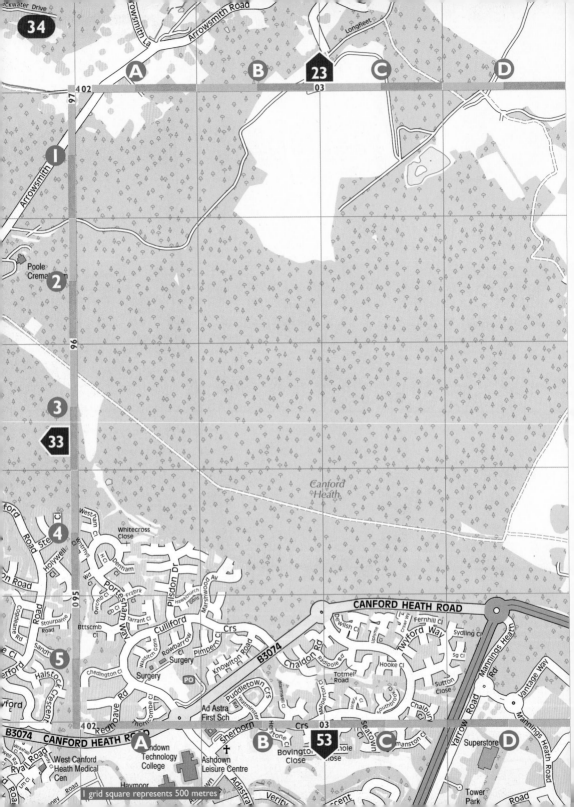

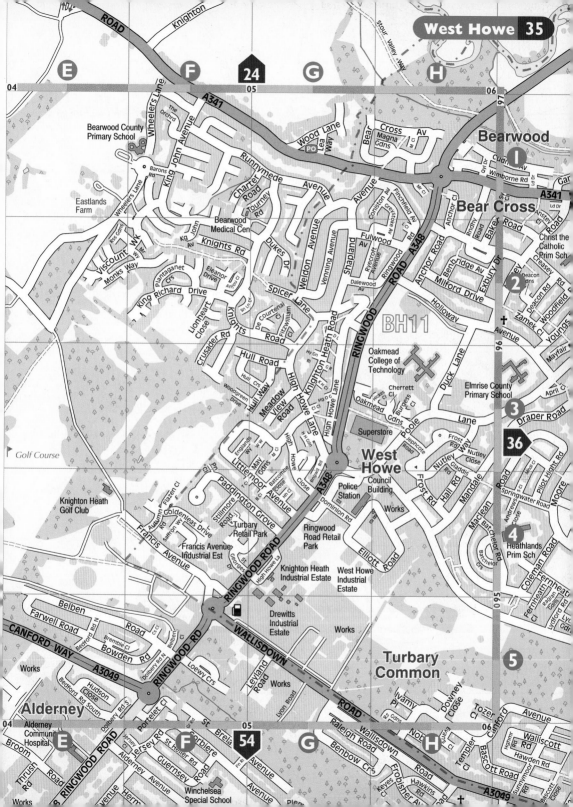

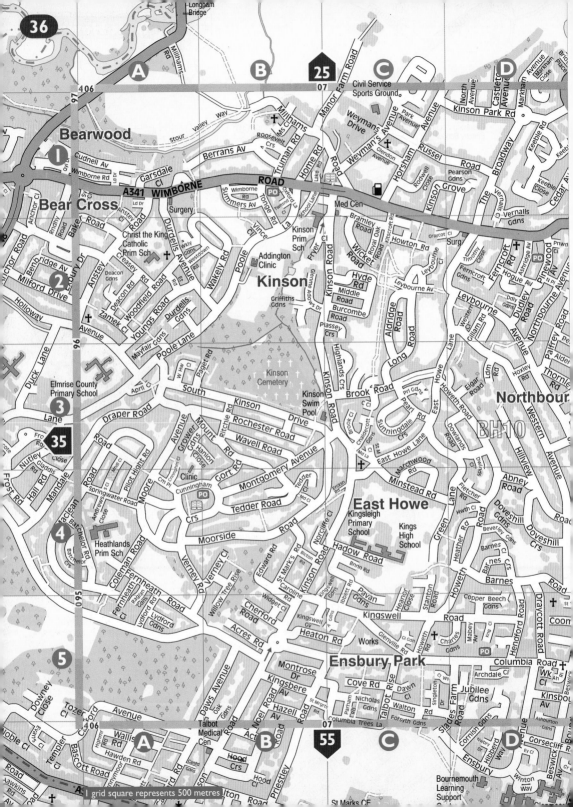

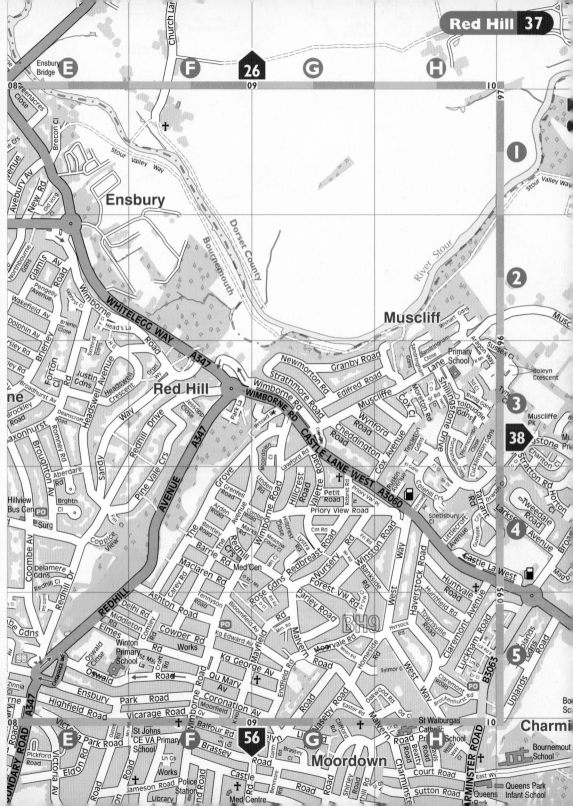

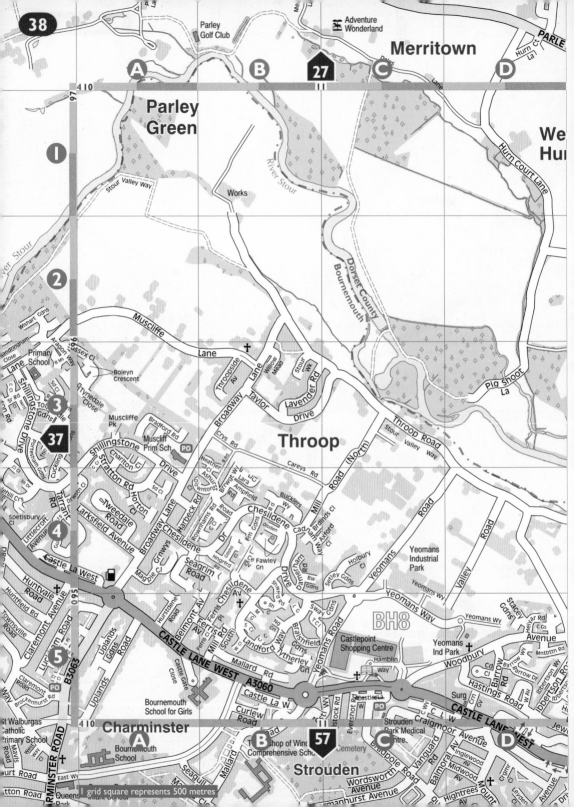

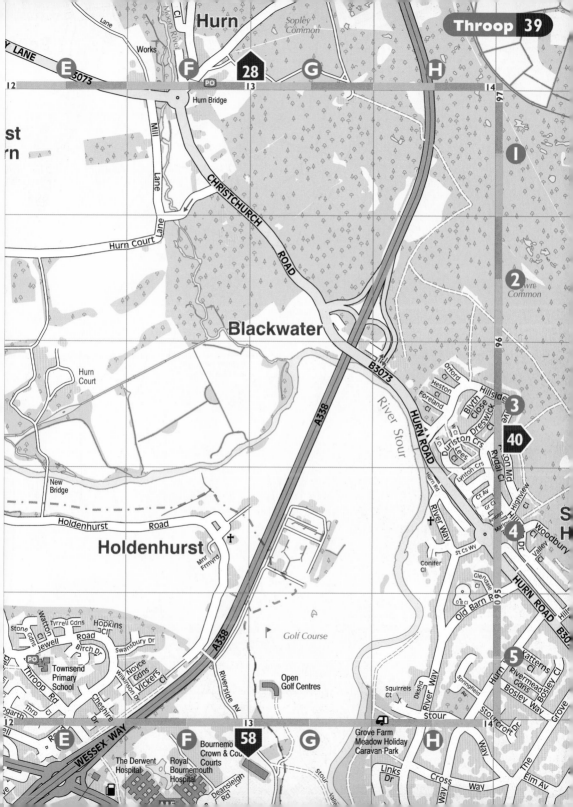

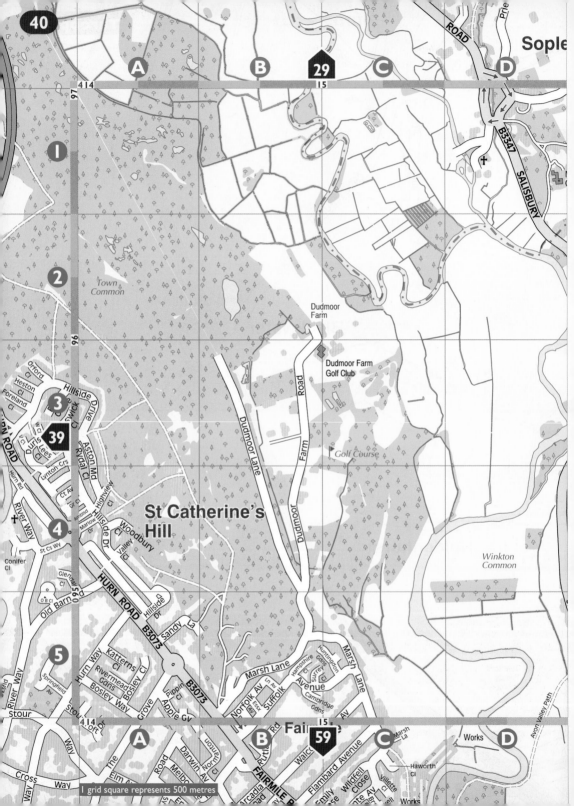

40

A   B   **29**   C   D

ROAD   Prie   **Sople**

414   15

97

B3347   SALISBURY

1

2

Town Common

Dudmoor Farm

Dudmoor Farm Golf Club

96

Hillside Drive

Orford Cl

Heston Cl

Foreland

3

Swick Cl

Durls

Lees

Wa

39

Lynton Crs

Hurn Rd

Aston Rd

Rydal Cl

Highview Cl

Ct Cl

Cl Cl

Ct AV

Ambled

Marlow

Cl

River Way

4

St Cs Wy

Hillside Dr

Woodbury Cl

Valley Cl

St Catherine's Hill

Dudmoor Lane

Dudmoor Farm Road

Golf Course

Winkton Common

Conifer Cl

Old Barn

Glenair

Cl

Cl

Cl Cl

HURN ROAD

Hillside Dr

Sandy La

5

River Way

Springfield

AV

Hurn Way

Katterns Cl

Bosley Cl

Rivermead Gdns

Bosley Way

Grove

Pippin Cl

Apple GV

B3073

B3073

Marsh Lane

Norfolk AV

Ln AV

Essex

Suffolk

Hampshire Gdns

Surrey

Cl

Huntingdon Gdns

Cambridge Gdns

Marsh Lane

AV

Avon Valley Path

stour

River Way

Way

Cross Way

The

Elm

Darwin Rd

Melboc

Road

Cannon

Arcadia

Rd

Ruffin

Fairmile   **59**

Walc

Flambard Avenue

Emily

Wildfell Close

AV

Villette

Haworth Cl

Works

Marsh La

Works

FAIRMILE R

15

A   B   **59**   C   D

1 grid square represents 500 metres

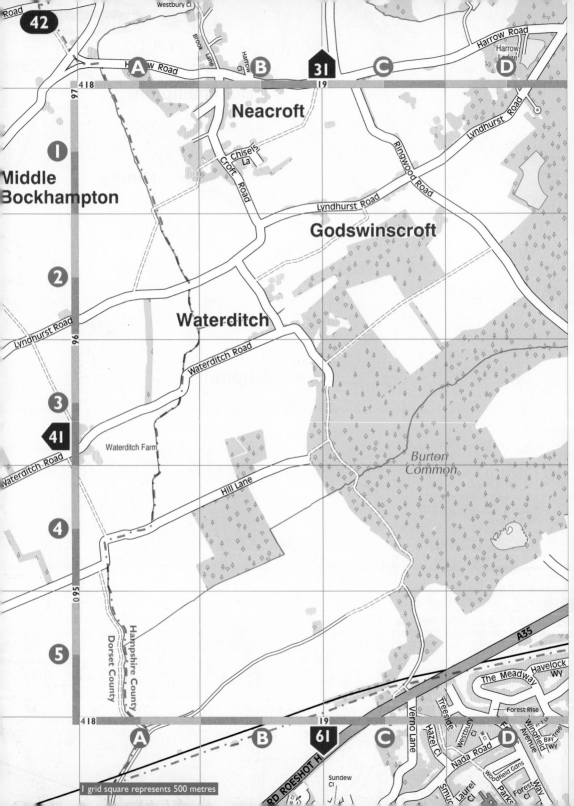

42

Westbury Cl

Harrow Road

A Harrow Road **B** **31** **C** **D**

418
97 19

Harrow Lodge

Neacroft

Brook Lane

Harrow Cl

Chisels La

1

Middle Bockhampton

Croft Road

Lyndhurst Road

Lyndhurst Road

Ringwood Road

Lyndhurst Road

Godswinscroft

2

Lyndhurst Road

96

Waterditch

Waterditch Road

3

41

Waterditch Farm

Burton Common

Waterditch Road

Hill Lane

4

095

5

A35

The Meadway

Havelock Wy

Forest Rise

Hampshire County

Dorset County

418
19

A **B** **61** **C** **D**

RD ROESHOT Hl

Verno Lane

Treeside

Hazel Cl

Westbury Cl

Nada Road

Wingfield Avenue

Bay Tree Wy

Laurel Cl

Woodfield Gdns

Parke

Forest Way

Sundew Cl

1 grid square represents 500 metres

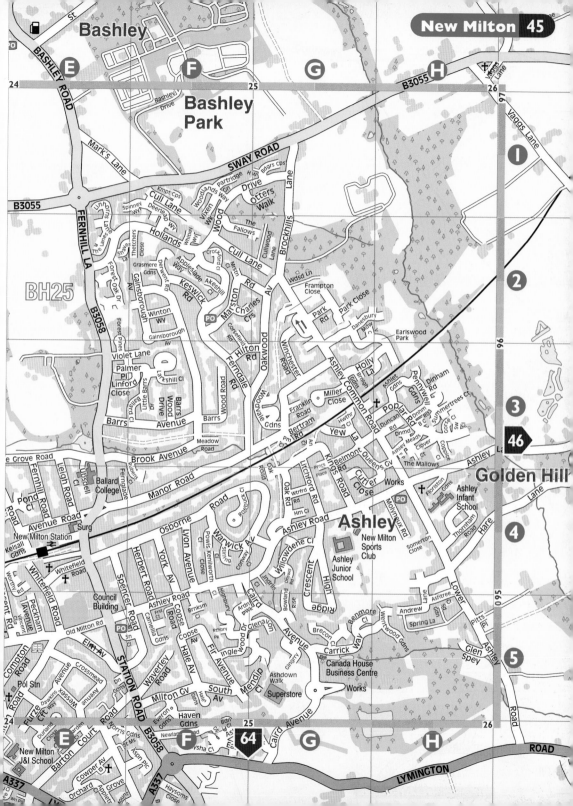

46

Northover Lane

ARNEWOOD   BRIDGE

A   B   C   Linnies   Lan   D

Barrows Lane

426   27   Agar's Lane

Little Arnewood House

I

Vaggs Lane

Arnewood Court

96

Hordle Grange

2

Vaggs Lane

Agar's Lane

Silver Street

Hordle Mews   Surgery

3   PO

Dinham Rd   Summertrees Ct   Laurel

Ashley La   Blenheim Crs   Holes Cl

45   Stoneleigh Av   Sycamore Rd   Everton Road   **Hordle**

Lane   Windsor   Elvin Cl   Stopples Lane   Acacia Rd   Lane   Sheldrake Gdns

Golden Hill   Firtree   Crs   Charnock   Cottagers   White Barn Crs   Woodcock Lane

Floriston Gdns   Pinewood Road   Stopples La   Yerville Gdns   Slade Cl   The Ostlr   Mallard Cl

Ashtree   Coppice   Lavender Rd   Heath Road   Cl   Yr Gdns   Woodlands   Heather Close   Everton Rd

4   Ashley Infant School   DaneCrest Rd   Dudley Av   Wisbech   Hordle CE Prim Sch

Thornham   Stopples Lane   Stanley St   Hordle Lane   Vcra Gdn   Longfield Road

090   Danes Stream   Ts Frm Bernfield   Fst Rd   Elizabeth Crs   Pegasus Av

5   Ashley   Vicarage Lane   St Mary Ld   Sylvan Ct   End La   Sky

426

A   B   **65**   C   D

ROAD

NGTON   Hordle Lane   Yeatton Ho

I grid square represents 500 metres

E   F   G   H

28   29   30   97

Mill Lane   Nor

Flexford Lane

Hazelhurst Farm

South Sway Lane

Works

Bowling Green

Hannah Way

Sway Road

Gordleton Industrial Park

Gordleton Industrial Estate

Gordleton Farm

Ramley Road

Ramley

Silver Street

Silver Street

Avon Water

I   Sway

2

96

3   Ramley Road   Northove

48

Hazel Road

Middle Common Rd   Common

Uppr Common Rd

4   Uppe   enning

Batchley Farm

Arnewood House

Wainsford House

Wainsford Road

5

095

Everton Road

Wainsford Road

Efford House

E   F   G   H

28   29   30

Greenm   66   Avenu

Buckstone Cl

Everlea   Cl   Centre Lane   East La

Everton

Manor Ho

Honeysuckle Gardens

Everton F   Frys Lane

Golden Crs   Beacon Cl   Firmou

Har   Cl   W La

Portmore

Hundred
Lane

E   F   G   H

32   33   MAIN   ROAD   34   97

B3054   MAIN   ROAD

I

Snooks Lane

Southlands
School

Vicars
Hill

Ampress
La →

La →

Works

Undershore

Hordle
Walhampton
School

MARSH   LANE   B3054

hill Dr

Marran

Sparrina Dr

Cl   Campion

Fd Cl   Sn

Colborne

Pl   Cl

Jonathan
Close

Wilm Rd

**Lower
Buckland**

WALHAMPTON HL

Clinton Road

Works

E'lery Gv

Tithe Barn

Broomfield
Road

Private

Fairlea

Brickfield
La

S041

Snooks Farm

2

96

Walhampton

Monument
Lane

3

South Baddesley Road

Shrubb's
Av

Lymington
Community
Hospitals

EAST HILL

North Close

Works

LC

BRIDGE RD

Waterford Rd

Lymington
Town Station

Solent
Way

Hillcroft

Ae

Brunswick

Cannon

Riverside
Bus Park

St

Station St

Works

Undershore

Solent   Way

Lisle

UE RD   Rd

Town Hall

NEW ST

AVENUE

Barfields

Gosport St

Mil La

Road

Lymington
Pier Station

Court

4

095

Macdonald
Elmers Court
Hotel

Eh Rd

School La

Anchor

Ms

Community
Cen Cinema

M

Z

Captain's Rw

Quay

St

Ferry
Terminal

St Thomas
Clinic Surg

St Barbe
Mus

High St

Stanwell
House
Hotel

Nelson's
Pl

W Hayes

Thomas's
St   Ch

PO

GV

Pastures

Grove Road

South GV

Fishrds

Qu Katherine Road

Solent
Way

Solent
Pl

Wm Pl
R'witt

LYMINGTON

Belmore

Fairfield
Cl

Webb Peploe
House Surg

Grove Pl

Lane

Waterford
Cl

Solent
Close

Works

Solent Av

Bath   Road

Springfield
Cl

Mayflower
Cl

Spring
Rd

YARMOUTH

5

Courtenay Pl

Daniell's
Cl

Bingham
Dr

Broad

Ambleside Rd

Pyrford MS

Victoria

Vitre Gdns

Daniell's
Walk

Lane

Old
Orchards

Burrard
Grove

Waterford Lane

Westfield Road

Spring Road

Kings
Rd

Kings Saltern Road

PH

Lane

Farnley

Lockerley Cl

Newenham
Rd

Vitre Gdns

By Cl

Prtt

Tranmere
Close

Cnfrnc
Pl

Brckns Wy

Stanley

Normandy

Solent   Way

All Saints Road

Mead
Chrch

We
Cl

Woodside
Av

Waterford

2

Woodside Lane

Viney Road

33   Lane   34

E   F   G   H

Woodside

Upton Heath

E   F   **32**   G   H

98   99   **I**

Spinde...
Sorrel Cl
Sorrel Gdns
...Dr
Gdns

Sundew Rd
Dogwood
Cl
Cdns
...Rd

Charlfinch Cl
Broadstone Way
Witchampt...
Rd
Keighley Av
Cannon Cl

Renault Dr
York Road
Whitby Av
Meldr Cl
Whitby Cl
Skipton Cl

Trailway

Cowslip Rd

Bullfinch Close
Hawthorn Dr

Snapdr...
Primrose Gdns

Rowan Dr
Spruce Close
Sycamore Cl

Creekmoor Lane
Rdshnk
Close
Clover Dr

Works

Wa

Larch
Beechbank
Avenue
Honeysuckle La
Hycnth
Bluebell Lane

Broadstone

94

Dorset County

Poole

Longmeadow Lane
Meadowsweet
Blackbird Cl
Goldfinch Rd
Linnet Rd
Swallow Cl
Swift

Pinetree Wk

Priors Rd

Balena

Creekm

Castleman Trailway
Castleman

A35

Meadows Close

Heights Road
Douglas
...Cl
Lwin
Hibbs
Cl
Ballam
Cl

Meadows
Dr
Dacombe
Drive

Gorse La
Palmerston Road
Upton Heath Estate
Dvnprt
strp Cl

Woodpecker Drive
Grebe Cl
Nightjar Cl

Northmead Drive

Woodpecker Drive
Pinetree Wk

Birchwood
Medical Cen
Martin
Close
Nuthatch
Close

Petersham Rd
Rdshnk

PO
Benmoor Rd
Petersham Road

Millstream

Creekmo...

2

Upton
Health Centre
Meadows
Heights
Upton
Court
Heights
DaC...
Prstn

Plmrstn
Close
Bridle
Porry Dr
Martingale Cl

Poole
Road

PO
The
Crossways

Old Kiln Road
Ropers La

Factory
Road

Ventura Pl

A350   UPTON ROAD   A35

93

3

52

A350

Millfield

Gwenlyn
Rd
Greenacre Cl
Yrls
Cl
Pine Vw
Cl
Sandy
Lane
Shore
Cl
Shore
La
Border Dr

BLANDFORD ROAD

Peters
Close

Allens
Oak
Rd
Brdr
Rd
Bld

B3068

Border
Road

Willow
Close

Factory
Road

Allens
Road
Allens
Road

Ind
Est

Allens Lane

Upton House

Upton
Country Park

Pergins
Island

4

5

092

98

99   400

Turlin Moor
Middle
School

E
Turlin Moor
Community
First School

Keysworth
Road

Turlin Road

Rice
Gardens

F   **69**

Symes Rd
Symes
Road

Symes
Rd

G

Hewitt Rd
Hewitt
Dr
Falconer
Dr

H

Hamworthy
Station

Galloway Rd
Carters
Rd

PO
Shipst...
...
Cl

Middlebere
Crs
Maryland
Rd

Avenue
Road

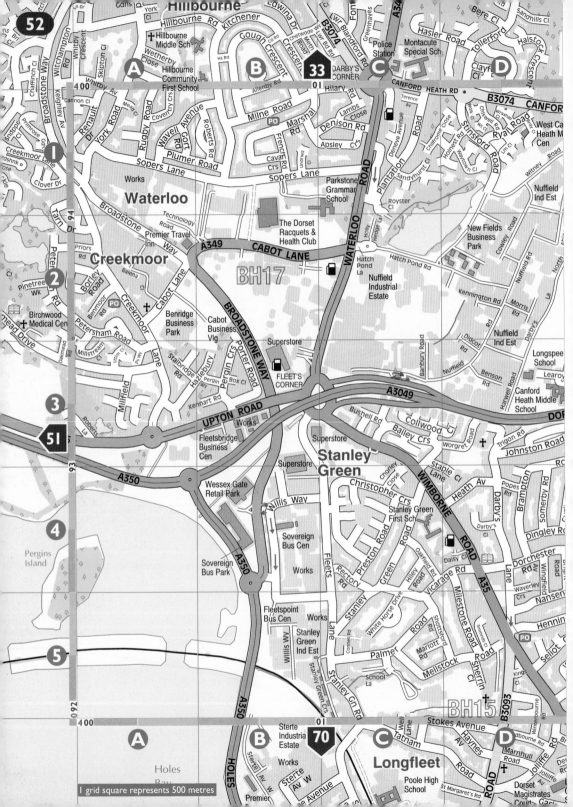

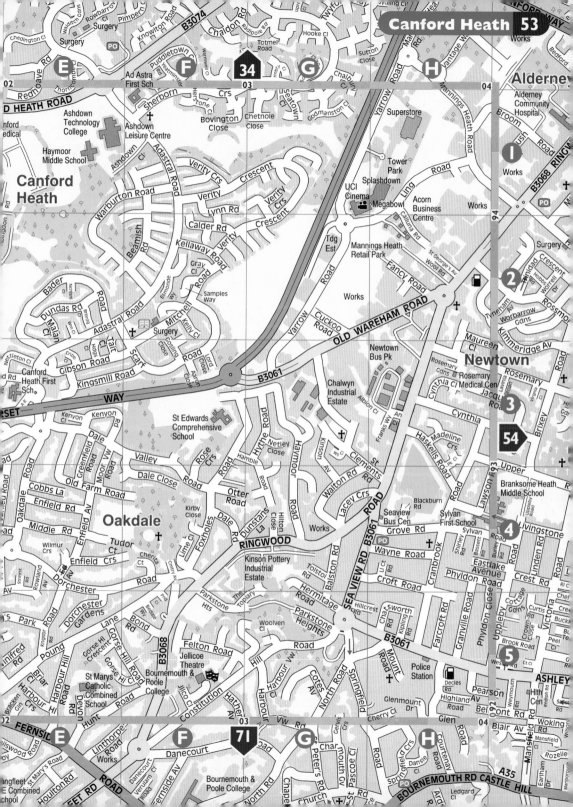

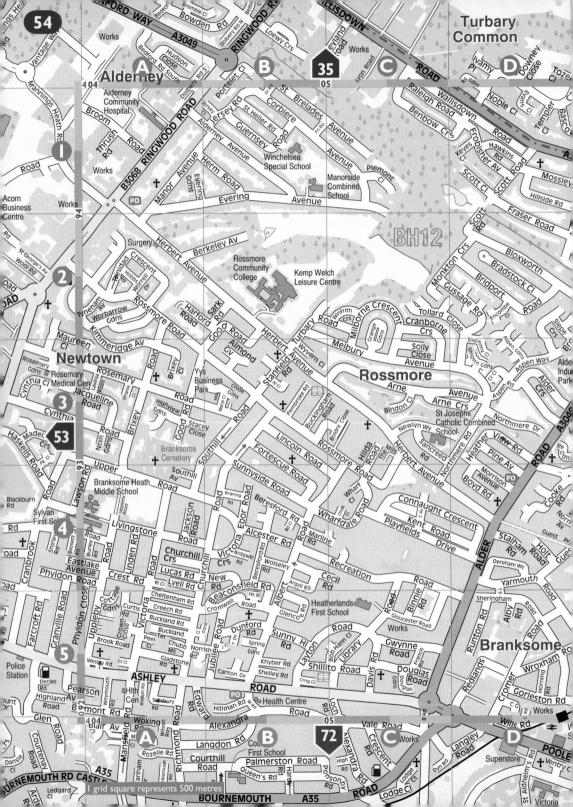

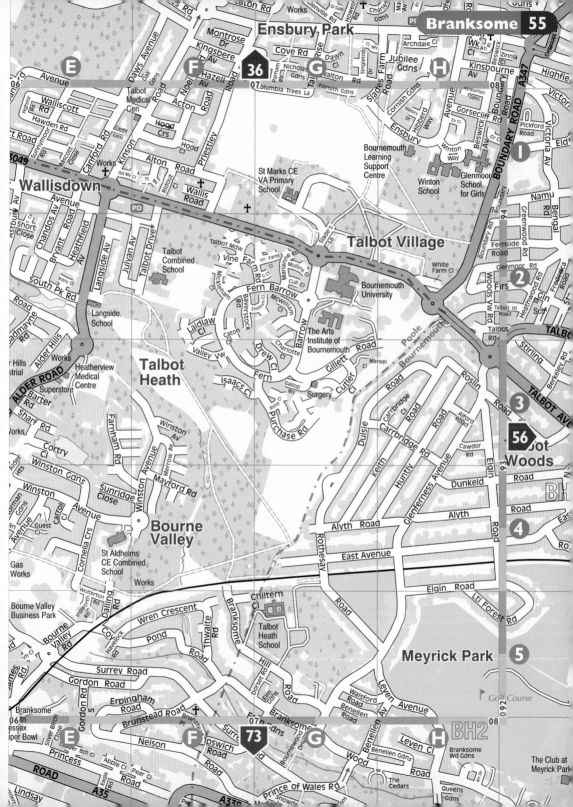

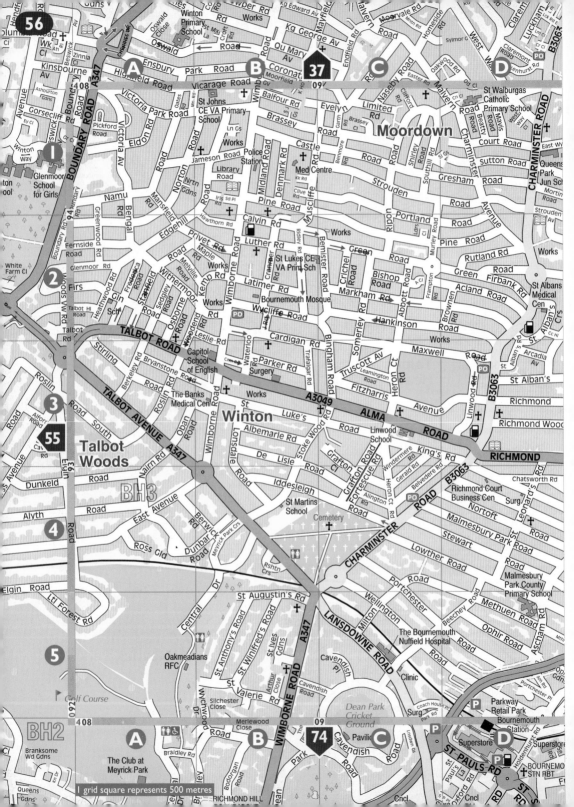

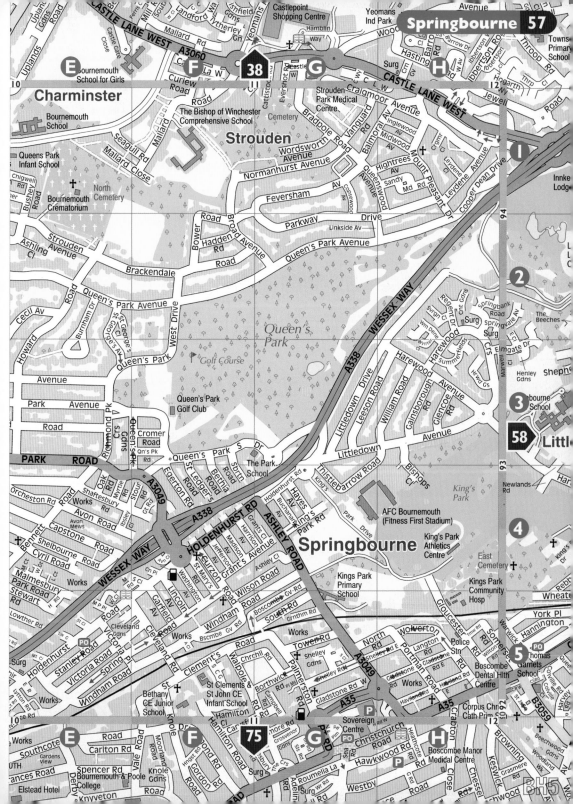

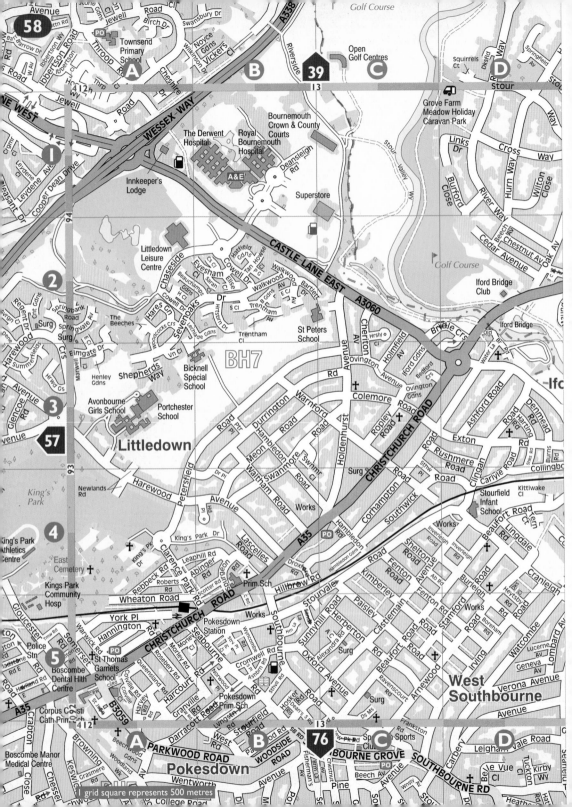

I grid square represents 500 metres

A35

Station

Dorset County

Hampshire Co.

E **F** **42** **G** **H**

18 19 20

The Meadway

Havelock Wy

Clive

Forest Rise

Fr T Le

Woodhayes Av

Buckland Grove

Langfield

Bay Tree Wy

Rossley Cl

Ashmore Gv

Terringten Av

Marston Grove

Birchwel Close

I

Roeshot Crs

94

Moonrakers Wy

Forest

LYNDHURST RD ROESHOT HILL

Garden Centre

Sundew Cl

Treeside

Verno Lane

Hazel Cl

Nada Road

Westbury

Woodfield Gdns

Forest Avenue

Wingfield Wy

Parkside

Forest Field Wy

Smugglers North

Ashmore

A35

Superstore

Westfield Gdns

Buttercup Cl

Snowdrop Gdns

Clover Ct

Drive

Cornflower Dr

Primrose Dr

Poppy La

Thstl Cl

Hoburne Gdns

Hoburne Lane

Smugglers Wd Rd

Laurel Cl

Highcliffe School

Ridgefield Gdns

S LN

Nea Cl

H Cl

Close

2

Smugglers La

St Josephs Primary School

Sorrell Wy

Saffron Cl

Yarrow Cl

Blue bell Cl

Vetch Cl

Mallow Cl

Manning Av

Balfour Cl

S Pl

Lane

Rowan Cl

North

Coose Cl

Pine Crs

Nea Cl

Premier Travel Inn

Somerford Av

Saffron

Celandine Cl

Hoburne Lane

Smugglers

PO

Saulfland Dr

Rowan Dr

Prstn Wy

Cornford Cl

Curzon Way

St Crgs

Woodland Wy

Woodland Way

Lymingt

Edward Rd

Surg

HIGHCLIFFE ROAD

Grange Road Business Centre

Grange Rd

Works

Barnfield

B3059

A337

Shelley Cl

LYMINGTON RD

SHELLEY HL

A337

Highcliffe Castle Golf Club

3

Sea Vixen Industrial Est

Alexander

Wessex

Wellington

Dunedin Av

Highcliffe Castle

Industrial Estate

Delta Cl

Priory Ind Pk

Airspeed Rd

Halifax Wy

Hunter

Wesley

Lancaster Cl

East Cliff Wy

Priors

93

Golf Course

62

Hughes Bus Cen

Pipers Dr

Vallant Cl

Austie Cl

Viscount Dr

Donnington

Bure Lane

Brook

Hynesbury Road

Seafield Road

Seaway

Avenue

Freshwater Rd

Somerford Bus Park

Brabazon Dr

Comet Wy

Blenheim

Stirling Cl

Tangmere Cl

Friars Cliff

Beaver Ind Est

Catalina Cl

Way

PO

Bure Pk

Southcliffe Road

Vecta Cl

Glengarry

Medina Wy

Seaway Av

Ambassador Ind Est

Kestrel Cl

Mallard Cl

Bure Homage Lane

Best-Western Waterford Lodge Hotel

Bure Rd

Cliff Dr

4

Curlew Rd

Havilland

Ricardo Crs

Mortimer Cl

Bure

Friars Road

Rook Hill Rd

Charlotte Cl

Hvn

Drive

Bure

Peregrine Rd

Sheldrake Road

Island View Av

Avon Run Rd

Run

Road

5

Mudeford

Merlin Way

Falcon Dr

D Cl

Bure Lane

Avon Run

Wren Cl

Raven Way

Osprey

Mude Gdns

Highcliffe Medical Centre

Robins Cl

Kingfisher Wy

Farm La

Fulmar Rd

Mudeford

Capesthorne

The Avonmouth Hotel

092

Viking Way

18 19 20

E **F** **79** **G** **H**

P

Chichester Way

Holly
Lane

Wick 2 Ind
Est

Williams
Ind Park

Wick Dr

Bus
Cen

Gore Road

Gore Road
Industrial
Est

E 22

F

44
23

G

New Milton
Recreation
Centre

H

The
Arnewood
School

Hurst Cl

Walkford

Road

Avenue

Seaview
Rd

Chewton
Farm

Road

I

Pol Stn

Milton Rd

Culver
Rd

Well Cl

Cemetery

Works

Old Milton

Furze Cft

New Milton
J&I School

Dorset County
Hampshire County

Golf Course

Moore

Th Pdn

**OLD
MILTON**

**OLD
MILTON GN**

Southlawns
Walk

Southern

Albany

Surg

A337

Chewton
Glen Hotel

Studley
Close

The Dell

Loraine

Abingdon Drive

Glendrive

Glendrive

Field Pl

The Crescent

Bartonside Rd

CHRISTCHURCH ROAD

Christchurch Rd

Chrst
Road

Hurst

Glen
Cl

East
Cl

Silwd
Way

Studley
Court

Burley

Sopley
Rd

Neacroft

Field Pl

Hengistbury Road

Western

Barton Lane

Byron
Road

Knighton
Park

Sea Road

Pine
Cl

Chilern Drive

Parkland
Drive

Heathwood
Av

Eldon
Av

Eldon
Cl

Three Acre Dr

Wavendon Avenue

Moorland Av

Lawn
Close

Heathy
Close

Barton Way

Barton
Dr

Barton
Court

Dilly

Highlands

Frlars
Walk

Chestnut

Farm Lane

Brtn
Ct Av

2

The Park

Pinecliffe
Road

East Av

Seaview Rd

Southcliffe Rd

Island Vw Rd

**Island View
Road**

The Crescent

Carlton
Av

Vectis Road

Naish Road

Avenue

Purbeck Rd

Cleveland
Cl

Powerscourt
Rd

Marine

Drive

West

Cliffe
Rd

Seacroft Av

Seafield Road

Fairfield Road

PO

Seaward
Rd

Woodlands
Rd

Arnolds
Close

Keysworth

Barton

Seafield
Close

Barton
Rd

Beach Avenue

Marine
Prospect

Avenue

Surg

Brckishm
Pl

Blythswd

Lynric Cl

Wht
Knight
Cl

Mitchell
Cl

3

64

Christchurch Bay

Marine Drive

Sandmartn

Cliff Cts

Crescent
Dr

First
Marine
Av

Marine

93 Av

Barton-on-Sea

4

5

092

E 22

F
23

G

H
24

Christchurch

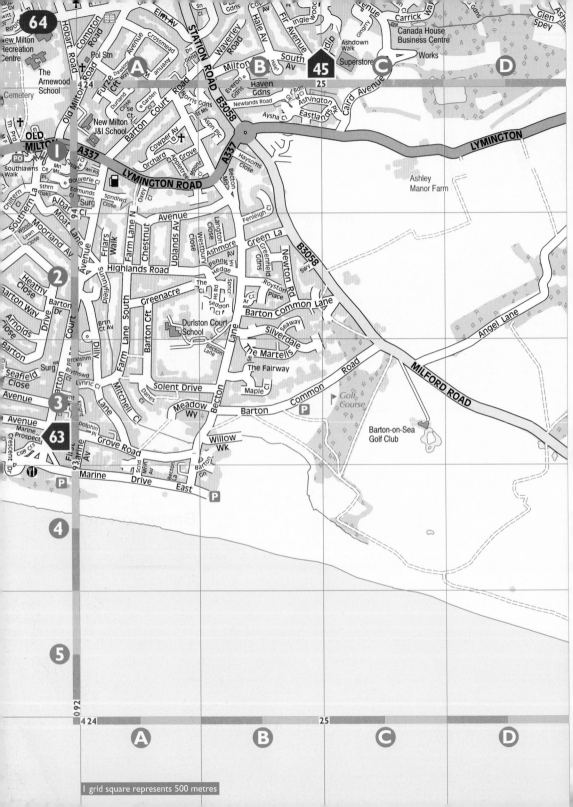

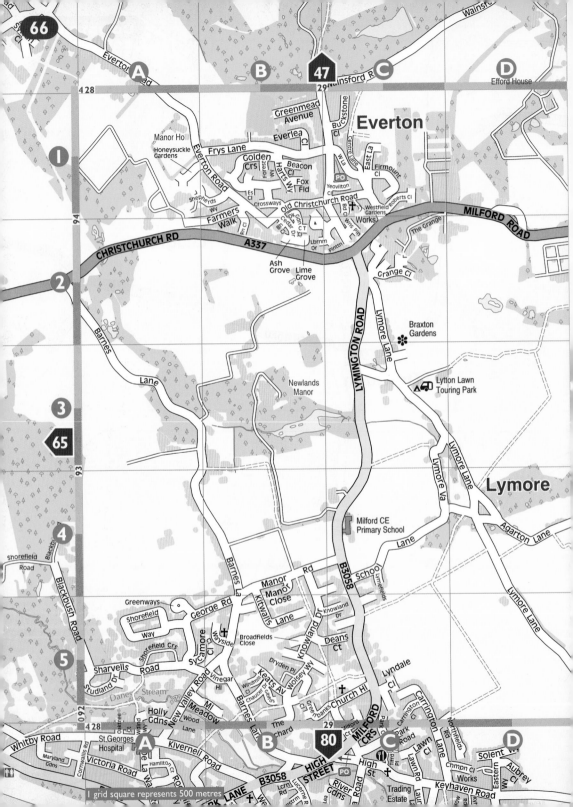

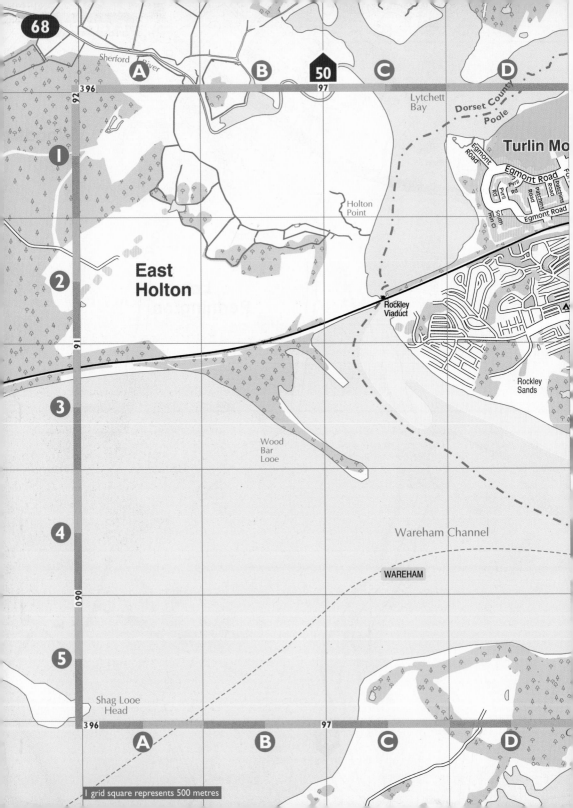

Sherford River

A   B   **50**   C   D

396   97

Lytchett
Bay

Dorset County
Poole

Turlin Mo

Egmont
Road

Egmont Road

Pvrll
Rd

Patchins Road

Road

Egmont Road

South
Rtin Cl

1

92

Holton
Point

East
Holton

2

91

Rockley
Viaduct

3

Rockley
Sands

Wood
Bar
Looe

4

Wareham Channel

WAREHAM

090

5

Shag Looe
Head

396   97

A   B   C   D

I grid square represents 500 metres

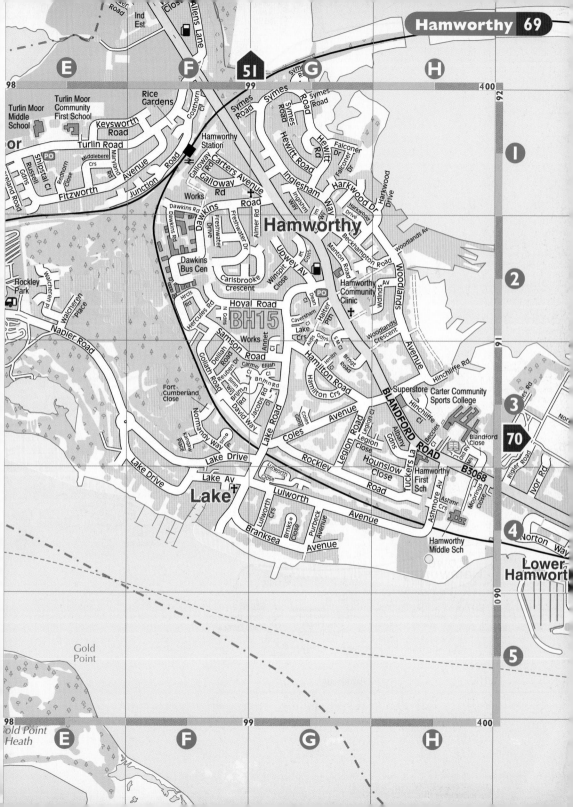

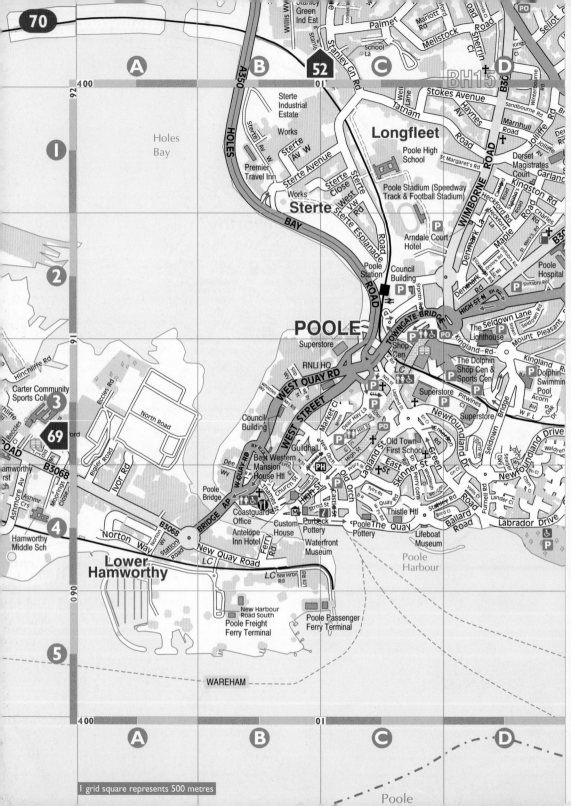

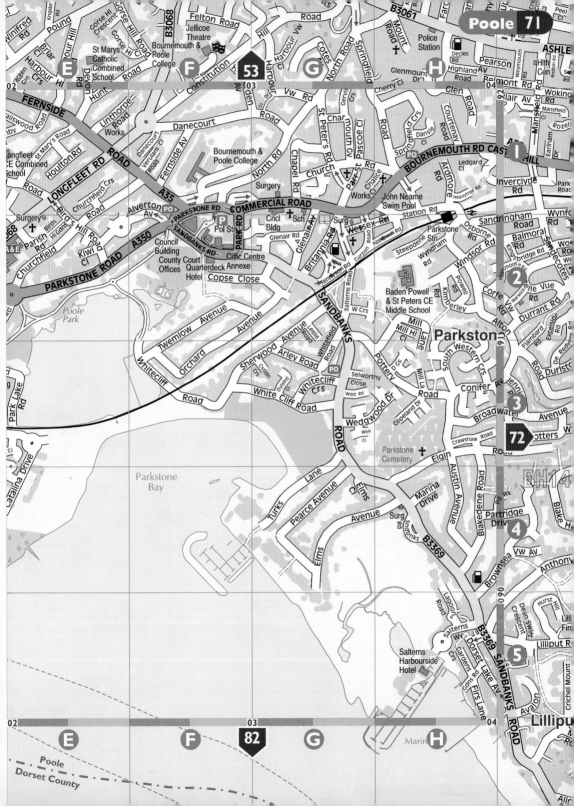

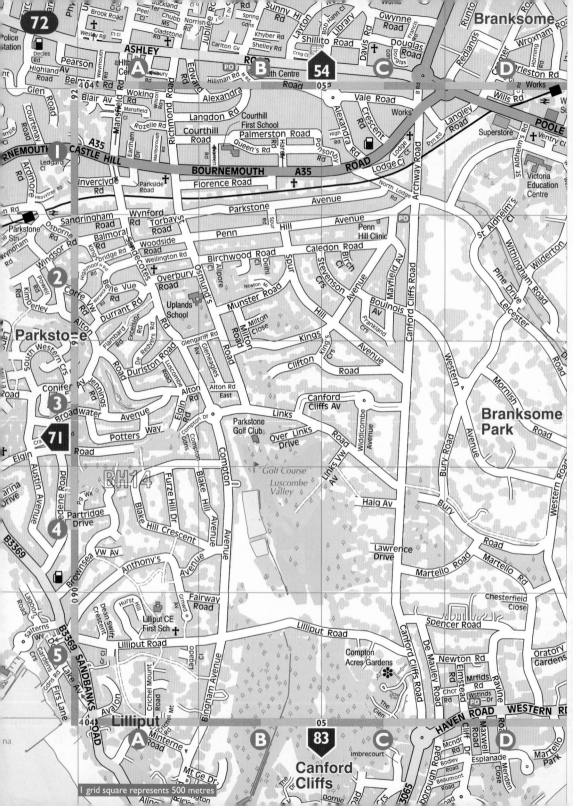

Christchurch

CHRISTCHURCH

E

Wessex
Complementary
Medical Cen

F

PO

Tuckton
Road

59

Wick Lane

G

H

Wick

I

Stour Valley Way

St Katharines
CE VA Prim Sch

Solent Meads
Golf Centre

Southbourne

VUE

BH6

St Peters
School

Church

St Catherine's Road

Southbourne

Coast

New
Horizons
College

Southbourne Coast Road

Golf Course

2

Broadway

3

78

4

5

E   **F**   **G**   **H**

78

A River Stour **B** **60** Stanpit Marsh **C** Chermin's Bank **D**

416 92 17

Wick

Wick La

Wicklea Rd

1

St Katharines
CE VA Prim Sch

Solent Meads
Golf Centre

Stour Valley Way

Rolls Drive

2

Golf Course

Broadway

3

77

Stour Valley Way

4

090

5

416 17

A **B** **C** **D**

Christchurch
Harbour

Dorset County
Bournemouth

Hengistbury
Head

Mudeford

Mudeford

Ledbury Rd

Argyle Rd

Fisherman's
Bank

Warren Av

Pinehurst
Av

Cricket Cl

Coastguard
Way

Rushford
Warren

Waterside

I grid square represents 500 metres

E
F
Capestho 61
G
H

The
Avonmouth
Hotel

Mudeford

Highcliffe
Medical
Centre

Raven Way
Falcon
Wren Cl
Bure L
Avon
Fulmar
Avon
Robins
Osprey

Farm La
Muse Cdrg

Viking Way

P

Chichester

Stour Valley Way

19
20

92

I

91

2

3

90

4

5

18
19
20

E
F
G
H

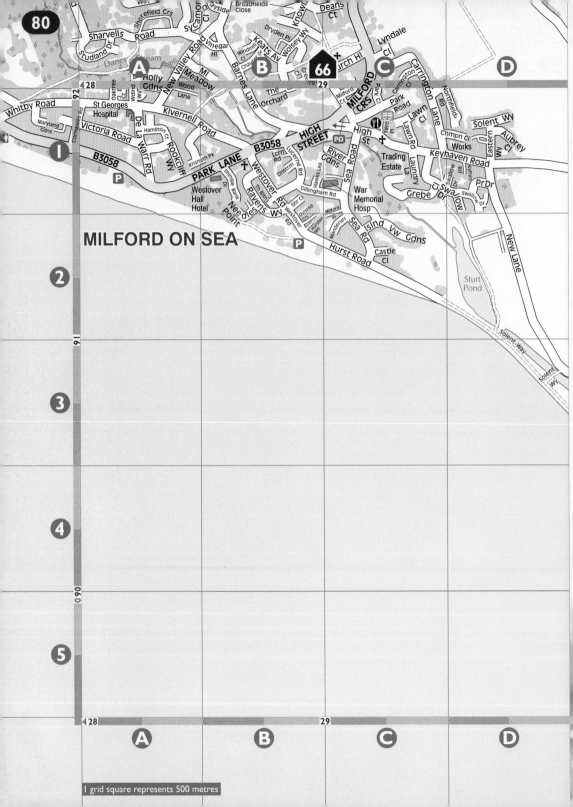

MILFORD ON SEA

80

Sharvells Road
Studland Dr
Shorefield Crs
Sycamore
Clayside
Broadfields Close
Knowle
Deans Ct
Dryden Pl
Windmill Cl
Keats Av
Wolsey Wy
Lyndale

A Holly Gdns
New Valley Road
Wood Lane
Barnes Lane
The Orchard
Chaveney Cl
Green
B
66 29
Church Hl
Milford
C
Carrington Lane
Northfields
D

428
92
Whitby Road
Cornwallis Rd
St Georges Hospital
Oaktree Cl
Upland
De La Warr Rd
Kiverneli Road
Maryland Gdns
Victoria Road
Hamilton Ct
Rookcliff Wy
Knington Pk
MILFORD CRS
Park Road
Lawn Cl
Lawn Rd
Solent Wy
Chmpn Cl
Works
Aubrey Cl
Eastern Wy
Keyhaven Road

1 B3058
PARK LANE
Shingle Bank Dr
Westover Rd
Lcrn Rd
Lucerne Rd
Dnstrm
B3058
River Gdns
Sea Road
High St
HIGH STREET
Trading Estate
Laundry La
Grebe Dr
Swallow
Pr Dr

Westover Hall Hotel
Needles Point
Ravens Wy
Shr Cl
Gillingham Rd
Lovrtnd Gdns
Manderley Pl
Milford
Hawks Lea
War Memorial Hosp
Isina Vw Gdns

MILFORD ON SEA

2 16
Hurst Road
Castle Cl
Sea Rd
Sturt Pond
New Lane
Solent Way
Solent Wy

3

4 0.90

5

428
29
A
B
C
D

1 grid square represents 500 metres

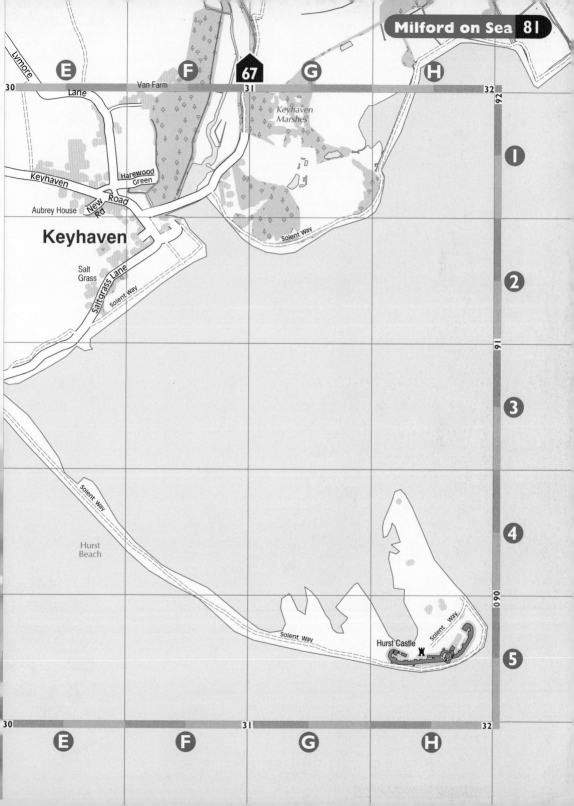

E F 67 G H

30 Van Farm 31 32 92

Lymore

Lane

Keyhaven
Marshes

I

Keyhaven Harewood
Green

Aubrey House New Rd Road

Keyhaven

Salt
Grass Saltgrass Lane Solent Way

Solent Way 2

91

3

Solent Way

4

Hurst
Beach 090

Solent Way

Hurst Castle ✕ 5

Solent Way

30 31 32

E F G H

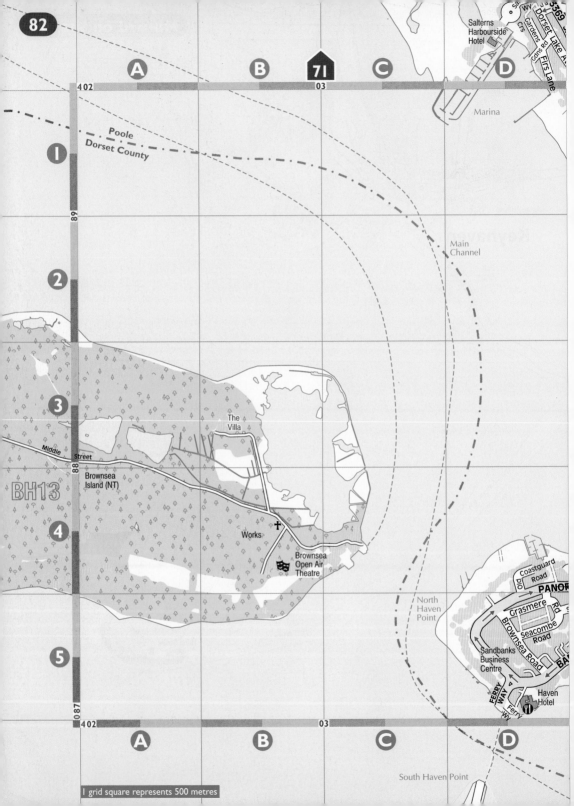

Salterns
Harbourside
Hotel

Dorset Lake Av.
Firs Lane
3369
WV
Gardens Rd
Cons Rd
Crs

(A)   (B)   (71)   (C)   (D)

402   03

Marina

Poole
Dorset County

1

89

Main
Channel

2

3

The
Villa

Middle   Street

88

Brownsea
Island (NT)

BH13

4

Works †

Brownsea
Open Air
Theatre

North
Haven
Point

Coastguard
Road

PANOR
Grasmere   Rd
Brownsea Road
Seacombe
Road
BA

Sandbanks
Business
Centre

FERRY WAY
Ferry
Haven
Hotel
WV

5

087

402   03

(A)   (B)   (C)   (D)

South Haven Point

1 grid square represents 500 metres

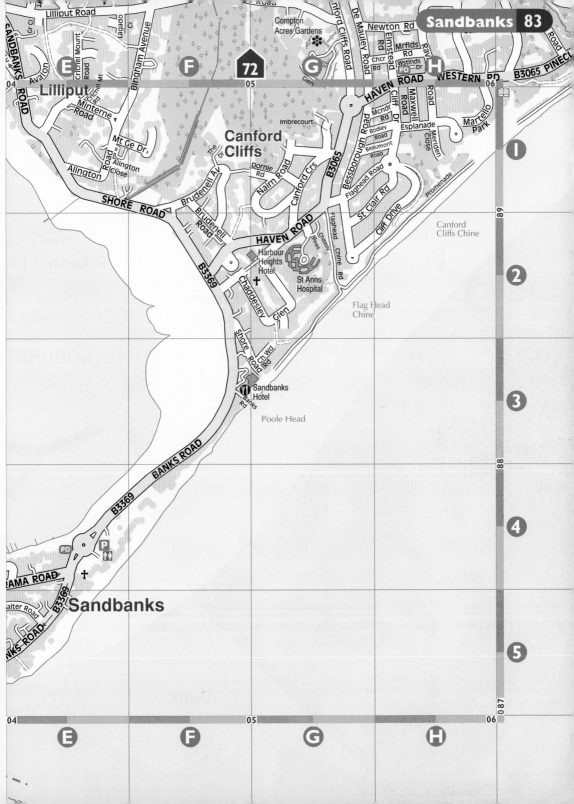

Lilliput Road

Lagado Cl

Grc Cl

SANDBANKS ROAD

Cricket Mount Road

Cricket Mt

Avalon

E

Lilliput

Bingham Avenue

Minterne Road

Mt Ge Dr

The Dr

Alington Close

Alington

Road

Alington

SHORE ROAD

B3369

Chaddesley

Shore Road

Ch Wd Rd

Glen

Banks Rd

Sandbanks Hotel

Poole Head

BANKS ROAD

B3369

PO

P

RAMA ROAD

B3369

Salter Road

KS ROAD

Sandbanks

F

Compton Acres/Gardens

72
05

Canford Cliffs

Imbrecourt

Brudenell Av

Dornie Rd

Nairn Road

Canford Crs

Brudenell Road

HAVEN ROAD

Harbour Heights Hotel

St Anns Hospital

Glen

Chadsly Pines

Flag Head Chine

G

mford Cliffs Road

De Mauley Road

Glen

Besborough Road

B3065

Flaghead Road

Flaghead Chine Rd

Chadsly Pines

St Clair Rd

Cliff Drive

Promenade

HAVEN ROAD

H

Newton Rd

Elmstead Rd

Mrflds Rd

Chcr Rd

PO

Wstnds Dr

WESTERN RD

Rav

Road

B3065 PINECl

Maxwell Road

Mcndr Rd

Bodley Road

Beaumont Road

Esplanade

Meriden Close

Martello Park

Canford Cliffs Chine

89

1

2

3

88

4

5

087

04

E

05

F

G

06

H

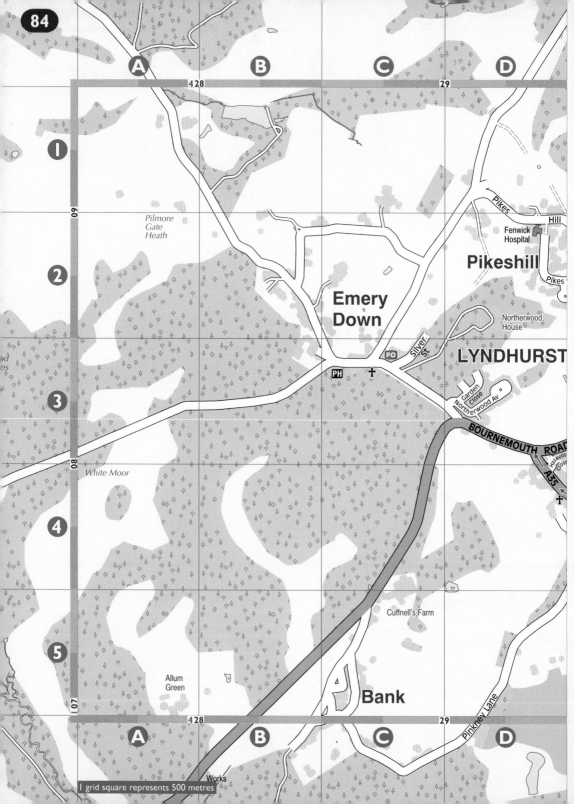

A B C D

4 28 29

I

60

Pilmore
Gate
Heath

2

Pikeshill

Fenwick
Hospital

Pikes
Hill

Pikes

**Emery
Down**

Northerwood
House

PO

Silver
St.

LYNDHURST

PH

✝

Garden
Close

Northerwood Av.

3

80

BOURNEMOUTH ROAD

Haskells
Close

A35

✝

White Moor

4

5

Cuffnell's Farm

Allum
Green

Bank

Pinkney Lane

1 07

A B C D

4 28 29

Works

1 grid square represents 500 metres

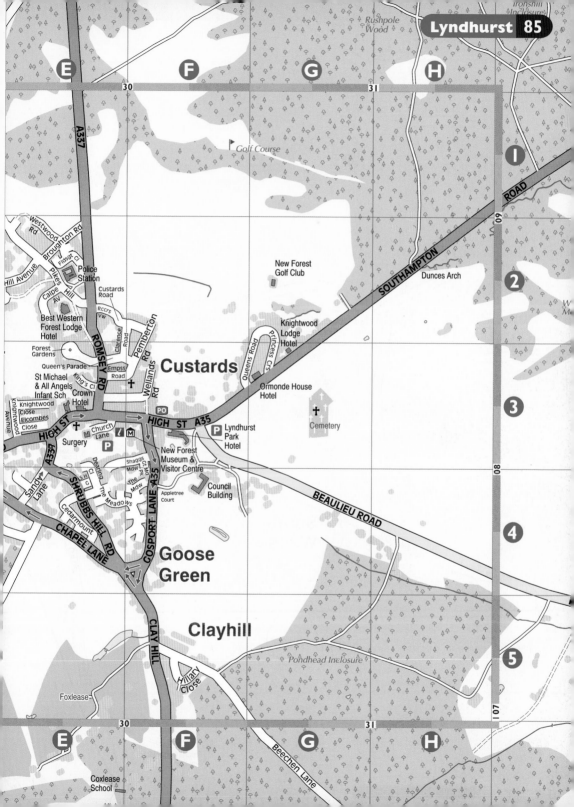

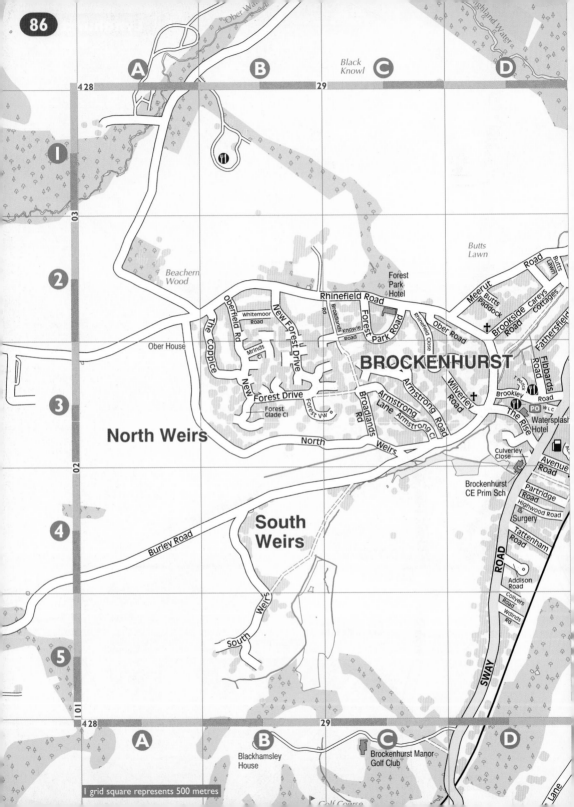

Ober Water

A   B   Black   C   D
Knowl

428   29

1

03

Beachern
Wood

2   Butts
Lawn

Forest
Park
Hotel   Meerut   Butts   Careys
Butts   Cottages
Paddock   Brookside
Road   Road

Rhinefield Road   Fathersfield

Oberfield Rd   Whitemoor   Ober House   Broadlands   Forest Park Road   Ober Road   Fibbards
Road   Rd   Knowle   Road   Rhinefield Close   Road   Brookley
The Coppice   Mrinds   Road   BROCKENHURST   Road
Cl   T Pitch   Brookley
New Forest Drive   Road   WLC   Waterplash
Forest Glade Cl   New Forest Drive   Forest VW   Broadlands Rd   Armstrong   Armstrong Road   Wilverley Road   PO   The Rise   Hotel
Lane   Armstrong Cl
Culverley
North Weirs   North   Weirs   Close

Brockenhurst   Avenue
CE Prim Sch   Road

Partridge
Road
Highwood Road
&
Surgery
South   Tattenham
Weirs   Road
Burley Road   Addison
Road
Collyers
Road
Walnds
South   Weirs   Rd
Weirs   SWAY   ROAD

5

101

428   29

A   B   C   D
Blackhamsley   Brockenhurst Manor
House   Golf Club   Lane

Golf Course

1 grid square represents 500 metres

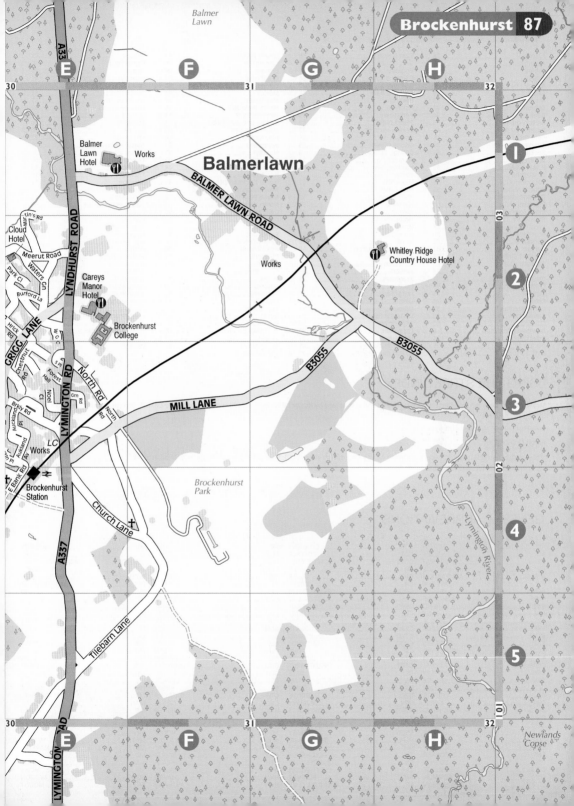

Balmer
Lawn

E   F   G   H

30   31   32

Balmer
Lawn
Hotel   Works

Balmerlawn

BALMER LAWN ROAD

Cloud
Hotel
Martin's Rd
Meerut Road
Waters Gn
Park Cl
Burford La

Works

Whitley Ridge
Country House Hotel

Careys
Manor
Hotel

Brockenhurst
College

GRIGG LANE

Chestnut

W C C

Forest
Hall

Noel
Cl

Grn
Rd

LYMINGTON RD

North Rd

North
Rd

S Pl

MILL LANE

B3055

B3055

Auckland
Pl

Aukland
Av

LC

Works

Brockenhurst
Station

A337

Church Lane

Brockenhurst
Park

Lymington River

E Bank Rd

Tilebarn Lane

LYMINGTON ROAD

Lymington River

Newlands
Copse

E   F   G   H

30   31   32

03

02

01

1

2

3

4

5

A33

LYNDHURST ROAD

Alderney 35 E5	East Howe 36 C4	Lower Pennington 67 G2	Shirley 31 E2
Ashington 22 A3	East Parley 27 G4	Lymington 49 E4	Somerford 60 C3
Ashley 12 D1	Ebblake 5 H3	Lymore 66 D4	Sopley 29 H5
Ashley 45 G4	Emery Down 84 C2	Lyndhurst 84 D3	South Bockhampton 41 F3
Ashley Heath 7 E5	Ensbury 37 E1	Lytchett Minster 50 A4	Southbourne 77 E2
Avon 29 F2	Ensbury Park 36 C5	Merley 23 E3	South Weirs 86 B4
Avon Castle 13 E4	Everton 66 C1	Merritown 27 G5	Springbourne 57 G4
Balmerlawn 87 F1	Fairmile 59 F1	Merry Field Hill 15 E1	Stanley Green 52 B3
Bank 84 C5	Ferndown 17 F4	Meyrick Park 55 H5	Stanpit 60 C4
Barton-on-Sea 63 H4	Friars Cliff 61 G4	Middle Bockhampton ...41 H1	Stapehill 16 C4
Bashley Park 45 F1	Godswinscroft 42 B2	Milford on Sea 80 A2	Sterte 70 B1
Bear Cross 35 H1	Golden Hill 45 H4	Moordown 56 C1	Strouden 57 F1
Bearwood 35 H1	Goose Green 85 F4	Mudeford 61 E5	Talbot Heath 55 F3
Beckley 44 A2	Grange Estate 19 H1	Muscliff 37 H2	Talbot Village 55 G2
Bisterne 21 F3	Hampreston 24 C2	Neacroft 42 B1	Talbot Woods 56 A3
Blackwater 39 F2	Hamworthy 69 G2	New Milton 44 C3	Throop 38 B3
Boscombe 75 G2	Hangersley 9 G1	Newtown 53 H3	Trickett's Cross 18 C2
Bournemouth 3 J4	Highcliffe 62 C2	North Bockhampton 30 C5	Tuckton 59 F5
Bourne Valley 55 F4	Hightown 9 F4	Northbourne 36 D3	Turbary Common 35 H5
Bowling Green 47 G1	Hillbourne 33 E5	North Poulner 9 F1	Turlin Moor 68 D1
Branksome 54 D5	Hill View 32 B3	North Weirs 86 A3	Upper Pennington 48 A4
Branksome Park 72 D3	Hinton 43 G3	Oakdale 53 E4	Upton 50 D3
Bransgore 31 F4	Holdenhurst 39 E4	Oakley 22 D3	Verwood 4 D3
Broadstone 33 F3	Hordle 46 C3	Old Milton 63 G1	Walhampton 49 G3
Brockenhurst 86 C3	Hurn 28 B5	Parkstone 71 H2	Walkford 62 D1
Buckland 48 C2	Iford 58 D3	Parley Green 38 A1	Wallisdown 55 E1
Burton 41 F5	Jumpers Common 59 E2	Pennington 48 C5	Waterditch 42 A2
Canford Cliffs 83 F1	Keyhaven 81 E2	Pikeshill 84 D2	Waterford 49 G5
Canford Heath 53 E1	Kingston 13 G5	Pilford 15 G1	Waterloo 52 A1
Canford Magna 23 G3	Kinson 36 B2	Pokesdown 76 A1	Westbourne 2 A5
Charminster 57 E1	Knighton 24 B5	Poole 70 B2	West Cliff 2 D6
Christchurch 59 H5	Lake 69 F4	Poulner 9 F3	West Howe 35 G3
Clayhill 85 F5	Leagreen 65 G2	Purewell 60 A3	West Hurn 38 D1
Colehill 15 F2	Leigh 15 F5	Red Hill 37 F3	West Moors 10 D4
Corfe Mullen 32 A1	Lilliput 83 E1	Ringwood 8 A3	West Parley 26 A4
Creekmoor 52 A2	Little Canford 16 A5	Ripley 30 A2	West Southbourne 58 D5
Custards 85 F3	Littledown 58 A3	Rossmore 54 C3	Wick 77 H1
Dewlands Common 4 B3	Longfleet 70 C1	St Catherine's Hill 40 A4	Wimborne Minster 14 C4
Downton 65 F3	Longham 25 F3	St Ives 12 B1	Winkton 41 E2
Dudsbury 25 G3	Lower Buckland 49 E2	St Leonards 12 A1	Winton 56 B3
East Holton 68 A2	Lower Hamworthy 70 A4	Sandbanks 83 E5	

USING THE STREET INDEX

Street names are listed alphabetically. Each street name is followed by its postal town or area locality, the Postcode District, the page number, and the reference to the square in which the name is found.

Standard index entries are shown as follows:

Aaron Cl *CFDH* BH17 ....**53** F3

Street names and selected addresses not shown on the map due to scale restrictions are shown in the index with an asterisk:

Admirals Wk *WCLF* BH2 * **2** D6

GENERAL ABBREVIATIONS

ACC ....ACCESS	CON ....CONVENT	FK ....FORK	IMP ....IMPERIAL
ALY ....ALLEY	COT ....COTTAGE	FLD ....FIELD	IN ....INLET
AP ....APPROACH	COTS ....COTTAGES	FLDS ....FIELDS	IND EST ....INDUSTRIAL ESTATE
AR ....ARCADE	CP ....CAPE	FLS ....FALLS	INF ....INFIRMARY
ASS ....ASSOCIATION	CPS ....COPSE	FM ....FARM	INFO ....INFORMATION
AV ....AVENUE	CR ....CREEK	FT ....FORT	INT ....INTERCHANGE
BCH ....BEACH	CREM ....CREMATORIUM	FTS ....FLATS	IS ....ISLAND
BLDS ....BUILDINGS	CRS ....CRESCENT	FWY ....FREEWAY	JCT ....JUNCTION
BND ....BEND	CSWY ....CAUSEWAY	FY ....FERRY	JTY ....JETTY
BNK ....BANK	CT ....COURT	GA ....GATE	KG ....KING
BR ....BRIDGE	CTRL ....CENTRAL	GAL ....GALLERY	KNL ....KNOLL
BRK ....BROOK	CTS ....COURTS	GDN ....GARDEN	L ....LAKE
BTM ....BOTTOM	CTYD ....COURTYARD	GDNS ....GARDENS	LA ....LANE
BUS ....BUSINESS	CUTT ....CUTTINGS	GLD ....GLADE	LDG ....LODGE
BVD ....BOULEVARD	CV ....COVE	GLN ....GLEN	LGT ....LIGHT
BY ....BYPASS	CYN ....CANYON	GN ....GREEN	LK ....LOCK
CATH ....CATHEDRAL	DEPT ....DEPARTMENT	GND ....GROUND	LKS ....LAKES
CEM ....CEMETERY	DL ....DALE	GRA ....GRANGE	LNDG ....LANDING
CEN ....CENTRE	DM ....DAM	GRG ....GARAGE	LTL ....LITTLE
CFT ....CROFT	DR ....DRIVE	GT ....GREAT	LWR ....LOWER
CH ....CHURCH	DRO ....DROVE	GTWY ....GATEWAY	MAG ....MAGISTRATE
CHA ....CHASE	DRY ....DRIVEWAY	GV ....GROVE	MAN ....MANSIONS
CHYD ....CHURCHYARD	DWGS ....DWELLINGS	HGR ....HIGHER	MD ....MEAD
CIR ....CIRCLE	E ....EAST	HL ....HILL	MDW ....MEADOWS
CIRC ....CIRCUS	EMB ....EMBANKMENT	HLS ....HILLS	MEM ....MEMORIAL
CL ....CLOSE	EMBY ....EMBASSY	HO ....HOUSE	MI ....MILL
CLFS ....CLIFFS	ESP ....ESPLANADE	HOL ....HOLLOW	MKT ....MARKET
CMP ....CAMP	EST ....ESTATE	HOSP ....HOSPITAL	MKTS ....MARKETS
CNR ....CORNER	EX ....EXCHANGE	HRB ....HARBOUR	ML ....MALL
CO ....COUNTY	EXPY ....EXPRESSWAY	HTH ....HEATH	MNR ....MANOR
COLL ....COLLEGE	EXT ....EXTENSION	HTS ....HEIGHTS	MS ....MEWS
COM ....COMMON	F/O ....FLYOVER	HVN ....HAVEN	MSN ....MISSION
COMM ....COMMISSION	FC ....FOOTBALL CLUB	HWY ....HIGHWAY	MT ....MOUNT

89

MTN MOUNTAIN
MTS MOUNTAINS
MUS MUSEUM
MWY MOTORWAY
N NORTH
NE NORTH EAST
NW NORTH WEST
O/P OVERPASS
OFF OFFICE
ORCH ORCHARD
OV OVAL
PAL PALACE
PAS PASSAGE
PAV PAVILION
PDE PARADE
PH PUBLIC HOUSE
PK PARK
PKWY PARKWAY
PL PLACE
PLN PLAIN
PLNS PLAINS
PLZ PLAZA
POL POLICE STATION
PR PRINCE
PREC PRECINCT
PREP PREPARATORY
PRIM PRIMARY
PROM PROMENADE
PRS PRINCESS
PRT PORT
PT POINT
PTH PATH
PZ PIAZZA
QD QUADRANT
QU QUEEN
QY QUAY
R RIVER
RBT ROUNDABOUT
RD ROAD
RDG RIDGE
REP REPUBLIC
RES RESERVOIR
RFC RUGBY FOOTBALL CLUB
RI RISE
RP RAMP
RW ROW
S SOUTH
SCH SCHOOL
SE SOUTH EAST
SER SERVICE AREA
SH SHORE
SHOP SHOPPING
SKWY SKYWAY
SMT SUMMIT
SOC SOCIETY
SP SPUR
SPR SPRING
SQ SQUARE
ST STREET
STN STATION
STR STREAM
STRD STRAND
SW SOUTH WEST
TDG TRADING
TER TERRACE
THWY THROUGHWAY
TNL TUNNEL
TOLL TOLLWAY
TPK TURNPIKE
TR TRACK
TRL TRAIL
TWR TOWER
U/P UNDERPASS
UNI UNIVERSITY
UPR UPPER
V VALE
VA VALLEY
VIAD VIADUCT
VIL VILLA
VIS VISTA
VLG VILLAGE
VLS VILLAS
VW VIEW
W WEST
WD WOOD
WHF WHARF
WK WALK
WKS WALKS
WLS WELLS
WY WAY
YD YARD
YHA YOUTH HOSTEL

POSTCODE TOWNS AND AREA ABBREVIATIONS

BDST Broadstone
BKME/WDN Branksome/Wallisdown
BMTH Bournemouth
BOSC Boscombe
BROC Brockenhurst
BWD Bearwood
CCLF Canford Cliffs
CFDH Canford Heath
CHAR Charminster
CHCH/BSGR Christchurch/Bransgore
FERN Ferndown/West Moors
LTDN Littledown
LYMN Lymington
LYND Lyndhurst
MOOR/WNTN Moordown/Winton
NBNE Northbourne
NMIL/BTOS New Milton/Barton on Sea
PLE Poole
PSTN Parkstone
RGWD Ringwood
SBNE Southbourne
TWDS Talbot Woods
UPTN Upton
VWD Verwood
WBNE Westbourne
WCLF West Cliff
WIMB Wimborne Minster

Index - streets

Aar - Ash

A

Aaron Cl *CFDH* BH17 53 F3
Abbey Gdns *WIMB* BH21 16 B4
Abbey Rd *FERN* BH22 18 C1
Abbotsbury Rd *BDST* BH18 32 C2
Abbots Cl *CHCH/BSGR* BH23 62 B3
Abbott Cl *MOOR/WNTN* BH9 56 C2
Abbott Rd *MOOR/WNTN* BH9 56 C2
Abbotts Wy *FERN* BH22 18 C1
Aberdare Rd *NBNE* BH10 37 E4
Abingdon Dr *CHCH/BSGR* BH23 63 E2
Abingdon Rd *CFDH* BH17 53 E2
Abinger Rd *LTDN* BH7 58 A4
Abney Rd *NBNE* BH10 36 D4
Acacia Av *VWD* BH31 5 G4
Acacia Rd *LYMN* SO41 46 B3
Acland Rd *MOOR/WNTN* BH9 56 D2
Acorn Av *PLE* BH15 70 D3
Acorn Cl *CHCH/BSGR* BH23 59 F2
NMIL/BTOS BH25 45 G3
RGWD BH24 11 H3
The Acorns *RGWD* BH24 18 D1
WIMB BH21 15 G5
Acorn Wy *VWD* BH31 5 E2
Acres Rd *BWD* BH11 36 B5
Acton Rd *NBNE* BH10 55 F1
Adamsfield Gdns *NBNE* BH10 36 C5
Adastral Rd *CFDH* BH17 53 E3
Addington Pl
CHCH/BSGR BH23 * 60 B4
Addiscombe Rd
CHCH/BSGR BH23 59 G3
Addison Rd *BROC* SO42 86 D4
Addison Sq *RGWD* BH24 8 D4
Adelaide Cl *CHCH/BSGR* BH23 59 F2
Adeline Rd *BMTH* BH1 75 G1
Admirals Wk *WCLF* BH2 * 2 D6
Admiralty Rd *SBNE* BH6 77 F2
Agar's La *LYMN* SO41 46 D2
Agarton La *LYMN* SO41 66 D4
LYMN SO41 67 E4
Aggis Farm Rd *VWD* BH31 4 C2
Airetons Cl *BDST* BH18 33 G4
Airfield Rd *CHCH/BSGR* BH23 60 D3
Airfield Wy *CHCH/BSGR* BH23 60 D3
Airspeed Rd *CHCH/BSGR* BH23 61 F3
Akeshill Cl *NMIL/BTOS* BH25 45 F2
Albany Cl *NMIL/BTOS* BH25 63 H1
Albany Gdns *PLE* BH15 69 H3
Albemarle Rd *TWDS* BH3 56 B3
Albert Rd *BKME/WDN* BH12 54 B5
BMTH BH1 3 G3
FERN BH22 17 H4
NMIL/BTOS BH25 44 D5
WIMB BH21 32 B2
Albion Cl *BKME/WDN* BH12 53 H3
Albion Rd *CHCH/BSGR* BH23 59 F1
Albion Wy *VWD* BH31 4 B1
Alby Rd *BKME/WDN* BH12 54 D5
Alcester Rd *BKME/WDN* BH12 54 B4
Alder Cl *CHCH/BSGR* BH23 60 B1
Alder Crs *BKME/WDN* BH12 54 D3
Alder Hts *BKME/WDN* BH12 55 E4
Alder Hills *BKME/WDN* BH12 55 E3
Alderley Rd *NBNE* BH10 36 D3
Alderney Av *BKME/WDN* BH12 54 A1
Alder Rd *BKME/WDN* BH12 54 D4
Aldis Gdns *PLE* BH15 69 G3
Aldridge Rd *FERN* BH22 26 A1
NBNE BH10 36 C2
Aldridge Wy *FERN* BH22 26 B1
Alexander Cl *CHCH/BSGR* BH23 60 C4
Alexandra Rd *LYMN* SO41 48 C2
PSTN BH14 72 C1
SBNE BH6 58 B5
Alford Rd *TWDS* BH3 55 H3
Alington Cl *PSTN* BH14 83 E1
Alington Rd *PSTN* BH14 83 E1
TWDS BH3 56 C4
Alipore Cl *PSTN* BH14 72 B2
Allenby Cl *CFDH* BH17 33 F5
Allenby Rd *CFDH* BH17 52 B1
Allen Ct *WIMB* BH21 14 C4
Allen Rd *WIMB* BH21 14 C5
Allens La *UPTN* BH16 51 F5
Allens Rd *UPTN* BH16 51 F5
Allenview Rd *WIMB* BH21 14 C4
All Saints Rd *LYMN* SO41 49 E5
Alma Rd *MOOR/WNTN* BH9 56 C3
Almer Rd *PLE* BH15 69 G2
Almond Gv *BKME/WDN* BH12 54 B3
Alpine Rd *RGWD* BH24 12 D4
Alton Rd *NBNE* BH10 55 F1
PSTN BH14 71 H2
Alton Rd East *PSTN* BH14 72 B3
Alum Chine Rd *WBNE* BH4 73 F2
Alumdale Rd *WBNE* BH4 73 F3
Alumhurst Rd *WBNE* BH4 73 F3
Alverton Av *PLE* BH15 71 F2
Alyth Rd *TWDS* BH3 55 H4
Ambassador Cl
CHCH/BSGR BH23 61 E4
Amberley Cl *CHCH/BSGR* BH23 62 A2
Amber Rd *WIMB* BH21 32 A3
Amberwood *FERN* BH22 18 A2
Amberwood Dr
CHCH/BSGR BH23 43 G5
Amberwood Gdns
CHCH/BSGR BH23 43 G5
Ambleside *CHCH/BSGR* BH23 39 H4
Ambleside Cl *BDST* BH18 33 G5
Ambleside Rd *LYMN* SO41 49 E5
Ambury La *CHCH/BSGR* BH23 60 D2
Amesbury Rd *SBNE* BH6 58 C4
Amethyst Rd *CHCH/BSGR* BH23 60 D3
Ameys La *FERN* BH22 18 B2
Ampfield Rd *CHAR* BH8 38 B4
Ampress La *LYMN* SO41 48 D1
Amsterdam Sq
CHCH/BSGR BH23 60 B3
Anchorage Wy *LYMN* SO41 48 D4
Anchor Cl *BWD* BH11 35 H2
CHCH/BSGR BH23 61 E5
Anchor Ms *LYMN* SO41 49 E3
Anchor Rd *BWD* BH11 35 H2
Andover Cl *CHCH/BSGR* BH23 61 G3
Andrew La *NMIL/BTOS* BH25 45 H5
Andrews Cl *BWD* BH11 36 A4
Angeline Cl *CHCH/BSGR* BH23 62 B2
Angel La *FERN* BH22 25 F1
NMIL/BTOS BH25 64 D2
Anjou Cl *BWD* BH11 35 F2
Anna La *CHCH/BSGR* BH23 21 G5
Anne Cl *CHCH/BSGR* BH23 59 G1
Annerley Rd *BMTH* BH1 75 E1
Annet Cl *PLE* BH15 69 G3
Anson Cl *CHCH/BSGR* BH23 60 D4
RGWD BH24 9 E3
Anstey Cl *BWD* BH11 36 A2
Anstey Rd *BWD* BH11 36 A2
Anthony's Av *PSTN* BH14 72 A4
Antler Dr *NMIL/BTOS* BH25 44 C3
Anvil Crs *BDST* BH18 32 C2
Apollo Cl *BKME/WDN* BH12 54 B3
Apple Cl *BKME/WDN* BH12 73 E1
Apple Gv *CHCH/BSGR* BH23 40 A5
Appleslade Wy
NMIL/BTOS BH25 45 F2
Appletree Cl *NMIL/BTOS* BH25 64 A1
SBNE BH6 58 C5
Appletree Ct *LYND* SO43 85 F4
Apple Tree Gv *FERN* BH22 18 A4
Approach Rd *PSTN* BH14 71 H2
April Cl *BWD* BH11 36 A3
Apsley Crs *CFDH* BH17 52 C1
Aragon Wy *MOOR/WNTN* BH9 37 H2
The Arcade *BMTH* BH1 3 G4
Arcadia Av *CHAR* BH8 56 D3
Arcadia Rd *CHCH/BSGR* BH23 59 F1
Archdale Cl *NBNE* BH10 36 D5
Archway Rd *PSTN* BH14 72 C1
Arden Rd *MOOR/WNTN* BH9 37 F4
Arden Wk *NMIL/BTOS* BH25 45 F5
Ardmore Rd *PSTN* BH14 71 H1
Argyle Rd *CHCH/BSGR* BH23 60 C5
Argyll Rd *BKME/WDN* BH12 54 B4
BOSC BH5 75 G1
Ariel Cl *SBNE* BH6 77 H1
Ariel Dr *SBNE* BH6 77 H1
Ark Dr *FERN* BH22 26 B1
Arley Rd *PSTN* BH14 71 G3
Arlington Ct *NMIL/BTOS* BH25 64 B2
Armstrong Cl *BROC* SO42 86 C3
Armstrong La *BROC* SO42 86 C3
Armstrong Rd *BROC* SO42 86 C3
Arne Av *BKME/WDN* BH12 54 C3
Arne Crs *BKME/WDN* BH12 54 C3
Arnewood Rd *SBNE* BH6 58 C5
Arnold Cl *FERN* BH22 10 B3
Arnold Rd *FERN* BH22 10 B3
Arnolds Cl *NMIL/BTOS* BH25 63 H2
Arran Wy *CHCH/BSGR* BH23 62 D1
Arrowsmith La *WIMB* BH21 23 E5
Arrowsmith Rd *CFDH* BH17 33 H1
WIMB BH21 23 E5
Arthur Cl *WCLF* BH2 56 B5
Arthur La *CHCH/BSGR* BH23 59 G3
Arthur Rd *CHCH/BSGR* BH23 59 G3
Arundel Cl *NMIL/BTOS* BH25 44 C4
Arundel Wy *CHCH/BSGR* BH23 62 B3
Ascham Rd *CHAR* BH8 56 D5
Ascot Rd *BDST* BH18 33 E3
Ashbourne Rd *BOSC* BH5 58 B5
Ashbrook Wk *UPTN* BH16 50 A4
Ashburn Garth *RGWD* BH24 9 F5
Ashburton Gdns *NBNE* BH10 55 H1
Ash Cl *UPTN* BH16 50 D2
Ashdene Cl *WIMB* BH21 14 D4
Ashdown Cl *CFDH* BH17 53 F1
Ashdown Wk
NMIL/BTOS BH25 45 G5
Ashford Rd *SBNE* BH6 58 D3
Ash Gv *LYMN* SO41 66 B2
RGWD BH24 9 E4
Ashington La *WIMB* BH21 22 A3
Ashington Pk *NMIL/BTOS* BH25 64 B1
Ashleigh Ri *NBNE* BH10 36 D5
Ashlet Gdns *NMIL/BTOS* BH25 45 H3
Ashley Cl *BMTH* BH1 57 G4
RGWD BH24 9 F5

Ashley Common Rd
NMIL/BTOS BH25 45 G3
Ashley Dr *RGWD* BH24 7 G3
Ashley Dr North *RGWD* BH24 6 D5
Ashley Dr South *RGWD* BH24 12 A1
Ashley Dr West *RGWD* BH24 12 A1
Ashley La *NMIL/BTOS* BH25 45 H3
Ashley Meads
NMIL/BTOS BH25 45 H3
Ashley Pk *RGWD* BH24 7 E5
Ashley Rd *BMTH* BH1 57 G4
NMIL/BTOS BH25 45 G4
PSTN BH14 54 A5
Ashling Cl *CHAR* BH8 57 E2
Ashmeads Cl *WIMB* BH21 15 G3
Ashmeads Wy *WIMB* BH21 15 G3
Ashmore *WIMB* BH21 14 D5
Ashmore Av *NMIL/BTOS* BH25 64 B2
PLE BH15 69 H4
Ashmore Crs *PLE* BH15 69 H4
Ashmore Gv *CHCH/BSGR* BH23 62 A1
Ashridge Av *NBNE* BH10 36 D2
Ashridge Gdns *NBNE* BH10 * 36 D2
Ashton Rd *MOOR/WNTN* BH9 37 F5
Ashtree Cl *NMIL/BTOS* BH25 45 H5
Ashurst Rd *CHAR* BH8 38 B4
FERN BH22 10 A3
Ashwood Dr *BDST* BH18 33 G2
Aspen Dr *VWD* BH31 5 F2
Aspen Gdns *BKME/WDN* BH12 54 D2
Aspen Pl *NMIL/BTOS* BH25 64 B1
Aspen Rd *BKME/WDN* BH12 54 D3
Aspen Wy *BKME/WDN* BH12 54 D3
Asquith Cl *CHCH/BSGR* BH23 60 B5
Astbury Av *BKME/WDN* BH12 55 E2
Aston Md *CHCH/BSGR* BH23 40 A3
Athelstan Rd *SBNE* BH6 59 E5
Aubrey Cl *LYMN* SO41 80 D1
Auckland Pl *BROC* SO42 86 D3
Auckland Rd
CHCH/BSGR BH23 61 G3
Audemer Ct *RGWD* BH24 9 E3
Aukland Av *BROC* SO42 87 E3
Austen Av *NBNE* BH10 * 36 D1
Auster Cl *CHCH/BSGR* BH23 61 F3
Austin Av *PSTN* BH14 71 H3
Austin Cl *BMTH* BH1 57 F5
Autumn Cl *FERN* BH22 17 F2
Autumn Rd *BWD* BH11 35 F4
Avalon *PSTN* BH14 72 A5
Avebury Av *NBNE* BH10 37 E1
Avenue La *WCLF* BH2 3 F4
Avenue Rd *BROC* SO42 86 D3
CHCH/BSGR BH23 59 F3
CHCH/BSGR BH23 63 E1
LYMN SO41 48 D3
NMIL/BTOS BH25 45 E4
WCLF BH2 2 E4
WIMB BH21 14 D5
The Avenue *CCLF* BH13 73 E5
FERN BH22 10 A3
MOOR/WNTN BH9 37 F4
RGWD BH24 18 D1
Aviation Pk West
CHCH/BSGR BH23 * 27 F3
Avon Av *RGWD* BH24 13 E3
Avon Buildings
CHCH/BSGR BH23 59 H3
Avon Castle Dr *RGWD* BH24 13 E3
Avon Cswy *CHCH/BSGR* BH23 29 E4
Avoncliffe Rd *SBNE* BH6 77 E2
Avon Cl *CHAR* BH8 57 F4
LYMN SO41 48 C4
Avon Gdns *CHCH/BSGR* BH23 31 F3
Avon Ms *CHAR* BH8 57 E4
Avon Pk *RGWD* BH24 7 H5
Avon Rd *CHAR* BH8 57 E4
FERN BH22 10 B5
Avon Rd East
CHCH/BSGR BH23 59 G2
Avon Rd West
CHCH/BSGR BH23 59 F2
Avon Run Cl
CHCH/BSGR BH23 61 F5
Avon Run Rd
CHCH/BSGR BH23 61 G5
Avon Valley Pth
CHCH/BSGR BH23 21 G5
CHCH/BSGR BH23 41 E1
RGWD BH24 8 B5
RGWD BH24 13 G4
Avon View Rd
CHCH/BSGR BH23 41 E4
Avon Whf *CHCH/BSGR* BH23 * 60 A4
Award Rd *WIMB* BH21 16 D4
Axford Cl *CHAR* BH8 38 C4
Aylesbury Rd *BMTH* BH1 75 F1
Aysha Cl *NMIL/BTOS* BH25 64 B1
Azalea Cl *RGWD* BH24 12 B1

B

Back Down La *RGWD* BH24 9 F4
Badbury Cl *BDST* BH18 33 G4
Badbury Vw *WIMB* BH21 14 D4
Baden Cl *NMIL/BTOS* BH25 64 B1
Bader Rd *CFDH* BH17 53 E2
Badgers Cl *RGWD* BH24 12 A1
Badgers Copse
NMIL/BTOS BH25 45 G1
Badgers Wk *FERN* BH22 18 A2
Badger Wy *VWD* BH31 4 D3
Bailey Cl *NMIL/BTOS* BH25 45 H3
Bailey Crs *PLE* BH15 52 C3
Bailey Dr *CHCH/BSGR* BH23 59 F3
Baiter Gdns *PLE* BH15 70 C4
Baker Rd *BWD* BH11 35 H2
Bakers Farm Rd *VWD* BH31 4 C1
Bakers Vw *WIMB* BH21 32 B2
Balcombe Rd *CCLF* BH13 73 E2
Baldwin Cl *CHCH/BSGR* BH23 60 C4
Balena Cl *CFDH* BH17 52 A2
Balfour Cl *CHCH/BSGR* BH23 61 H2
Balfour Rd *MOOR/WNTN* BH9 56 B1
Ballam Cl *UPTN* BH16 51 E3
Ballard Cl *NMIL/BTOS* BH25 45 F3
PLE BH15 70 C4
Ballard Rd *PLE* BH15 70 D4
Balmer Lawn Rd *BROC* SO42 87 F1
Balmoral Av *CHAR* BH8 57 G1
Balmoral Rd *PSTN* BH14 72 A2
Balmoral Wk *NMIL/BTOS* BH25 44 D4
Balston Rd *PSTN* BH14 53 G4
Balston Ter *PLE* BH15 * 70 B3
Banbury Rd *CFDH* BH17 52 C3
Bankhill Dr *LYMN* SO41 48 D2
Bank Pde *BKME/WDN* BH12 * 55 E1
Bankside *LYMN* SO41 48 D1
Bankside Rd *MOOR/WNTN* BH9 37 G4
Banks Rd *CCLF* BH13 82 D5
Bankview *LYMN* SO41 48 D1
Banstead Rd *BDST* BH18 33 E2
Barberry Wy *VWD* BH31 5 G3
Barbers Piles *PLE* BH15 70 B4
Barfields *LYMN* SO41 49 E3
Bargates *CHCH/BSGR* BH23 59 G3
Baring Rd *SBNE* BH6 77 G1
Barlands Cl *CHCH/BSGR* BH23 41 E5
Barn Cl *UPTN* BH16 50 C3
Barnes Cl *NBNE* BH10 36 D4
Barnes Crs *NBNE* BH10 36 D4
WIMB BH21 15 E5
Barnes La *LYMN* SO41 66 A2
Barnes Rd *NBNE* BH10 36 D4
Barnfield *CHCH/BSGR* BH23 61 H2
Barn Rd *BDST* BH18 33 F4
Barnsfield Rd *RGWD* BH24 12 B5
Barns Rd *FERN* BH22 18 C3
Barons Rd *BWD* BH11 35 F1
Barrack Rd *CHCH/BSGR* BH23 59 F3
FERN BH22 26 C2
Barrie Rd *MOOR/WNTN* BH9 37 F4
Barrow Dr *CHAR* BH8 38 D5
Barrowgate Rd *CHAR* BH8 38 B3
Barrowgate Wy *CHAR* BH8 38 B4
Barrow Rd *CHAR* BH8 38 D5
Barrows La *LYMN* SO41 46 D2
Barrow Vw *FERN* BH22 17 E3
Barrow Wy *CHAR* BH8 38 D5
Barrs Av *NMIL/BTOS* BH25 45 E3
Barrs Wood Dr
NMIL/BTOS BH25 45 F3
Barrs Wood Rd
NMIL/BTOS BH25 45 F3
Barry Gdns *BDST* BH18 32 D2
Barter Rd *BKME/WDN* BH12 55 E3
Barters La *BDST* BH18 32 D3
Bartlett Dr *LTDN* BH7 58 B2
Barton Cha *NMIL/BTOS* BH25 * 63 H3
Barton Common La
NMIL/BTOS BH25 64 B2
Barton Common Rd
NMIL/BTOS BH25 64 C3
Barton Court Av
NMIL/BTOS BH25 63 H3
Barton Court Rd
NMIL/BTOS BH25 64 A1
Barton Cft *NMIL/BTOS* BH25 64 A3
Barton Dr *NMIL/BTOS* BH25 63 H3
Barton Gn *NMIL/BTOS* BH25 64 B4
Barton La *NMIL/BTOS* BH25 63 F2
Bartonside Rd *NMIL/BTOS* BH25 63 E2
Barton Wy *NMIL/BTOS* BH25 63 H2
Barton Wood Rd
NMIL/BTOS BH25 63 G3
Bascott Cl *BWD* BH11 55 E1
Bascott Rd *BWD* BH11 54 D1
Bashley Cross Rd
NMIL/BTOS BH25 44 C2
Bashley Dr *NMIL/BTOS* BH25 45 F1
Bassett Rd *BKME/WDN* BH12 53 H4
Batchelor Crs *BWD* BH11 35 H4
Batchelor Rd *BWD* BH11 35 H4
Batcombe Cl *BWD* BH11 35 G4
Bath Hill Rbt *BMTH* BH1 3 H5
Bath Rd *LYMN* SO41 49 F4
WCLF BH2 3 H5
Batstone Wy *FERN* BH22 17 F3
Batten Cl *CHCH/BSGR* BH23 60 B2
Baverstock Rd
BKME/WDN BH12 55 F2
Bay Cl *UPTN* BH16 50 D4
Bay Hog La *PLE* BH15 70 B3
Bays Rd *LYMN* SO41 48 C4
Bay Tree Wy *CHCH/BSGR* BH23 61 H1
Beach Av *NMIL/BTOS* BH25 63 H3
Beach Rd *CCLF* BH13 73 E5
UPTN BH16 50 C4
Beacon Cl *LYMN* SO41 66 B1
Beacon Dr *CHCH/BSGR* BH23 62 B3
Beacon Gdns *BDST* BH18 32 C4
Beacon Park Crs *UPTN* BH16 50 D2
Beacon Park Rd *UPTN* BH16 50 D3
Beacon Rd *BDST* BH18 32 B4
UPTN BH16 50 D3
WCLF BH2 3 G6
Beaconsfield Rd
BKME/WDN BH12 54 B5
CHCH/BSGR BH23 59 H3
Beacon Wy *BDST* BH18 32 C4
Beamish Rd *CFDH* BH17 53 F2
Bear Cross Av *BWD* BH11 35 H1
Beatty Cl *RGWD* BH24 9 E3
Beatty Rd *MOOR/WNTN* BH9 56 D1
Beauchamp Pl *CHCH/BSGR* BH23 59 G3
Beauchamps Gdns *LTDN* BH7 58 A2
Beaucroft La *WIMB* BH21 15 E3
Beaucroft Rd *WIMB* BH21 14 D3
Beaufort Cl *CHCH/BSGR* BH23 61 F3
Beaufort Dr *WIMB* BH21 14 C4
Beaufort Rd *SBNE* BH6 58 C5
Beaufoys Av *FERN* BH22 17 G2
Beaufoys Cl *FERN* BH22 17 G2
Beaulieu Av *CHCH/BSGR* BH23 59 E3
Beaulieu Cl *NMIL/BTOS* BH25 44 C4
Beaulieu Rd *CHCH/BSGR* BH23 59 E3
LYND SO43 85 G4
WBNE BH4 73 F4
Beaumont Rd *CCLF* BH13 83 G1
Beccles Cl *PLE* BH15 69 H3
Becher Rd *PSTN* BH14 72 C1
Beckhampton Rd *PLE* BH15 69 G2
Beckley Copse
CHCH/BSGR BH23 43 G5
Becton La *NMIL/BTOS* BH25 64 B3
Becton Md *NMIL/BTOS* BH25 64 B1
Bedale Wy *PLE* BH15 53 F5
Bedford Crs *LTDN* BH7 58 C3
Bedford Rd North
BKME/WDN BH12 35 E5
Bedford Rd South
BKME/WDN BH12 35 E5
Beech Av *CHCH/BSGR* BH23 58 D2
SBNE BH6 76 C1
Beechbank Av *CFDH* BH17 51 G1
Beech Cl *BDST* BH18 32 B3
LYMN SO41 66 B2
VWD BH31 4 C3
Beech Ct *WIMB* BH21 15 E5
Beechcroft La *RGWD* BH24 8 D3
The Beeches *LTDN* BH7 58 A2
Beechey Rd *CHAR* BH8 56 D5
Beech La *RGWD* BH24 11 H4
Beechleigh Pl *RGWD* BH24 * 8 C3
Beechwood Av *BOSC* BH5 75 H1
NMIL/BTOS BH25 44 C3
Beech Wood Cl *BDST* BH18 33 E4
Beechwood Gdns *BOSC* BH5 76 A1
Beechwood Rd *FERN* BH22 10 C5
Belben Cl *BKME/WDN* BH12 35 F5
Belben Rd *BKME/WDN* BH12 35 E5
Belfield Rd *SBNE* BH6 77 G1
Belgrave Rd *CCLF* BH13 73 E3
Belle Vue Cl *SBNE* BH6 76 D1
Belle Vue Crs *SBNE* BH6 77 F1
Belle Vue Gv *FERN* BH22 10 C4
Belle Vue Rd *PSTN* BH14 72 A2
SBNE BH6 76 D2
Belle Vue Wk *FERN* BH22 26 A2
Bellflower Cl *CHCH/BSGR* BH23 61 F2
Bell Heather Cl *UPTN* BH16 * 50 D2
Belmont Av *CHAR* BH8 38 B5
Belmont Cl *VWD* BH31 5 E3
Belmont Rd *NMIL/BTOS* BH25 45 G3
PSTN BH14 53 H5
Belmore La *LYMN* SO41 49 E4
Belmore Rd *LYMN* SO41 48 D4
Belvedere Rd *CHCH/BSGR* BH23 59 G3
TWDS BH3 56 C4
Bemister Rd *MOOR/WNTN* BH9 56 C2
Benbow Crs *BKME/WDN* BH12 54 C1
Benbridge Av *BWD* BH11 35 H2
Bendigo Rd *CHCH/BSGR* BH23 59 E2
Benellen Av *WBNE* BH4 2 B1
Benellen Gdns *WBNE* BH4 2 B1
Benellen Rd *WBNE* BH4 55 G5
Bengal Rd *MOOR/WNTN* BH9 56 A1
Benjamin Rd *PLE* BH15 69 G3
Benmoor Rd *CFDH* BH17 52 A2
Benmore Cl *NMIL/BTOS* BH25 45 G5
Benmore Rd *MOOR/WNTN* BH9 56 C1
Bennett Rd *CHAR* BH8 57 E4
Bennion Rd *NBNE* BH10 36 C4
Benridge Cl *BDST* BH18 33 F4
Benson Cl *CHCH/BSGR* BH23 31 F3
Benson Rd *CFDH* BH17 52 D3
Bentley Rd *MOOR/WNTN* BH9 37 F4
Bently Wy *LYMN* SO41 48 D1
Bere Cl *CFDH* BH17 33 H5
Beresford Cl *BKME/WDN* BH12 54 B4
Beresford Gdns
CHCH/BSGR BH23 60 C4
Beresford Rd *BKME/WDN* BH12 54 B4
LYMN SO41 48 C3
SBNE BH6 76 C1
Berkeley Av *BKME/WDN* BH12 54 A2
Berkeley Cl *VWD* BH31 4 C1
Berkeley Rd *TWDS* BH3 56 A3
Berkley Av *FERN* BH22 25 H2
Bernards Cl *CHCH/BSGR* BH23 59 E2
Berrans Av *BWD* BH11 36 B1
Berryfield Rd *LYMN* SO41 46 C5
Bertram Rd *NMIL/BTOS* BH25 45 G3
Berwick Rd *TWDS* BH3 56 A4
Bessborough Rd *CCLF* BH13 83 G1
Bessemer Cl *VWD* BH31 5 G4
Beswick Av *NBNE* BH10 36 D5
Bethia Cl *CHAR* BH8 * 57 F4
Bethia Rd *CHAR* BH8 57 F4
Betsy Cl *CHCH/BSGR* BH23 31 F3
Betsy La *CHCH/BSGR* BH23 31 F3
Bettiscombe Cl *CFDH* BH17 33 H5
Beverley Gdns *NBNE* BH10 36 D4
Bexington Cl *BWD* BH11 35 G4
Bickerley Gdns *RGWD* BH24 8 B5
Bickerley Rd *RGWD* BH24 8 B5
Bicton Rd *BWD* BH11 36 B4
Bindon Cl *BKME/WDN* BH12 54 C3
Bingham Av *PSTN* BH14 83 F1
Bingham Dr *LYMN* SO41 49 E4
Bingham Rd *CHCH/BSGR* BH23 60 C3
MOOR/WNTN BH9 56 C2
VWD BH31 5 E4
Binnie Rd *BKME/WDN* BH12 54 C5
Birch Av *CHCH/BSGR* BH23 41 E4
FERN BH22 26 B3
NMIL/BTOS BH25 44 B1
Birch Cl *PSTN* BH14 72 C2
RGWD BH24 11 G3
WIMB BH21 32 B1
Birchdale Rd *WIMB* BH21 14 D4
Birch Dr *CHAR* BH8 39 E5
Birch Gv *FERN* BH22 10 A4
Birch Rd *RGWD* BH24 12 C2
Birch Wk *FERN* BH22 26 B1
Birchwood Cl *CHCH/BSGR* BH23 62 A2
Birchwood Rd *PSTN* BH14 72 B2
UPTN BH16 50 D4
Birds Hill Gdns *PLE* BH15 71 E2
Bird's Hill Rd *PLE* BH15 71 E1
Birkdale Ct *BDST* BH18 33 E2
Birkdale Rd *BDST* BH18 33 E2
Bishop Cl *BKME/WDN* BH12 55 G3
Bishop Ct *RGWD* BH24 8 C4
Bishop Rd *MOOR/WNTN* BH9 56 C2
Bishops Cl *LTDN* BH7 57 H4
Bitterne Wy *LYMN* SO41 48 D5
VWD BH31 5 E3
Blackberry La *CHCH/BSGR* BH23 60 D4
Blackbird Cl *CFDH* BH17 51 G2
Blackbird Wy *CHCH/BSGR* BH23 31 G4
Blackburn Rd *BKME/WDN* BH12 53 H4
Blackbush Rd *LYMN* SO41 65 H4
Blackfield La *FERN* BH22 10 B3
Blackfield Rd *CHAR* BH8 38 B4
Black Hl *VWD* BH31 5 E2
Black Moor Rd *VWD* BH31 5 H4
Blacksmith Cl *WIMB* BH21 32 B2
Blackthorn Cl *LYMN* SO41 48 B5
Blackthorn Wy *VWD* BH31 5 F3
Blackwater Dr *WIMB* BH21 22 D5
Blair Av *PSTN* BH14 72 A1
Blair Cl *NMIL/BTOS* BH25 44 C4
Blakedene Rd *PSTN* BH14 71 H4
Blake Hill Av *PSTN* BH14 72 B4

Blake Hill Crs *PSTN* BH14 ....**72** A4
Blandford Cl *PLE* BH15.............**69** H3
Blandford Rd *UPTN* BH16.........**51** E4
Blandford Rd North
UPTN BH16 ....**50** D2
Blaney Wy *WIMB* BH21 ....**32** A1
Blenheim Crs *LYMN* SO41........**46** B3
Blenheim Dr *CHCH/BSGR* BH23...**61** F3
Blind La *WIMB* BH21 ....**14** B3
Bloomfield Av
MOOR/WNTN BH9 ....**37** F5
Bloxworth Rd
BKME/WDN BH12 ....**54** D2
Bluebell Cl *CHCH/BSGR* BH23...**61** F2
Bluebell La *CFDH* BH17............**51** H1
Blyth Cl *CHCH/BSGR* BH23 ......**39** H3
Blythe Rd *WIMB* BH21 ....**32** B1
Blythswood Ct
NMIL/BTOS BH25 ....**63** H3
Bob Hann Cl *BKME/WDN* BH12...**54** C5
Bockhampton Rd
CHCH/BSGR BH23................**41** G2
Bodley Rd *CCLF* BH13 ....**83** H1
Bodorgan Rd *WCLF* BH2............**3** G2
Bodowen Cl *CHCH/BSGR* BH23...**41** F5
Bodowen Rd *CHCH/BSGR* BH23...**41** F5
Bognor Rd *BDST* BH18 ....**33** G3
Boldre Cl *BKME/WDN* BH12......**54** C3
NMIL/BTOS BH25 ....**63** F2
Boleyn Crs *MOOR/WNTN* BH9...**38** A3
Bolton Crs *FERN* BH22.............**18** C3
Bolton Rd *SBNE* BH6 ....**77** E2
The Boltons *LYMN* SO41..........**80** B1
Bond Av *FERN* BH22................**10** A2
Bond Rd *PLE* BH15..................**53** F5
Bonham Rd *MOOR/WNTN* BH9...**56** B3
Bonington Cl *CHCH/BSGR* BH23...**60** C2
Border Dr *UPTN* BH16..............**51** E5
Border Rd *UPTN* BH16 ....**51** F5
Boreham Rd *SBNE* BH6 ....**58** D5
Borley Rd *CFDH* BH17..............**52** A2
Borthwick Rd *BMTH* BH1..........**57** C5
Boscombe Cliff Rd *BOSC* BH5...**75** H2
Boscombe Grove Rd *BMTH* BH1...**57** C5
Boscombe Overcliff Dr *BOSC* BH5**75** H2
Boscombe Spa Rd *BOSC* BH5....**75** F1
Bosley Cl *CHCH/BSGR* BH23 .....**40** A5
Bosley Wy *CHCH/BSGR* BH23 ....**40** A5
Bosworth Ms
MOOR/WNTN BH9................**37** H3
Boulnois Av *PSTN* BH14 ....**72** C2
Boundary Dr *WIMB* BH21 ....**14** D3
Boundary La *RGWD* BH24.........**11** G5
Boundary Rd *MOOR/WNTN* BH9...**55** H2
NBNE BH10..........................**55** H1
Bourne Av *WCLF* BH2...............**2** E5
Bourne Av *WCLF* BH2...............**2** C3
Bourne Ct *WIMB* BH21.............**14** C1
Bournemouth Ar *BMTH* BH1 *...**3** G4
Bournemouth International
Centre Rbt *WCLF* BH2..........**3** G5
Bournemouth Rd *LYND* SO43.....**84** D3
PSTN BH14 ....**72** A1
Bournemouth Rd Castle HI
PSTN BH14 ....**71** H1
Bournemouth Station Rbt
BMTH BH1 ....**74** D1
Bourne Valley Rd
BKME/WDN BH12 ....**55** E5
Bournewood Dr *WBNE* BH4.......**2** A1
Bourton Gdns *LTDN* BH7...........**58** B2
Bouverie Rd *NMIL/BTOS* BH25...**63** H1
Boveridge Gdns
MOOR/WNTN BH9................**37** H3
Bovington Cl *CFDH* BH17..........**53** F1
Bowden Rd *BKME/WDN* BH12...**35** E5
Bower Rd *CHAR* BH8 ....**57** F2
Bowland Ri *NMIL/BTOS* BH25....**45** G5
Box Cl *CFDH* BH17 ....**52** B3
Boyd Rd *BKME/WDN* BH12.......**54** D4
Brabazon Dr *CHCH/BSGR* BH23...**61** F3
Brabazon Rd *WIMB* BH21..........**23** F3
Brabourne Av *FERN* BH22.........**17** G5
Bracken Cl *RGWD* BH24............**11** G2
Brackendale Rd *CHAR* BH8.......**57** E2
Bracken Gln *PLE* BH15 ....**53** E5
Brackenhill *CCLF* BH13.............**73** E4
Brackenhill Rd *WIMB* BH21.......**15** G2
Bracken Rd *FERN* BH22............**17** F2
SBNE BH6.............................**76** C1
Brackens Wy *LYMN* SO41.........**49** F5
Bracken Wy *CHCH/BSGR* BH23...**62** D1
Bracklesham Pl
NMIL/BTOS BH25 ....**63** H3
Brackley Cl *CHCH/BSGR* BH23...**28** A4
Bradburne Rd *WCLF* BH2..........**2** E3
Bradford Rd *MOOR/WNTN* BH9...**38** A3
Bradpole Rd *CHAR* BH8 ....**57** G1
Bradstock Cl *BKME/WDN* BH12...**54** D2

Braemar Av *SBNE* BH6.............**77** G1
Braemar Cl *SBNE* BH6..............**77** G1
Braemar Dr *CHCH/BSGR* BH23...**62** B1
Braeside Rd *FERN* BH22...........**10** B3
RGWD BH24..........................**11** H2
Braidley Rd *WCLF* BH2.............**3** G2
Brailswood Rd *PLE* BH15..........**70** D1
Braishfield Gdns *CHAR* BH8......**38** B5
Bramble Ct *FERN* BH22............**10** B3
Bramble La *CHCH/BSGR* BH23...**62** D1
Bramble Wk *LYMN* SO41...........**48** C3
Bramble Wy *CHCH/BSGR* BH23...**31** F3
Bramley Cl *LYMN* SO41............**49** E5
Bramley Rd *FERN* BH22 ....**17** G3
NBNE BH10 ....**36** C2
Brampton Rd *PLE* BH15............**52** D4
Bramshaw Gdns *CHAR* BH8......**38** B4
Bramshaw Wy
NMIL/BTOS BH25 ....**63** H3
Branders Cl *SBNE* BH6.............**77** G1
Branders La *SBNE* BH6.............**59** H5
Branksea Av *PLE* BH15............**69** F4
Branksea Cl *PLE* BH15.............**69** G4
Branksome Dene Rd
WBNE BH4............................**73** F4
Branksome Hill Rd *WBNE* BH4...**55** G5
Branksome Towers *CCLF* BH13...**73** F5
Branksome Wood Gdns
WBNE BH4............................**2** D1
Branksome Wood Rd
WBNE BH4............................**55** G5
Bransgore Gdns
CHCH/BSGR BH23................**31** F3
Branwell Cl *CHCH/BSGR* BH23...**29** F2
Branwood Cl *LYMN* SO41.........**66** C1
Brassey Cl *MOOR/WNTN* BH9...**56** B1
Brassey Rd *MOOR/WNTN* BH9...**56** B1
Brassey Ter *MOOR/WNTN* BH9 *...**56** B1
Breamore Cl *NMIL/BTOS* BH25...**44** C4
Brecon Cl *NBNE* BH10..............**37** E1
NMIL/BTOS BH25 ....**45** G5
Bredy Cl *CFDH* BH17................**52** A3
Bremble Cl *BKME/WDN* BH12...**35** E5
Brendon Cl *CHAR* BH8 *...........**38** C5
Briar Cl *CHCH/BSGR* BH23........**60** D4
PLE BH15.............................**53** E5
Briarswood Rd *UPTN* BH16.......**51** E3
Briar Wy *WIMB* BH21...............**15** H4
Brickfield La *LYMN* SO41..........**49** F2
Brickyard La *WIMB* BH21..........**17** E3
Bridge Ap *PLE* BH15 ....**70** B4
Bridge Pl *NBNE* BH10...............**25** H5
Bridge Rd *LYMN* SO41.............**49** F3
Bridges Cl *FERN* BH22.............**10** C3
The Bridges *RGWD* BH24..........**8** A4
Bridge St *CHCH/BSGR* BH23.....**60** A4
Bridgewater Rd
BKME/WDN BH12 ....**54** B4
Bridle Cl *CHCH/BSGR* BH23 ......**51** F3
Bridle Crs *LTDN* BH7...............**58** D2
Bridle Wy *WIMB* BH21.............**15** H3
Bridport Rd *BKME/WDN* BH12...**54** D2
VWD BH31............................**4** D3
Brierley Av *FERN* BH22............**26** A3
Brierley Rd *NBNE* BH10............**37** G5
Brierley Rd *NBNE* BH10............**37** E3
Brightlands Av *SBNE* BH6.........**77** F1
Bright Rd *PLE* BH15.................**52** D4
Brinsons Cl *CHCH/BSGR* BH23...**41** H5
Brisbane Rd *CHCH/BSGR* BH23...**59** E1
Britannia Rd *PSTN* BH14..........**71** G2
Britannia Wy *CHCH/BSGR* BH23...**41** F3
Brixey Cl *BKME/WDN* BH12......**54** A3
Brixey Rd *BKME/WDN* BH12......**54** A3
Broad Av *CHAR* BH8................**38** A5
Broadfields Cl *LYMN* SO41.......**66** B5
Broadhurst Av *NBNE* BH10.......**37** E1
Broadlands Cl *CHAR* BH8 ....**38** B4
CHCH/BSGR BH23................**43** H5
Broadlands Rd *BROC* SO42.......**86** C3
Broad La *LYMN* SO41...............**49** F4
Broadly Cl *LYMN* SO41 ....**48** B5
Broadmayne Rd
BKME/WDN BH12 ....**54** D3
Broadmoor Rd *WIMB* BH21......**32** A1
Broadshard La *RGWD* BH24......**8** D2
The Broads *WIMB* BH21 ....**14** A3
Broadstone Wy *BDST* BH18......**51** H1
CFDH BH17...........................**52** B2
Broadwater Av *PSTN* BH14.......**71** H3
Broadway *SBNE* BH6...............**77** C1
Broadway La *CHAR* BH8...........**38** A4
The Broadway *NBNE* BH10.......**36** D1
Brockenhurst Rd
MOOR/WNTN BH9................**37** H5
Brockhills La *NMIL/BTOS* BH25...**45** G2

Brockley Rd *NBNE* BH10...........**37** E3
Brocks Pine *RGWD* BH24..........**12** A3
Brockway *VWD* BH31................**4** C1
Brockwood *RGWD* BH24...........**11** G4
Bronte Av *CHCH/BSGR* BH23.....**59** G1
Brook Av *NMIL/BTOS* BH25.......**45** F3
Brook Cl *NBNE* BH10................**36** C3
Brookdale Cl *BDST* BH18..........**33** E3
Brook Dr *VWD* BH31................**5** F4
Brookland Cl *LYMN* SO41.........**48** C4
Brook La *CHCH/BSGR* BH23......**31** F5
WIMB BH21...........................**32** A1
Brookley Rd *BROC* SO42...........**86** D3
Brooklyn Ct *NMIL/BTOS* BH25...**44** D4
Brook Rd *BKME/WDN* BH12......**54** A5
LYMN SO41...........................**49** F5
NBNE BH10..........................**36** C3
WIMB BH21...........................**15** E5
Brooks Cl *RGWD* BH24.............**8** D5
Brookside Cl *CHCH/BSGR* BH23...**31** E3
CHCH/BSGR BH23................**31** E4
WIMB BH21...........................**15** E4
Brookside Rd *BROC* SO42.........**86** D2
Brookside Wy
CHCH/BSGR BH23................**62** A1
Brook Wy *CHCH/BSGR* BH23.....**61** G3
Broomfield La *LYMN* SO41........**49** E3
Broomhill Cl *LYMN* SO41..........**48** B5
Broom La *SBNE* BH6.................**76** B1
Broom Rd *BKME/WDN* BH12.....**54** A1
Broughton Av *NBNE* BH10........**37** E3
Broughton Cl *NBNE* BH10.........**37** E4
Broughton Rd *LYND* SO43........**85** E2
Brownen Rd *MOOR/WNTN* BH9...**56** D2
Browning Av *BOSC* BH5............**75** H1
Browning Rd *BKME/WDN* BH12...**54** B4
Brownings Cl *LYMN* SO41.........**48** A3
Brownsea Av *WIMB* BH21.........**32** B1
Brownsea Cl *NMIL/BTOS* BH25...**44** D4
Brownsea Rd *CCLF* BH13..........**82** D5
Brownsea View Av *PSTN* BH14...**71** H4
Brudenell Av *CCLF* BH13..........**83** F1
Brudenell Rd *CCLF* BH13..........**83** F2
Brunel Cl *VWD* BH31................**5** G4
Brune Wy *FERN* BH22..............**25** H1
Brunstead Pl *BKME/WDN* BH12...**73** F1
Brunstead Rd
BKME/WDN BH12 ....**73** E1
Brunswick Pl *LYMN* SO41.........**49** E3
Bryanstone Rd *TWDS* BH3........**56** A3
Bryant Rd *BKME/WDN* BH12.....**55** E2
Bryon Rd *WIMB* BH21...............**14** C3
Bryony Cl *BDST* BH18...............**32** D4
Bub La *CHCH/BSGR* BH23.........**60** C4
Buccaneers Cl
CHCH/BSGR BH23................**60** B4
Buccleuch Rd *CCLF* BH13.........**73** E5
Bucehayes Cl *CHCH/BSGR* BH23...**62** D2
Buchanan Av *LTDN* BH7...........**57** G4
Buckingham Rd
BKME/WDN BH12 ....**54** B3
Buckland Dene *LYMN* SO41......**48** D2
Buckland Gv *CHCH/BSGR* BH23...**43** E5
Buckland Rd *BKME/WDN* BH12...**54** A5
Buckland Ter *BKME/WDN* BH12...**54** A5
The Bucklers *LYMN* SO41.........**65** G5
Bucklers Wy *CHAR* BH8............**38** B4
Buckstone Cl *LYMN* SO41.........**66** C1
Buckthorn Cl *BDST* BH18..........**32** D5
Buddens Meadow *WIMB* BH21...**32** A3
Bugdens La *VWD* BH31............**4** D2
Bullfinch Cl *CFDH* BH17............**51** H1
Bunting Rd *FERN* BH22............**17** F1
Burbridge Cl *CFDH* BH17..........**53** E2
Burcombe La *RGWD* BH24........**9** G2
Burcombe Rd *NBNE* BH10........**36** C2
Burdock Cl *CHCH/BSGR* BH23...**61** F1
Bure Cl *CHCH/BSGR* BH23........**61** F4
Bure Haven Dr
CHCH/BSGR BH23................**61** F4
Bure Homage Gdns
CHCH/BSGR BH23................**61** F4
Bure Homage La
CHCH/BSGR BH23................**61** E4
Bure La *CHCH/BSGR* BH23.......**61** F5
Bure Pk *CHCH/BSGR* BH23.......**61** F5
Bure Rd *CHCH/BSGR* BH23.......**61** F4
Burford Cl *CHCH/BSGR* BH23....**58** D1
Burford La *BROC* SO42.............**87** E2
Burgess Cl *BWD* BH11.............**35** F4
Burleigh Rd *SBNE* BH6.............**58** D4
Burley Cl *NMIL/BTOS* BH25......**63** F2
VWD BH31............................**4** C3
Burley Rd *BKME/WDN* BH12.....**54** A4
CHCH/BSGR BH23................**31** G3
CHCH/BSGR BH23................**41** E2
Burlington Ar *BMTH* BH1 *........**3** H3
Burnaby Rd *WBNE* BH4............**2** A7

Burnbake Rd *VWD* BH31..........**4** D3
Burnbrae Rd *FERN* BH22..........**25** H3
Burn Cl *VWD* BH31..................**5** F4
Burnett Av *CHCH/BSGR* BH23...**59** E3
Burnett Rd *CHCH/BSGR* BH23...**59** F5
Burngate Rd *PLE* BH15............**69** D3
Burnham Dr *CHAR* BH8............**57** E3
Burnham Rd *CHCH/BSGR* BH23...**41** E5
Burnleigh Gdns
NMIL/BTOS BH25 ....**45** G3
Burnside *CHCH/BSGR* BH23......**60** C3
Burns Rd *SBNE* BH6.................**58** D3
Burnt House La
CHCH/BSGR BH23................**31** G2
Burrard Gv *LYMN* SO41...........**49** F5
Burtley Rd *SBNE* BH6...............**77** E2
Burton Cl *CHCH/BSGR* BH23.....**60** A1
RGWD BH24..........................**11** G1
Burtoncroft *CHCH/BSGR* BH23...**41** E4
Burton Hall Pl
CHCH/BSGR BH23................**41** F4
Burton Rd *CCLF* BH13..............**73** E2
CHCH/BSGR BH23................**60** C3
Burt's HI *WIMB* BH21...............**14** C3
Bury Rd *CCLF* BH13.................**72** D4
Bushell Rd *PLE* BH15...............**53** H2
Bushey Rd *CHAR* BH8..............**57** E1
Bushmead Dr *RGWD* BH24.......**11** H1
Bute Dr *CHCH/BSGR* BH23.......**62** D3
Butlers La *RGWD* BH24............**9** E2
Buttercup Dr *CHCH/BSGR* BH23...**61** F1
The Buttery *CHCH/BSGR* BH23...**60** B3
Butts Lawn *BROC* SO42............**86** D2
Butts Paddock *BROC* SO42.......**86** D2
Byron Cl *BOSC* BH5..................**75** H1
NMIL/BTOS BH25 ....**63** G2

C

Cabot La *CFDH* BH17...............**52** B2
Cabot Wy *NMIL/BTOS* BH25......**44** C4
Cadhay Cl *NMIL/BTOS* BH25.....**44** C4
Cadnam Wy *CHAR* BH8............**38** B4
Cadogan Rd *RGWD* BH24.........**8** D4
Caesar's Wy *BDST* BH18..........**32** C3
Caird Av *NMIL/BTOS* BH25.......**45** F4
Cairns Cl *CHCH/BSGR* BH23.....**59** F2
Caister Cl *FERN* BH22..............**17** G3
Calder Rd *CFDH* BH17.............**53** F2
Caledonia Cl *CHCH/BSGR* BH23...**61** H1
Caledon Rd *PSTN* BH14...........**72** B2
Calkin Cl *CHCH/BSGR* BH23.....**59** C1
Calluna Rd *BKME/WDN* BH12...**53** H1
Calmore Cl *CHAR* BH8..............**38** B4
Calpe Av *LYND* SO43................**85** E2
Calvin Rd *MOOR/WNTN* BH9....**56** B2
Cambridge Gdns
CHCH/BSGR BH23................**40** B5
Cambridge Rd *WCLF* BH2.........**2** D3
Camden Cl *MOOR/WNTN* BH9...**56** C1
Camellia Gdns *NMIL/BTOS* BH25...**45** F5
Cameron Rd *CHCH/BSGR* BH23...**60** B3
Cammel Rd *FERN* BH22...........**25** H2
Campbell Rd *BMTH* BH1...........**57** G5
CHCH/BSGR BH23................**40** B5
Campion Cl *LYMN* SO41 *.........**49** E2
Campion Gv *CHCH/BSGR* BH23...**60** D4
Campion Wy *LYMN* SO41.........**49** E2
Canberra Rd *CHCH/BSGR* BH23...**59** E1
Canford Av *BWD* BH11.............**54** D1
Canford Bottom *WIMB* BH21.....**16** A3
Canford Cliffs Av *PSTN* BH14....**72** B3
Canford Cliffs Rd *CCLF* BH13....**72** C2
Canford Crs *CCLF* BH13...........**83** G1
Canford Gdns *BWD* BH11.........**54** D1
Canford Heath Rd *CFDH* BH17...**33** G5
CFDH BH17...........................**34** C5
Canford Magna *WIMB* BH21.....**23** F2
Canford Rd *BWD* BH11.............**54** D1
PLE BH15.............................**70** D1
Canford View Dr *WIMB* BH21....**15** H3
Canford Wy *BKME/WDN* BH12...**35** E5
Cannon Cl *BDST* BH18.............**51** H1
Cannon Hill Gdns *WIMB* BH21...**15** H2
Cannon Hill Rd *WIMB* BH21......**15** G2
Cannon St *LYMN* SO41............**49** F3
Canterbury Cl *FERN* BH22........**10** B5
Canute Dr *CHCH/BSGR* BH23...**31** F3
Capesthorne
CHCH/BSGR BH23................**61** F5
Capstone Pl *CHAR* BH8............**57** F4
Capstone Rd *CHAR* BH8...........**57** F4
Captain's Rw *LYMN* SO41.........**49** F3
Caradon Pl *VWD* BH31.............**4** D2
Carbery Av *SBNE* BH6..............**76** D1
Carbery Gdns *SBNE* BH6..........**59** E5
Carbery Rw *SBNE* BH6 *...........**76** C1

Cardigan Rd BKME/WDN BH12 72 D1
MOOR/WNTN BH9 56 B2
Carey Rd MOOR/WNTN BH9 37 F5
Careys Cottages BROC SO42 86 D2
Careys Rd CHAR BH8 38 B3
Carisbrooke Ct
NMIL/BTOS BH25 44 D4
Carisbrooke Crs PLE BH15 69 F2
Carisbrooke Wy
CHCH/BSGR BH23 62 A1
Carlton Av NMIL/BTOS BH25 63 F3
Carlton Gv PSTN BH14 54 B5
Carlton Rd BMTH BH1 75 E1
Carlyle Rd SBNE BH6 58 D4
Carmel Cl PLE BH15 69 F3
Carnarvon Rd BMTH BH1 75 G1
Carnegie Cl BKME/WDN BH12 54 B5
Caroline Av CHCH/BSGR BH23 60 C5
Caroline Rd BWD BH11 36 B5
Carpenter Cl LYMN SO41 48 D2
Carrbridge Cl TWDS BH3 55 H3
Carrbridge Rd TWDS BH3 55 H3
Carrick Wy NMIL/BTOS BH25 45 G5
Carrington Cl LYMN SO41 80 C1
Carrington La LYMN SO41 66 C5
Carroll Av FERN BH22 17 H4
Carroll Cl BKME/WDN BH12 55 E4
Carsworth Wy CFDH BH17 34 C5
Carters Av PLE BH15 69 F1
Carter's La PLE BH15 70 C3
Cartref Cl VWD BH31 4 D2
Cartwright Cl NBNE BH10 36 C3
Carvers La RGWD BH24 8 C4
Carysfort Rd BMTH BH1 75 F1
Cashmoor Cl BKME/WDN BH12 54 D3
Caslake Cl NMIL/BTOS BH25 63 H1
Cassel Av CCLF BH13 73 F4
Casterbridge Rd FERN BH22 25 G1
Castle Av CHCH/BSGR BH23 62 A2
Castle Cl LYMN SO41 80 C2
Castledene Crs PSTN BH14 71 G3
Castle Gate Cl CHAR BH8 38 A5
Castle La East LTDN BH7 58 B2
Castle La West CHAR BH8 38 B5
MOOR/WNTN BH9 37 H4
Castlemain Av SBNE BH6 58 C5
Castleman Trailway
BDST BH18 33 E4
CFDH BH17 51 G2
RGWD BH24 7 E5
WIMB BH21 11 E2
WIMB BH21 16 B2
WIMB BH21 22 C4
Castleman Wy RGWD BH24 8 C5
Castlemews RGWD BH24 12 D1
Castle Point CHAR BH8 * 38 C5
Castle Rd MOOR/WNTN BH9 56 B1
Castle St CHCH/BSGR BH23 59 H4
PLE BH15 70 C4
Castleton Av NBNE BH10 36 D1
Castle Wy CHAR BH8 57 F1
Castlewood RGWD BH24 13 E1
Catalina Cl CHCH/BSGR BH23 61 E4
Catalina Dr PLE BH15 71 E4
Caton Cl BKME/WDN BH12 55 F2
Cattistock Rd CHAR BH8 57 G1
Cavan Crs CFDH BH17 52 B1
Cavendish Pl BMTH BH1 56 C5
Cavendish Rd WCLF BH2 56 B5
Caversham Cl PLE BH15 69 G2
Cawdor Rd TWDS BH3 55 H3
Caxton Cl CHCH/BSGR BH23 60 D3
Cecil Av CHAR BH8 57 E2
Cecil Cl WIMB BH21 32 C1
Cecil Hl CHAR BH8 56 D2
Cecil Rd BKME/WDN BH12 54 B4
BOSC BH5 75 G1
Cedar Av CHCH/BSGR BH23 58 D2
NBNE BH10 36 D1
RGWD BH24 11 H3
Cedar Cl UPTN BH16 50 D2
Cedar Dr LYMN SO41 66 B2
WIMB BH21 15 H4
Cedarmount LYND SO43 85 E4
Cedar Pl CHCH/BSGR BH23 31 F3
The Cedars WBNE BH4 2 B1
Cedar Wy FERN BH22 17 G1
Celandine Cl CHCH/BSGR BH23 61 F2
Cellars Farm Rd SBNE BH6 77 G2
Cemetery Av PLE BH15 53 F4
Cemetery Rd WIMB BH21 14 B4
Central Av BKME/WDN BH12 54 C4
Central Dr RGWD BH24 18 D1
WCLF BH2 3 F2
Centre La LYMN SO41 66 C1
Centre Pl RGWD BH24 8 B4
Cerne Abbas CCLF BH13 73 E4
Cerne Cl MOOR/WNTN BH9 37 H3
Chaddesley Gln CCLF BH13 83 F2
Chaddesley Pines CCLF BH13 83 G2
Chaddesley Wood Rd
CCLF BH13 83 G3
Chaffey Cl RGWD BH24 9 E3
Chaffinch Cl CFDH BH17 51 H1
NMIL/BTOS BH25 44 D5
Chalbury Cl CFDH BH17 34 C5
Chaldecott Gdns NBNE BH10 36 C3
Chaldon Rd CFDH BH17 34 B5
Chalfont Av CHCH/BSGR BH23 39 H4
Chalice Cl PSTN BH14 71 G1
Champion Cl LYMN SO41 80 C1
Chander Cl FERN BH22 17 H5
Chandlers Cl LTDN BH7 58 B2
Chandos Av BKME/WDN BH12 55 E2
Chant Cl CHCH/BSGR BH23 60 B3
Chantry Cl CHCH/BSGR BH23 62 B1
Chapel Cl WIMB BH21 32 A2
Chapel La CHCH/BSGR BH23 27 E1
CHCH/BSGR BH23 31 E4
LYND SO43 85 E4
PLE BH15 70 C3
WIMB BH21 14 B4
WIMB BH21 32 A2
Chapel Ri RGWD BH24 13 E4
Chapel Rd PSTN BH14 71 G1
Charborough Rd BDST BH18 33 F4
Charing Cl RGWD BH24 8 C5
Charles Crs NMIL/BTOS BH25 45 F2
Charles Gdns NBNE BH10 36 C5
Charles Keightley Ct
WIMB BH21 14 D5
Charles Rd CHCH/BSGR BH23 60 D2
PLE BH15 70 D2
Charlotte Cl BKME/WDN BH12 55 G3
CHCH/BSGR BH23 61 E4
Charlton Cl LYMN SO41 46 B4
MOOR/WNTN BH9 38 A3
Charminster Av
MOOR/WNTN BH9 56 D1
Charminster Cl CHAR BH8 37 H5
Charminster Pl CHAR BH8 * 38 A5
Charminster Rd CHAR BH8 56 D1
Charmouth Gv PSTN BH14 71 G1
Charnock Cl LYMN SO41 46 B4
Charnwood Av
MOOR/WNTN BH9 37 H4
Charnwood Cl FERN BH22 10 B4
Charter Rd BWD BH11 35 F1
Chaseside LTDN BH7 58 A2
The Chase RGWD BH24 13 E1
VWD BH31 5 G2
Chatsworth Rd CHAR BH8 56 D4
PSTN BH14 53 H5
Chatsworth Wy
NMIL/BTOS BH25 44 C4
Chaucer Cl WIMB BH21 14 C3
Chaucer Dr LYMN SO41 66 B5
Chaucer Rd CCLF BH13 72 C5
Chaucombe Pl
NMIL/BTOS BH25 63 H1
Cheam Rd BDST BH18 32 D3
Cheddington Rd
MOOR/WNTN BH9 37 G3
Chedington Cl CFDH BH17 34 A5
Chelmsford Rd UPTN BH16 50 D3
Cheltenham Rd
BKME/WDN BH12 54 A5
Chene Rd WIMB BH21 14 D5
Chequers Cl LYMN SO41 48 B4
Cherford Rd BWD BH11 36 B5
Cherita Ct PLE BH15 53 F4
Cheriton Av LTDN BH7 58 C2
Cheriton Wy WIMB BH21 14 C3
Cherrett Cl BWD BH11 35 H3
Cherries Dr MOOR/WNTN BH9 37 E5
Cherry Cl PSTN BH14 71 H1
Cherry Gv FERN BH22 17 G3
Cherry Hill Gv UPTN BH16 50 D4
Cherry Tree Cl LYMN SO41 66 B2
RGWD BH24 11 G3
Cherry Tree Dr
NMIL/BTOS BH25 44 C2
Cheshire Dr CHAR BH8 39 E5
Chesilbourne Gv CHAR BH8 38 B4
Chesildene Av CHAR BH8 38 B5
Chesildene Dr CHAR BH8 38 B4
Chessel Av BOSC BH5 75 H1
Chesterfield Cl CCLF BH13 72 D5
Chester Rd CCLF BH13 73 E3
Chestnut Av CHCH/BSGR BH23 58 D2
NMIL/BTOS BH25 64 A2
SBNE BH6 76 C1
Chestnut Gv WIMB BH21 16 C3
Chestnut Rd BROC SO42 87 E3
Chestnut Wy
CHCH/BSGR BH23 41 E4
Chetnole Cl CFDH BH17 53 F1
Chetwode Wy BDST BH18 33 F5
Cheviot Wy VWD BH31 4 D3
Chewton Common Rd
CHCH/BSGR BH23 62 C1
Chewton Farm Rd
CHCH/BSGR BH23 44 A5
Chewton Ldg CHCH/BSGR BH23 62 D2
Chewton Wy CHCH/BSGR BH23 62 D1
Cheyne Gdns WBNE BH4 2 B5
Chichester Rd RGWD BH24 9 E3
Chichester Wk WIMB BH21 23 F3
Chichester Wy
CHCH/BSGR BH23 79 E1
Chickerell Cl MOOR/WNTN BH9 37 H4
Chideock Cl BKME/WDN BH12 54 C4
Chigwell Rd CHAR BH8 57 E1
Chilcombe Rd SBNE BH6 * 58 B5
Chilfrome Cl CFDH BH17 52 C1
Chiltern Cl NMIL/BTOS BH25 63 H1
WBNE BH4 55 F5
Chiltern Dr NMIL/BTOS BH25 63 G2
VWD BH31 4 D2
Chine Crs WCLF BH2 2 D5
Chine Crescent Rd WCLF BH2 2 D5
Chine Rd WBNE BH4 73 F2
Chine Wk FERN BH22 26 A3
Chisels La CHCH/BSGR BH23 42 B1
Chiswell Rd CFDH BH17 52 D1
Chloe Gdns BKME/WDN BH12 54 B3
Chorley Cl PLE BH15 52 C4
Chris Crs UPTN BH16 51 E3
Christchurch Bay Rd
NMIL/BTOS BH25 63 H3
Christchurch By-Pass
CHCH/BSGR BH23 59 H3
Christchurch Rd BMTH BH1 74 D2
CHCH/BSGR BH23 39 F1
FERN BH22 25 F2
LTDN BH7 58 A5
NMIL/BTOS BH25 63 G2
RGWD BH24 8 B4
RGWD BH24 13 H2
Christopher Crs PLE BH15 52 C4
Chubb Ms BKME/WDN BH12 54 A5
Churchfield VWD BH31 4 C2
Churchfield Crs PLE BH15 71 E1
Churchfield Rd PLE BH15 71 E2
Church Hl LYMN SO41 66 C5
VWD BH31 4 C2
Churchill Crs BKME/WDN BH12 54 A4
Churchill Gdns
BKME/WDN BH12 54 A5
Churchill Rd BKME/WDN BH12 54 A4
BMTH BH1 57 F5
WIMB BH21 22 D1
Church La BROC SO42 87 E4
CHCH/BSGR BH23 59 H4
FERN BH22 26 B5
LYMN SO41 49 E4
LYND SO43 85 E3
Church Md LYMN SO41 49 E5
Churchmoor Rd WIMB BH21 15 G4
Church Rd FERN BH22 17 G4
PSTN BH14 71 G1
SBNE BH6 77 F2
Church St CHCH/BSGR BH23 59 H4
PLE BH15 70 B4
WIMB BH21 14 B4
Cinnamon La PLE BH15 70 B4
The Circle MOOR/WNTN BH9 * 37 G3
Clare Lodge Cl
CHCH/BSGR BH23 31 E4
Claremont Av
MOOR/WNTN BH9 37 H5
Claremont Rd
MOOR/WNTN BH9 37 H5
Clarence Gdns BDST BH18 33 E5
Clarence Park Rd LTDN BH7 58 A4
Clarence Rd LYND SO43 85 F3
PSTN BH14 * 71 G2
Clarendon Cl BDST BH18 33 E3
Clarendon Pk LYMN SO41 48 D5
Clarendon Rd BDST BH18 32 C4
CHCH/BSGR BH23 59 G3
WBNE BH4 2 C5
Clark's Cl RGWD BH24 8 C4
Clausen Wy LYMN SO41 67 G1
Clayford Av FERN BH22 17 F2
Clayford Cl CFDH BH17 33 H5
Claylake Dr VWD BH31 5 E3
Cleeves Cl BKME/WDN BH12 35 F5
Clematis Cl CHCH/BSGR BH23 61 G2
Cleveland Cl NMIL/BTOS BH25 63 F3
Cleveland Gdns BMTH BH1 57 E5
Cleveland Rd BMTH BH1 57 F5
Cliff Crs NMIL/BTOS BH25 63 H3
Cliff Dr CCLF BH13 83 H2
CHCH/BSGR BH23 61 G4
Cliffe Rd NMIL/BTOS BH25 63 G3
Clifford Rd MOOR/WNTN BH9 56 C1
Cliff Ter NMIL/BTOS BH25 * 63 H4
Clifton Gdns FERN BH22 17 G5
Clifton Rd PSTN BH14 72 B3
SBNE BH6 76 D2
Clingan Rd SBNE BH6 58 D4
Clinton Cl CHCH/BSGR BH23 43 H5
Clinton Rd LYMN SO41 49 E2
Cliveden Cl FERN BH22 17 G2
Clive Rd CHCH/BSGR BH23 43 E5
MOOR/WNTN BH9 56 B1
The Cloisters LYMN SO41 * 49 E4
RGWD BH24 9 E5
The Close BDST BH18 32 C4
NMIL/BTOS BH25 64 A2
RGWD BH24 8 B4
RGWD BH24 12 B2
RGWD BH24 13 E2
Clough's Rd RGWD BH24 8 D4
Clover Cl CHCH/BSGR BH23 61 F2
Clover Ct NMIL/BTOS BH25 45 H3
Clover Dr CFDH BH17 51 H1
The Clovers BKME/WDN BH12 55 E2
Clowes Av SBNE BH6 77 H2
Clyde Rd CFDH BH17 33 F5
Coach House Ms FERN BH22 18 B2
Coach House Pl BMTH BH1 56 C5
Coastguard Wy
CHCH/BSGR BH23 78 C1
Cobbs La PLE BH15 53 E4
Cobb's Rd WIMB BH21 15 E3
Cobham Rd FERN BH22 17 F1
MOOR/WNTN BH9 37 G4
WIMB BH21 16 D2
Cobham Wy WIMB BH21 23 E3
Cockerell Cl WIMB BH21 23 F3
Cogdeane Rd CFDH BH17 33 H5
Colborne Av WIMB BH21 15 F4
Colborne Cl LYMN SO41 49 E2
PLE BH15 70 D4
Colbourne Cl CHCH/BSGR BH23 31 E4
Colehill Crs MOOR/WNTN BH9 37 H4
Colehill La WIMB BH21 15 E3
Coleman Rd BWD BH11 36 A4
Colemere Gdns
CHCH/BSGR BH23 62 B1
Colemore Rd LTDN BH7 58 C3
Coleridge Gn CHCH/BSGR BH23 60 D2
Coles Av PLE BH15 69 G3
Coles Gdns PLE BH15 69 G3
Colin Cl WIMB BH21 32 B2
College Rd BOSC BH5 76 A1
RGWD BH24 8 C4
Collingbourne Av SBNE BH6 58 D4
Collins La RGWD BH24 8 C4
Collwood Cl PLE BH15 52 C3
Collyers Rd BROC SO42 86 D5
Colonnade Rd BOSC BH5 58 A5
Colonnade Rd West BOSC BH5 58 A5
Colt Cl WIMB BH21 15 H3
Columbian Wy NBNE BH10 36 C5
Columbia Rd NBNE BH10 36 D5
Columbia Trees La NBNE BH10 55 G1
Columbine Cl CHCH/BSGR BH23 61 F1
Colville Cl BOSC BH5 58 A5
Colville Rd LTDN BH7 58 A5
Comber Rd MOOR/WNTN BH9 37 F4
Comet Wy CHCH/BSGR BH23 61 E4
Comley Rd MOOR/WNTN BH9 37 F5
Commercial Rd PSTN BH14 71 F1
WCLF BH2 2 E4
Compton Av PSTN BH14 72 B3
Compton Beeches RGWD BH24 12 B1
Compton Cl VWD BH31 4 D2
Compton Crs FERN BH22 10 D5
Compton Dr PSTN BH14 72 A3
Compton Gdns PSTN BH14 72 A3
Compton Rd NMIL/BTOS BH25 45 E5
Condor Cl WIMB BH21 11 E1
Coneygar La FERN BH22 25 E1
Conference Pl LYMN SO41 49 F5
Conifer Av PSTN BH14 71 H3
Conifer Cl CHCH/BSGR BH23 39 H4
FERN BH22 26 B3
RGWD BH24 11 G2
Conifer Crs LYMN SO41 48 B5
Coniston Av BWD BH11 35 H1
Coniston Cl VWD BH31 4 C3
Coniston Rd RGWD BH24 * 8 D5
Connaught Cl NMIL/BTOS BH25 63 G2
Connaught Crs
BKME/WDN BH12 54 C4
Connaught Rd LTDN BH7 58 B5
Connell Rd PLE BH15 52 C5
Consort Cl BKME/WDN BH12 54 A5
Constable Cl FERN BH22 17 G5
Constitution Hill Rd PSTN BH14 71 F1
Conway Cl NMIL/BTOS BH25 45 F4
Conways Dr PSTN BH14 71 G1
Cook Cl RGWD BH24 9 E3

Cooke Rd BKME/WDN BH12....54 D4
Cook Rw WIMB BH21....14 B5
Coombe Av NBNE BH10....37 E4
Coombe Gdns NMIL/BTOS BH25....36 D5
Cooper Dean Dr CHAR BH8....57 H1
Coopers La VWD BH31....4 D1
Copeland Dr PSTN BH14....71 H3
Copper Beech Cl
  BKME/WDN BH12....73 E1
Copper Beech Gdns
  NBNE BH10....36 D5
Coppice Av FERN BH22....17 F2
Coppice Cl NMIL/BTOS BH25....45 H3
  RGWD BH24....12 A3
The Coppice BROC SO42....86 B2
  CHCH/BSGR BH23....61 F4
Coppice Vw NBNE BH10....37 E4
Copse Cl PSTN BH14....71 F2
Copse Rd NMIL/BTOS BH25....45 F5
  VWD BH31....4 D2
The Copse RGWD BH24....18 D1
Copse Wy CHCH/BSGR BH23....62 A2
Copsewood Av CHAR BH8....57 G1
Copythorne Cl CHAR BH8....38 B5
Corbar Rd CHCH/BSGR BH23....59 E2
Corbiere Av BKME/WDN BH12....54 B5
Corbin Av CHCH/BSGR BH23....18 C3
Corbin Rd LYMN SO41....48 B5
Corfe Lodge Rd BDST BH18....32 B4
Corfe View Rd PSTN BH14....71 H2
  WIMB BH21....32 B2
Corfe Wy BDST BH18....32 C4
Corhampton Rd SBNE BH6....58 C4
Cornelia Crs BKME/WDN BH12....55 E4
Cornflower Dr
  CHCH/BSGR BH23....61 G1
Cornford Wy CHCH/BSGR BH23....61 H2
Cornish Gdns NBNE BH10....55 H1
Coronation Av
  MOOR/WNTN BH9....37 F5
  UPTN BH16....50 D3
Coronation Rd VWD BH31....4 D1
Corporation Rd BMTH BH1....57 E5
Corscombe Cl CFDH BH17....34 A5
Cortry Cl BKME/WDN BH12....55 E3
Cotes Av PSTN BH14....53 C5
Cotlands Rd BMTH BH1....74 D1
Cotswold Cl VWD BH31....4 D3
Cottage Gdns
  BKME/WDN BH12....54 A5
Cottage Ms RGWD BH24....8 B4
Cottagers La LYMN SO41....46 C4
Cotton Cl BDST BH18....32 D2
Countess Cl WIMB BH21....23 E4
Countess Gdns LTDN BH7....57 H2
County Gates La WBNE BH4....73 F1
Court Cl CHCH/BSGR BH23....60 C3
  LYMN SO41....48 D5
Courtenay Cl WIMB BH21....14 C3
Courtenay Pl LYMN SO41....49 E5
Courtenay Rd PSTN BH14....71 H1
Courthill Rd PSTN BH14....72 A1
Court Ldg LYMN SO41 *....48 C5
Court Rd MOOR/WNTN BH9....56 D1
Covena Rd SBNE BH6....58 D4
Coventry Cl WIMB BH21....32 A3
Coventry Crs CFDH BH17....52 C4
Cove Rd NBNE BH10....36 C5
Cowdrey Gdns CHAR BH8....38 D5
Cowdrys Fld WIMB BH21....14 B3
Cowell Dr LTDN BH7....58 B2
Cowgrove Rd WIMB BH21....14 A4
Cowley Rd CFDH BH17....52 D2
  LYMN SO41....66 A2
Cowpitts La RGWD BH24....9 F1
Cowper Av NMIL/BTOS BH25....64 A1
Cowper Rd MOOR/WNTN BH9....37 F5
Cowslip Rd BDST BH18....51 G1
Cox Av MOOR/WNTN BH9....37 H4
Cox Cl MOOR/WNTN BH9....37 H3
Coxstone La RGWD BH24....8 C5
Coy Pond Rd BKME/WDN BH12....55 F5
Crabton Close Rd BOSC BH5....75 H1
  LTDN BH7....57 H5
Crabtree Cl CHCH/BSGR BH23....41 E5
Cracklewood Cl FERN BH22....18 C2
Craigmoor Av CHAR BH8....57 G1
Craigmoor Cl CHAR BH8....57 H1
Craigmoor Wy CHAR BH8....38 C5
Craigside Rd RGWD BH24....11 G2
Craigwood Dr FERN BH22....18 A5
Cranborne Crs
  BKME/WDN BH12....54 C2
  WIMB BH21....14 C1
Cranbrook Rd
  BKME/WDN BH12....53 H4

Crane Cl VWD BH31....4 C1
Crane Dr VWD BH31....4 C2
Cranemoor Av
  CHCH/BSGR BH23....43 E5
Cranemoor Cl
  CHCH/BSGR BH23....43 E5
Cranemoor Gdns
  CHCH/BSGR BH23....43 F5
Cranes Ms PLE BH15....70 D2
Cranleigh Av WIMB BH21....14 D4
Cranleigh Cl SBNE BH6....59 E5
Cranleigh Gdns SBNE BH6....59 E5
Cranleigh Rd SBNE BH6....58 D4
Cranmer Rd MOOR/WNTN BH9....56 B2
Crantock Gv CHAR BH8....38 D5
Cranwell Cl BWD BH11....35 G3
  CHCH/BSGR BH23....31 F3
Crawshaw Rd PSTN BH14....71 H3
Creasey Rd BWD BH11....36 B4
Creech Rd BKME/WDN BH12....54 A5
Creedy Dr CHCH/BSGR BH23....59 G5
Creekmoor La CFDH BH17....51 H1
Crescent Dr NMIL/BTOS BH25....63 H3
Crescent Rd PSTN BH14....72 C1
  VWD BH31....5 E2
  WCLF BH2....2 E3
  WIMB BH21....14 C5
The Crescent BMTH BH1....75 G1
  NMIL/BTOS BH25....63 F2
  RGWD BH24....18 D1
Crescent Wk FERN BH22....26 A2
Cresta Gdns FERN BH22....26 A2
Crest Rd BKME/WDN BH12....54 A4
Cribb Cl CFDH BH17....52 E3
Crichel Mount Rd PSTN BH14....72 A5
Crichel Rd MOOR/WNTN BH9....56 B2
Cricket Cl CHCH/BSGR BH23....60 D5
Crimea Rd MOOR/WNTN BH9....56 B3
Cringle Av SBNE BH6....77 G1
Crispin Cl CHCH/BSGR BH23....62 B2
Criterion Ar BMTH BH1 *....3 G4
Crockford Cl NMIL/BTOS BH25....45 F2
Crofton Cl CHCH/BSGR BH23....59 E2
Croft Cl BKME/WDN BH12....53 H4
  CHCH/BSGR BH23....42 B1
  CHCH/BSGR BH23....60 D3
  MOOR/WNTN BH9....37 F5
  RGWD BH24....9 E2
Cromer Gdns BKME/WDN BH12....54 D5
Cromer Rd BKME/WDN BH12....54 D5
  CHAR BH8....57 F3
Cromwell Pl BOSC BH5....58 B5
Cromwell Rd BKME/WDN BH12....54 B5
  BOSC BH5....58 B5
  WIMB BH21....14 D5
Crosby Rd WBNE BH4....73 G4
Crossmead Av
  NMIL/BTOS BH25....45 E5
Cross Wy CHCH/BSGR BH23....58 D1
Crossways LYMN SO41....66 B1
The Crossways UPTN BH16....51 E3
Crow Arch La RGWD BH24....8 D5
Crown Cl BKME/WDN BH12....54 A5
Crown Md WIMB BH21....14 C5
Crusader Rd BWD BH11....35 F3
Cucklington Gdns
  MOOR/WNTN BH9....37 H4
Cuckoo Hill Wy
  CHCH/BSGR BH23....31 C3
Cuckoo Rd BKME/WDN BH12....53 G2
Cudnell Av BWD BH11....35 H1
The Cul-de-Sac
  NMIL/BTOS BH25 *....63 E2
Culford Cl CHAR BH8....38 D5
Cull Cl BKME/WDN BH12....55 G2
Culliford Crs CFDH BH17....34 A5
Cull La NMIL/BTOS BH25....45 F2
Cullwood La NMIL/BTOS BH25....45 G2
Culverhayes Pl WIMB BH21....14 B3
Culverhayes Rd WIMB BH21....14 B3
Culverley Cl BROC SO42....86 D3
Culver Rd NMIL/BTOS BH25....44 D5
Cumnor Rd BMTH BH1....3 J3
Cunningham Cl BWD BH11....36 A4
  CHCH/BSGR BH23....61 E3
  RGWD BH24....9 E3
Cunningham Crs BWD BH11....36 A4
Cunningham Pl BWD BH11....36 A4
Curlew Cl FERN BH22....17 F2
Curlew Rd CHAR BH8....38 B5
  CHCH/BSGR BH23....61 E4
The Curlews VWD BH31....5 E3
Curlieu Rd PLE BH15....53 E4
Curtis Rd BKME/WDN BH12....54 A5
Curzon Pl LYMN SO41....48 D5
Curzon Rd BMTH BH1....57 F4
  PSTN BH14....71 G2
Curzon Wy CHCH/BSGR BH23....61 H2
Custards Rd LYND SO43....85 E2

Cuthburga Rd WIMB BH21....14 C4
Cuthbury Cl WIMB BH21....14 A5
Cuthbury Gdns WIMB BH21....14 A4
Cutler Cl BKME/WDN BH12....55 G3
  NMIL/BTOS BH25....45 G4
Cutlers Pl WIMB BH21....15 C4
Cynthia Cl BKME/WDN BH12....53 H3
Cynthia Rd BKME/WDN BH12....53 H3
Cyril Rd CHAR BH8....57 E4

D

Dacombe Cl UPTN BH16....51 E3
Dacombe Dr UPTN BH16....51 E3
Dairy Cl CHCH/BSGR BH23....60 B4
Daisy Cl PLE BH15....52 D4
Dale Cl PLE BH15....53 F4
Dale Rd PLE BH15....53 F4
Dales Cl WIMB BH21....16 A3
Dales Dr WIMB BH21....15 H4
Dales La CHCH/BSGR BH23....27 G5
Dale Valley Rd PLE BH15....53 F3
Dalkeith Rd CCLF BH13....73 E4
  WIMB BH21....32 B3
Dalkeith Steps BMTH BH1 *....3 H3
Dalling Rd BKME/WDN BH12....55 E5
Dalmeny Rd SBNE BH6....77 G2
Damerham Rd CHAR BH8....38 B4
Danecourt Cl PSTN BH14....71 F1
Danecourt Rd PSTN BH14....71 F1
Danecrest Rd LYMN SO41....46 B4
Dane Dr FERN BH22....26 A1
Dane Rd LYMN SO41....65 G4
Danesbury Av SBNE BH6....77 F1
Danesbury Mdw
  NMIL/BTOS BH25....45 G2
Danes Cl NMIL/BTOS BH25....64 A3
Danestream Cl LYMN SO41....80 B1
Daneswood Rd
  NMIL/BTOS BH25....45 G4
Daniell's Cl LYMN SO41....49 E4
Daniell's Wk LYMN SO41....49 E5
Dansie Cl PSTN BH14....71 H1
Darby's Cl PLE BH15....52 D4
Darby's Cnr CFDH BH17....33 G5
Darby's La PLE BH15....52 D4
Darby's La North CFDH BH17....52 D3
Dark La CHCH/BSGR BH23....43 G3
Darley Rd FERN BH22....25 G1
Darracott Rd BOSC BH5....76 A1
Darwin Av CHCH/BSGR BH23....59 E1
Davenport Cl UPTN BH16....51 E3
David's La RGWD BH24....12 D1
Davis Fld NMIL/BTOS BH25....44 D5
Davis Rd BKME/WDN BH12....54 C5
Dawkins Rd PLE BH15....69 F2
Dawkins Wy NMIL/BTOS BH25....45 E5
Dawn Cl NBNE BH10....36 C5
Daws Av BWD BH11....36 B5
Daylesford Cl PSTN BH14....71 G3
Day's Ct WIMB BH21....14 D5
Deacon Gdns BWD BH11....36 A2
Deacon Rd BWD BH11....36 A2
Dean Cl PLE BH15....69 G2
Dean Park Crs BMTH BH1....3 H3
Dean Park Rd WCLF BH2....3 G2
Deans Ct LYMN SO41....66 B5
Deans Court La WIMB BH21....14 B5
Deanscroft Rd NBNE BH10....37 E3
Deans Gv WIMB BH21....14 D2
Deansleigh Rd LTDN BH7....58 B1
Dean's Rd BOSC BH5....58 B5
The Deans BMTH BH1....3 H1
Dean Swift Crs PSTN BH14....72 A5
Dear Hay La PLE BH15....70 C3
Dearing Cl LYND SO43....85 E4
Decies Rd PSTN BH14....53 H5
De Courtenai Cl BWD BH11....35 G2
Deerleap Wy NMIL/BTOS BH25....45 F2
Deer Park Cl NMIL/BTOS BH25....44 D3
Dee Wy PLE BH15....70 B3
De Haviland Wy WIMB BH21....23 F2
De Havilland Wy
  CHCH/BSGR BH23....61 E3
Delamere Gdns NBNE BH10....37 E4
De La Warr Rd LYMN SO41....80 A1
Delft Ms CHCH/BSGR BH23....60 B3
Delhi Cl PLE BH15....52 B2
Delhi Rd MOOR/WNTN BH9....37 E5
Delilah Rd PLE BH15....69 F3
De Lisle Rd TWDS BH3....56 B3
Dell Cl BDST BH18....32 C3
The Dell CHCH/BSGR BH23....63 E2
Delph Rd WIMB BH21....22 D4
Delta Cl CHCH/BSGR BH23....61 E3

De Mauley Rd CCLF BH13....72 C5
De Montfort Rd WIMB BH21....22 D3
De Mowbray Wy LYMN SO41....48 D5
Denby Rd PLE BH15....70 D1
Dene Cl RGWD BH24....9 F2
Deneside Copse LYMN SO41....67 F1
Deneside Gdns LYMN SO41....48 C5
Deneve Av CFDH BH17....52 C1
Dene Wk FERN BH22....26 A3
Denewood Copse FERN BH22....10 A3
Denewood Rd FERN BH22....10 A2
  WBNE BH4....73 F3
Denham Cl CFDH BH17....34 A4
Denham Dr CHCH/BSGR BH23....62 B1
Denholm Cl RGWD BH24....9 F2
Denison Rd CFDH BH17....52 C1
Denmark La PLE BH15....70 D2
Denmark Rd MOOR/WNTN BH9....56 B1
  PLE BH15....70 D2
Denmead NMIL/BTOS BH25....45 H3
Denmead Rd SBNE BH6....58 D3
Dennis Rd PLE BH15....32 B2
Dennistoun Av
  CHCH/BSGR BH23....60 D3
Derby Rd BMTH BH1....75 E1
De Redvers Rd PSTN BH14....72 A3
Dereham Wy BKME/WDN BH12....54 D4
Derritt La CHCH/BSGR BH23....30 A5
Derrybrian Gdns
  NMIL/BTOS BH25....45 E5
Derwent Cl FERN BH22....18 C3
  MOOR/WNTN BH9....37 G5
Derwent Rd NMIL/BTOS BH25....45 F2
Derwentwater Rd WIMB BH21....22 D2
Deverel Cl CHCH/BSGR BH23....59 G2
Devon Cl CHCH/BSGR BH23....59 E2
  PLE BH15....53 E5
Dewlands Rd VWD BH31....4 B2
Dewlands Wy VWD BH31....4 C2
Dewlish Cl CFDH BH17....34 C5
Dial Cl CHCH/BSGR BH23....31 G2
Dibden Cl CHAR BH8....38 B4
Dickens Rd SBNE BH6....58 D3
Didcot Rd CFDH BH17....52 D3
Dilly La NMIL/BTOS BH25....64 A3
Dingle Rd BOSC BH5....76 B1
Dingley Rd PLE BH15....52 D4
Dinham Rd NMIL/BTOS BH25....45 H3
Disraeli Rd CHCH/BSGR BH23....60 B4
Ditchbury LYMN SO41....48 D1
Doe Copse Wy NMIL/BTOS BH25....44 C3
Dogdean WIMB BH21....14 C1
Dogwood Rd BDST BH18....32 C5
Dolberry Rd South
  BKME/WDN BH12....54 A1
Dolphin Av NBNE BH10....37 E2
Dolphin Pl NMIL/BTOS BH25....63 H3
Dominion Rd BWD BH11....35 G4
Donnelly Rd SBNE BH6....59 F5
Donnington Dr
  CHCH/BSGR BH23....61 F3
Donoughmore Rd BMTH BH1....75 F1
Dorchester Gdns PLE BH15....53 E5
Dorchester Rd PLE BH15....53 E4
  UPTN BH16....50 C3
Dornie Rd CCLF BH13....83 C1
Dorset Av FERN BH22....17 H5
Dorset Lake Av PSTN BH14....71 H5
Dorset Rd CHCH/BSGR BH23....60 D2
  WBNE BH4....55 C5
Dorset Wy PLE BH15....52 D3
Douglas Av CHCH/BSGR BH23....59 F4
Douglas Cl UPTN BH16....51 E3
Douglas Gdns BKME/WDN BH12....54 C5
Douglas Ms SBNE BH6....58 C5
Douglas Rd BKME/WDN BH12....54 C5
  SBNE BH6....77 E2
Doulton Gdns PSTN BH14....71 H3
Doussie Cl UPTN BH16....50 C3
Dover Cl CCLF BH13....73 E2
Dover Rd CCLF BH13....73 E2
Doveshill Crs NBNE BH10....36 D4
Doveshill Gdns NBNE BH10....36 D4
Dowlands Cl NBNE BH10....36 D3
Dowlands Rd NBNE BH10....36 D3
Downey Cl BWD BH11....35 H5
Downland Pl CFDH BH17 *....53 E2
Downton Cl CHAR BH8....38 A4
Downton La LYMN SO41....65 F4
Doyne Rd PSTN BH14....72 C1
Dpdn La RGWD BH24....35 G2
Dragon La RGWD BH24....21 G1
Dragoon Wy CHCH/BSGR BH23....59 F3
Drake Cl CHCH/BSGR BH23....60 D4
  NMIL/BTOS BH25....44 D4
  RGWD BH24....9 E2
Drake Rd PLE BH15....70 C4
Drakes Rd FERN BH22....26 B1

Draper Rd *BWD* BH11 ....36 A3
CHCH/BSGR BH23 ....60 C3
Draycott Rd *NBNE* BH10 ....36 D5
Dreswick Cl *CHCH/BSGR* BH23 .....39 H3
Drew Cl *BKME/WDN* BH12 ....15 H2
The Drive *BKME/WDN* BH12 ....54 B5
CCLF BH13 ....83 F1
Droxford Rd *LTDN* BH7 ....58 B4
Druids Cl *FERN* BH22 ....25 H2
Druitt Rd *CHCH/BSGR* BH23 ....60 D3
Drummond Rd *BMTH* BH1 ....75 F1
Drury Rd *WBNE* BH4 ....73 F3
Dryden Cl *RGWD* BH24 ....11 H1
Dryden Pl *LYMN* SO41 ....66 B5
Ducking Stool La
CHCH/BSGR BH23 ....59 H4
Duck Island La *RGWD* BH24 ....8 B5
Duck La *BWD* BH11 ....35 H3
Dudley Av *LYMN* SO41 ....46 B5
Dudley Gdns *NBNE* BH10 ....36 D2
Dudley Rd *NBNE* BH10 ....36 D2
Dudmoor Farm Rd
Dudmoor La *CHCH/BSGR* BH23....40 B4
Dudsbury Av *FERN* BH22 ....17 H5
Dudsbury Crs *FERN* BH22 ....17 H5
Dudsbury Gdns *FERN* BH22 ....26 A4
Dudsbury Rd *FERN* BH22 ....25 H3
Dugdell Cl *FERN* BH22 ....18 B3
Dukes Cl *SBNE* BH6 ....58 D5
Dukes Dr *BWD* BH11 ....35 G2
Dukesfield *CHCH/BSGR* BH23 ......39 H5
Dulsie Rd *TWDS* BH3 ....55 C3
Dunbar Crs *CHCH/BSGR* BH23 .....43 F5
Dunbar Rd *TWDS* BH3 ....56 A4
Duncan Rd *NMIL/BTOS* BH25 ......45 H3
Duncliff Rd *SBNE* BH6 ....77 G1
Duncombe Dr *RGWD* BH24 ....7 F1
Dundas Rd *CFDH* BH17 ....53 E2
Dunedin Cl *FERN* BH22 ....25 F1
Dunedin Dr *FERN* BH22 ....25 F1
Dunedin Gdns *FERN* BH22 ....25 F1
Dunedin Gv *CHCH/BSGR* BH23 ....61 G3
Dunford Cl *NMIL/BTOS* BH25 ....63 G2
Dunford Rd *BKME/WDN* BH12 .....54 B5
Dunkeld Rd *TWDS* BH3 ....55 H4
Dunlin Cl *CHCH/BSGR* BH23 ....61 F5
Dunnock Cl *FERN* BH22 ....17 F1
Dunstans La *PSTN* BH14 ....53 G4
Dunyeats Rd *BDST* BH18 ....33 F3
Dunyeats Rbt *BDST* BH18 ....33 H2
Durdells Av *BWD* BH11 ....36 A2
Durdells Gdns *BWD* BH11 ....36 A2
Durland Cl *NMIL/BTOS* BH25 ....64 A1
Durley Chine Rd *WCLF* BH2 ....2 D5
Durley Chine Rd South
WCLF BH2 ....2 D6
Durley Gdns *WCLF* BH2 ....2 D6
Durley Rd *WCLF* BH2 ....2 E5
Durley Rd South *WCLF* BH2 ....2 E5
Durley Rbt *WCLF* BH2 ....2 E5
Durlston Crs *CHCH/BSGR* BH23 ...39 H3
Durlston Rd *PSTN* BH14 ....72 A3
Durrant Rd *PSTN* BH14 ....72 A2
WCLF BH2 ....3 F2
Durrell Wy *PLE* BH15 ....70 D3
Durrington Pl *LTDN* BH7 ....58 B4
Durrington Rd *LTDN* BH7 ....58 B3
Durweston Cl
MOOR/WNTN BH9 ....37 H4

E

Eagle Rd *BKME/WDN* BH12 ....73 E1
Earle Rd *WBNE* BH4 ....2 A7
Earlham Dr *PSTN* BH14 ....72 A1
Earlsdon Wy *CHCH/BSGR* BH23 ...62 B2
Earlswood Pk *NMIL/BTOS* BH25 ...45 H1
East Av *NMIL/BTOS* BH25 ....63 E3
TWDS BH3 ....55 G4
East Bank Rd *BROC* SO42 ....87 E4
East Beach *BMTH* BH1 * 3 H5
East Borough *WIMB* BH21 ....14 C4
Eastbrook Rw *WIMB* BH21 * 14 C4
East Cliff Wy *CHCH/BSGR* BH23 ..61 G3
East Cl *NMIL/BTOS* BH25 ....63 F2
Eastcott Cl *LTDN* BH7 ....58 A2
East Dr *RGWD* BH24 ....18 D1
Eastern Av *NMIL/BTOS* BH25 ......48 D3
Eastern Wy *LYMN* SO41 ....80 D1
Easter Rd *MOOR/WNTN* BH9 ......37 E5
Eastfield Ct *RGWD* BH24 ....9 E3
Eastfield La *RGWD* BH24 ....9 E4
East Hl *LYMN* SO41 ....49 E3
East Howe La *NBNE* BH10 ....36 C3
Eastlake Av *BKME/WDN* BH12 .....53 H4
Eastlands *NMIL/BTOS* BH25 ....64 B1

East La *LYMN* SO41 ....66 C1
East Overcliff Dr *BMTH* BH1 ....3 K5
BMTH BH1 ....75 L2
East Quay Rd *PLE* BH15 ....70 C4
East St *PLE* BH15 ....70 C3
WIMB BH21 ....14 C5
East View Rd *RGWD* BH24 ....8 D4
East Wy *CHAR* BH8 ....56 D1
WIMB BH21 ....32 B2
Eastwood Av *FERN* BH22 ....18 A3
Eastworth Rd *VWD* BH31 ....4 C1
Eaton Rd *CCLF* BH13 ....73 E5
Ebblake Cl *VWD* BH31 ....5 C5
Ebor Cl *FERN* BH22 ....26 A2
Ebor Rd *BKME/WDN* BH12 ....54 B4
Eccles Rd *PLE* BH15 ....70 A3
Eden Gv *WIMB* BH21 ....22 D1
Edgarton Rd *CFDH* BH17 ....33 H4
Edgehill Rd *MOOR/WNTN* BH9 .....56 A2
Edgemoor Rd *FERN* BH22 ....11 E5
Edifred Rd *MOOR/WNTN* BH9 ......37 G3
Edmunds Cl *NMIL/BTOS* BH25 .....63 H1
Edward Rd *BWD* BH11 ....36 B4
CHCH/BSGR BH23 ....60 D2
PSTN BH14 ....54 A5
Edwards Cl *LYMN* SO41 ....48 B4
Edwina Cl *RGWD* BH24 ....9 E2
Edwina Dr *CFDH* BH17 ....33 F5
Efford Wy *LYMN* SO41 ....48 B5
Egdon Cl *FERN* BH22 ....25 F2
Egdon Ct *UPTN* BH16 ....50 D3
Egdon Dr *WIMB* BH21 ....23 E4
Egerton Gdns *CHAR* BH8 * 57 F4
Egerton Rd *CHAR* BH8 ....57 F4
Egmont Cl *RGWD* BH24 ....12 D4
Egmont Dr *RGWD* BH24 ....13 E4
Egmont Gdns *RGWD* BH24 ....13 E4
Egmont Rd *UPTN* BH16 ....68 D1
Eicombes Cl *LYND* SO43 ....85 E3
Elderberry La *CHCH/BSGR* BH23...60 D4
Eldon Av *NMIL/BTOS* BH25 ....63 G2
Eldon Cl *NMIL/BTOS* BH25 ....63 G2
Eldon Pl *WBNE* BH4 * 73 F2
Eldon Rd *MOOR/WNTN* BH9 ....56 A1
Eleanor Dr *BWD* BH11 ....35 F2
Eleanor Gdns *CHCH/BSGR* BH23 .59 E2
Elfin Dr *FERN* BH22 ....17 G2
Elgar Rd *NBNE* BH10 ....36 D3
Elgars Ct *LYMN* SO41 * 49 F3
Elgin Rd *PSTN* BH14 ....71 H1
WBNE BH4 ....55 H5
Elijah Cl *PLE* BH15 ....69 G3
Elise Cl *LTDN* BH7 ....58 B2
Elizabeth Av *CHCH/BSGR* BH23 ..59 F3
Elizabeth Pl *PLE* BH15 ....70 D2
Elizabeth Crs *LYMN* SO41 ....46 D5
Elkhams Cl *LYMN* SO41 ....66 B1
Ellery Gv *LYMN* SO41 ....49 E2
Ellesdale Dr *FERN* BH22 ....25 H1
Ellingham Rd *NMIL/BTOS* BH25 ...63 F2
Elliott Rd *BWD* BH11 ....35 G4
Elm Av *CHCH/BSGR* BH23 ....59 E1
LYMN SO41 ....67 G1
NMIL/BTOS BH25 ....45 E5
Elmers Wy *CHCH/BSGR* BH23 .....31 F3
Elmes Rd *MOOR/WNTN* BH9 ......37 E5
Elm Gdns *WBNE* BH4 ....55 G5
Elmgate Dr *LTDN* BH7 ....57 H3
Elmhurst Rd *BWD* BH11 ....36 A2
FERN BH22 ....10 C5
Elmhurst Wy *LYMN* SO41 ....10 C4
Elmore Dr *RGWD* BH24 ....6 C5
Elms Av *PSTN* BH14 ....71 G4
Elms Cl *PSTN* BH14 ....71 G4
Elmstead Rd *CCLF* BH13 ....72 D5
Elms Wy *SBNE* BH6 ....77 E1
Elm Tree Wk *FERN* BH22 ....26 A4
Elmwood Wy
CHCH/BSGR BH23 ....62 B3
Elphinstone Rd
CHCH/BSGR BH23 ....62 D2
Eltham Cl *LTDN* BH7 ....58 B2
Elvin Cl *LYMN* SO41 ....46 B4
Elwyn Rd *CHAR* BH8 ....57 E5
Embankment Wy *RGWD* BH24 ......8 D5
Emberley Cl *FERN* BH22 ....18 C3
Emerald Cl *RGWD* BH24 ....6 C5
Emerson Cl *PLE* BH15 ....70 C5
Emerson Rd *PLE* BH15 ....70 C5
Emily Cl *CHCH/BSGR* BH23 ....59 E1
Empress Rd *LYND* SO43 ....85 E3
Emsworth Rd *LYMN* SO41 ....49 E3
Encombe Cl *BKME/WDN* BH12 ....54 D2
Endfield Cl *CHCH/BSGR* BH23 .....59 F1
Endfield Rd *CHCH/BSGR* BH23 ....59 F2
MOOR/WNTN BH9 ....37 G5
Enfield Av *PLE* BH15 ....53 E4

Enfield Crs *PLE* BH15 ....53 E4
Enfield Rd *PLE* BH15 ....53 E4
Englands Wy *BWD* BH11 ....35 F3
Ensbury Av *NBNE* BH10 ....55 H1
Ensbury Br *NBNE* BH10 ....26 A5
Ensbury Cl *NBNE* BH10 ....55 H1
Ensbury Park Rd
MOOR/WNTN BH9 ....37 F5
Enterprise Wy
CHCH/BSGR BH23 ....27 F4
Erica Dr *WIMB* BH21 ....32 B1
Ericksen Rd *BWD* BH11 ....36 C4
Erpingham Rd
BKME/WDN BH12 ....55 E5
Esmonde Wy *CFDH* BH17 ....53 F2
Esplanade *CCLF* BH13 ....83 H1
Essex Av *CHCH/BSGR* BH23 ......40 B5
Ethelbert Rd *WIMB* BH21 ....14 C5
Eton Gdns *WBNE* BH4 ....2 A1
Ettrick Rd *CCLF* BH13 ....73 E4
Eucalyptus Av *RGWD* BH24 ....12 B4
Euston Gv *RGWD* BH24 ....8 D5
Evans Cl *BWD* BH11 ....54 D1
BWD BH11 ....6 C5
Evelyn Rd *MOOR/WNTN* BH9 ......56 C1
Evening Gld *FERN* BH22 ....26 A1
Everest Rd *CHCH/BSGR* BH23 ....60 C2
Everglades *FERN* BH22 ....17 H2
Evergreens *RGWD* BH24 ....11 H1
Evering Av *BKME/WDN* BH12 ......54 B1
Evering Gdns *BKME/WDN* BH12 ...54 A1
Everlea Cl *LYMN* SO41 ....66 B1
Everon Gdns *NMIL/BTOS* BH25 ...64 B1
Evershot Rd *CHAR* BH8 ....57 G1
Everton Rd *LYMN* SO41 ....46 B3
Evesham Cl *LTDN* BH7 ....58 A2
Exbury Dr *BWD* BH11 ....35 H2
Excelsior Rd *PSTN* BH14 ....72 A3
Exeter Crs *WCLF* BH2 ....3 G5
Exeter Park Rd *WCLF* BH2 ....3 G5
Exeter Rd *WCLF* BH2 ....3 G5
Exton Rd *SBNE* BH6 ....58 D3

F

Factory Rd *UPTN* BH16 ....51 F4
Fairfield *CHCH/BSGR* BH23 ....59 H3
Fairfield Cl *CHCH/BSGR* BH23 .....59 H3
LYMN SO41 ....49 E4
WIMB BH21 ....15 E4
Fairfield Rd *NMIL/BTOS* BH25 .....63 G3
WIMB BH21 ....14 D5
Fairies Dr *FERN* BH22 ....26 B3
Fairlea Rd *LYMN* SO41 ....49 E3
Fairlie *RGWD* BH24 ....9 E2
Fairlie Pk *RGWD* BH24 ....8 D2
Fairmile Rd *CHCH/BSGR* BH23 ....59 F1
Fairview Crs *BDST* BH18 ....33 E2
Fairview Rd *BDST* BH18 ....33 E2
Fairway Dr *CHCH/BSGR* BH23 .....59 G4
Fairway Rd *PSTN* BH14 ....72 A5
Fairways *FERN* BH22 ....18 B3
The Fairway *NMIL/BTOS* BH25 ....64 B3
Fairwood Rd *VWD* BH31 ....5 C3
Falcon Dr *CHCH/BSGR* BH23 ......61 F5
Falconer Dr *PLE* BH15 ....69 G1
The Fallows *NMIL/BTOS* BH25 .....45 F2
Fancy Rd *BKME/WDN* BH12 ....53 H2
Farcroft Rd *BKME/WDN* BH12 .....53 H5
Farm Cl *RGWD* BH24 ....8 C3
Farm Ct *WIMB* BH21 ....15 C5
Farmdene Cl
CHCH/BSGR BH23 * 61 H2
Farmers Wk *LYMN* SO41 ....66 B2
WIMB BH21 ....14 B3
Farm La North
NMIL/BTOS BH25 ....64 A2
Farm La South
NMIL/BTOS BH25 ....64 A3
Farm Rd *FERN* BH22 ....10 A4
Farnham Rd *BKME/WDN* BH12 ....55 H5
Farnleys Md *LYMN* SO41 ....49 E5
Farriers Cl *WIMB* BH21 ....15 H3
Farwell Cl *CHCH/BSGR* BH23 .....41 E4
Farwell Rd *BKME/WDN* BH12 .....35 E5
Fathersfield *BROC* SO42 ....86 D3
Fawcett Rd *NMIL/BTOS* BH25 .....44 D5
Fawley Gn *CHAR* BH8 ....38 B4
Fawn Gdns *NMIL/BTOS* BH25 .....44 D3
Fir Cl *LYND* SO43 * 85 E4
Felton Crs *CHCH/BSGR* BH23 .....62 B2
Felton Rd *PSTN* BH14 ....53 F5
Fenleigh Cl *NMIL/BTOS* BH25 .....64 B2
Fennel Gdns *LYMN* SO41 ....48 D2
Fenton Rd *SBNE* BH6 ....58 C4

Fern Barrow *BKME/WDN* BH12 ....55 F2
Fern Cl *CHCH/BSGR* BH23 ....41 E5
Ferncroft Gdns *NBNE* BH10 ....36 D2
Ferncroft Rd *NBNE* BH10 ....36 D2
Ferndale Rd *NMIL/BTOS* BH25 ....45 F3
Ferndown, Stour & Forest Trail
FERN BH22 ....17 F3
FERN BH22 ....25 E3
WIMB BH21 ....16 A2
Fernglade *NMIL/BTOS* BH25 ....45 E4
Fernheath Cl *BWD* BH11 ....36 A5
Fernheath Rd *BWD* BH11 ....36 A4
Fernhill Cl *CFDH* BH17 ....34 C5
Fernhill La *NMIL/BTOS* BH25 ......45 E1
Fernhill Rd *NMIL/BTOS* BH25 ......45 E1
Fernlea Av *FERN* BH22 ....17 H5
Fernlea Cl *FERN* BH22 ....17 H5
RGWD BH24 ....11 H2
Fernlea Gdns *FERN* BH22 ....17 H5
Fernside Av *PSTN* BH14 ....71 F1
Fernside Rd *FERN* BH22 ....10 B4
MOOR/WNTN BH9 ....55 H2
PLE BH15 ....71 E1
Fernway Cl *WIMB* BH21 ....15 H5
Fernwood Cl *RGWD* BH24 ....12 C1
Ferris Av *CHAR* BH8 ....38 A5
Ferris Cl *CHAR* BH8 ....38 B5
Ferris Pl *CHAR* BH8 ....38 B5
Ferry Point *LYMN* SO41 * 49 G3
Ferry Rd *PLE* BH15 ....70 B4
SBNE BH6 ....77 F2
Ferry Wy *CCLF* BH13 ....82 D5
Feversham Av *CHAR* BH8 ....57 G1
Fibbards Rd *BROC* SO42 ....86 D3
Field Pl *NMIL/BTOS* BH25 ....63 F2
VWD BH31 ....4 C1
Field Wk *LYMN* SO41 ....48 D2
Field Wy *CHCH/BSGR* BH23 ....61 H1
Fieldway *RGWD* BH24 ....9 E3
Filton Rd *LYMN* SO41 ....48 D3
Finchfield Av *BWD* BH11 ....35 H1
Firbank Rd *MOOR/WNTN* BH9 .....55 D2
Fir Cl *FERN* BH22 ....10 B3
Firmain Rd *BKME/WDN* BH12 ......54 B1
Firmount Cl *LYMN* SO41 ....66 C1
Firs Glen Rd *FERN* BH22 ....10 C4
MOOR/WNTN BH9 ....55 H2
VWD BH31 ....4 D3
Firshill *CHCH/BSGR* BH23 ....62 A1
Firside Rd *WIMB* BH21 ....32 A3
Firs La *PSTN* BH14 ....71 H5
The Firs *BMTH* BH1 ....3 K2
First Marine Av
NMIL/BTOS BH25 ....63 H3
Fir Tree Cl *RGWD* BH24 ....11 G4
Firtree Crs *LYMN* SO41 ....46 B4
Fir Tree La *CHCH/BSGR* BH23 .....61 H1
Fir Vale Rd *BMTH* BH1 ....3 H3
Fisherman's Av *BOSC* BH5 ....76 B1
Fisherman's Bank
CHCH/BSGR BH23 ....60 C5
Fishermans Quay *LYMN* SO41 * ..49 F3
Fishermans Rd *PLE* BH15 ....70 C4
Fitzharris Av *MOOR/WNTN* BH9 ..56 C3
Fitzmaurice Rd
CHCH/BSGR BH23 ....59 E2
Fitzpain Cl *FERN* BH22 ....25 H2
Fitzpain Rd *FERN* BH22 ....25 H2
Fitzwilliam Cl *BWD* BH11 ....35 G2
Fitzworth Av *UPTN* BH16 ....69 E1
Flaghead Chine Rd *CCLF* BH13 ...83 G3
Flaghead Rd *CCLF* BH13 ....83 G3
Flambard Av *CHCH/BSGR* BH23 ..59 F1
Flambard Rd *PSTN* BH14 ....72 A2
Flazen Cl *BWD* BH11 ....35 F4
Fleet's Cnr *CFDH* BH17 ....52 B3
Fleets La *PLE* BH15 ....52 C4
Fletcher Cl *NBNE* BH10 * 36 D4
Fletcher Rd *NBNE* BH10 ....36 D4
Flexford La *LYMN* SO41 ....47 E1
Floral Farm *WIMB* BH21 ....23 F2
Florence Rd *BOSC* BH5 ....75 G1
PSTN BH14 ....72 A1
Floriston Gdns
NMIL/BTOS BH25 ....45 H4
Flushards *LYMN* SO41 ....49 F4
Foldsgate Cl *LYND* SO43 ....85 E2
Folly Farm La *RGWD* BH24 ....7 C5
Fontmell Rd *BDST* BH18 ....33 C5
Footners La *CHCH/BSGR* BH23....41 E5
Ford Cl *FERN* BH22 ....18 B2
Ford La *FERN* BH22 ....18 C2
Foreland Cl *CHCH/BSGR* BH23 ...39 H3
Foreland Rd *UPTN* BH16 ....68 D1
Forest Cl *NMIL/BTOS* BH25 ....45 F5
VWD BH31 ....5 H4
Forest Ct *NMIL/BTOS* BH25 ....45 F5
Forest Edge Cl *RGWD* BH24 ....6 B3

Forest Gdns LYND SO43 ....85 E3
Forest Gate Gdns LYMN SO41 ....67 H1
Forest Glade Cl BROC SO42 ....86 B3
Forest Hall BROC SO42 ....87 E3
Forest Hills Ct RGWD BH24 ....9 F5
Forestlake Av RGWD BH24 ....9 F5
Forest La RGWD BH24 ....9 H5
VWD BH31 ....4 C1
Forest Oak Dr NMIL/BTOS BH25 ....45 E2
Forest Park Rd BROC SO42 ....86 C3
Forest Pines NMIL/BTOS BH25 ....45 E2
Forest Ri CHCH/BSGR BH23 ....42 D5
Forest Rd CCLF BH13 ....73 E3
FERN BH22 ....10 C3
Forestside Gdns RGWD BH24 ....9 E2
The Forestside VWD BH31 ....5 H3
Forest Vw BROC SO42 ....86 B3
Forest View Cl
MOOR/WNTN BH9 ....37 G5
Forest View Dr WIMB BH21 ....17 E3
Forest View Rd
MOOR/WNTN BH9 ....37 G4
Forest Wk NMIL/BTOS BH25 ....44 B2
Forest Wy CHCH/BSGR BH23 ....61 H1
LYMN SO41 ....66 B1
WIMB BH21 ....17 E4
Forsyth Gdns NBNE BH10 ....36 C5
Fort Cumberland Cl PLE BH15 ....69 F3
Fortescue Rd BKME/WDN BH12 ....54 B3
TWDS BH3 ....56 C4
Forton Cl NBNE BH10 ....37 E3
Forward Dr LYMN SO41 ....48 C5
Fountain Wy CHCH/BSGR BH23 ....59 H4
Four Wells Rd WIMB BH21 ....15 G2
Foxbury Rd RGWD BH24 ....19 G3
Foxcote Gdns
NMIL/BTOS BH25 * 44 D4
Foxcroft Dr WIMB BH21 ....15 H4
Foxes Cl VWD BH31 ....4 D3
Fox Fld LYMN SO41 ....66 B1
Foxglove Cl CHCH/BSGR BH23 ....61 G2
Foxglove Pl NMIL/BTOS BH25 ....45 H3
Foxgloves UPTN BH16 ....50 D3
Foxhills VWD BH31 ....5 F2
Foxholes Rd PLE BH15 ....53 F4
SBNE BH6 ....77 F1
Fox La WIMB BH21 ....16 B4
Fox Pond La LYMN SO41 ....48 C5
Foxwood Av CHCH/BSGR BH23 ....60 D5
Frampton Cl NMIL/BTOS BH25 ....45 G2
Frampton Pl RGWD BH24 ....8 C4
Frampton Rd
MOOR/WNTN BH9 ....56 C2
Frances Rd BMTH BH1 ....74 D1
Francis Av BWD BH11 ....35 F4
Francis Rd BKME/WDN BH12 ....54 C5
Frankland Crs PSTN BH14 ....72 C2
Franklin Rd MOOR/WNTN BH9 ....37 G4
NMIL/BTOS BH25 ....45 G3
Franklyn Cl UPTN BH16 ....50 D3
Frankston Rd SBNE BH6 ....76 C1
Franks Wy BKME/WDN BH12 ....53 H3
Fraser Rd BKME/WDN BH12 ....54 D1
Freda Rd CHCH/BSGR BH23 ....59 F4
Frederica Rd
MOOR/WNTN BH9 ....56 A2
Freemans Cl WIMB BH21 ....15 H3
Freemans La WIMB BH21 ....15 H4
French Rd CFDH BH17 ....52 B1
French's Farm Rd UPTN BH16 ....50 C3
Frensham Cl NBNE BH10 ....37 E4
Freshwater Dr PLE BH15 ....69 F2
Freshwater Rd
CHCH/BSGR BH23 ....61 G4
Friars Rd CHCH/BSGR BH23 ....61 F4
Friars Wk NMIL/BTOS BH25 ....64 A2
Fritham Gdns CHAR BH8 ....38 B4
Frobisher Av
BKME/WDN BH12 ....54 D1
Frobisher Cl
CHCH/BSGR BH23 ....60 D4
RGWD BH24 ....9 E3
Fromond Cl LYMN SO41 ....49 E2
Frost Rd BWD BH11 ....35 H4
Froud Wy WIMB BH21 ....32 A3
Fryer Cl BWD BH11 ....36 B2
Fryer's Copse WIMB BH21 ....16 A3
Frys La LYMN SO41 ....66 B1
Fullerton Rd LYMN SO41 ....48 C3
Fulmar Rd CHCH/BSGR BH23 ....61 E5
Fulwood Av BWD BH11 ....35 G2
The Furlong RGWD BH24 ....8 B4
Furnell Rd PLE BH15 ....70 D4
Furzebrook Cl CFDH BH17 ....34 A5
Furze Cft NMIL/BTOS BH25 ....64 A1
Furze Hill Dr PSTN BH14 ....72 A4
Furzey Rd UPTN BH16 ....50 D4
Furzy Whistlers Cl
CHCH/BSGR BH23 ....31 F3

G

Gainsborough Av
NMIL/BTOS BH25 ....45 F3
Gainsborough Rd LTDN BH7 ....57 H3
RGWD BH24 ....11 H1
Gallop Wy BKME/WDN BH12 ....55 G3
Galloway Rd PLE BH15 ....69 F1
Gallows Dr FERN BH22 ....25 H3
Galton Av CHCH/BSGR BH23 ....59 F4
Garden Cl LYND SO43 ....84 D3
NMIL/BTOS BH25 ....64 A1
Garden La RGWD BH24 ....11 H3
Gardens Crs PSTN BH14 ....71 H5
Gardens Rd PSTN BH14 ....71 H5
Gardens Vw BMTH BH1 ....75 E1
Garden Wk FERN BH22 ....18 A2
Gardner Rd CHCH/BSGR BH23 ....59 E2
RGWD BH24 ....8 D5
Garfield Av BMTH BH1 ....57 F5
Garland Rd PLE BH15 ....70 D1
Garrow Dr LYMN SO41 ....49 E2
Garsdale Cl BWD BH11 ....36 A1
Garth Cl RGWD BH24 ....11 G2
Garth Rd MOOR/WNTN BH9 ....56 C1
Gaydon Ri BWD BH11 ....35 G3
Geneva Av SBNE BH6 ....58 D5
Genoa Cl LYMN SO41 ....67 G1
George Rd LYMN SO41 ....66 A5
Georgian Cl RGWD BH24 ....8 C3
Georgian Wy NBNE BH10 ....37 F3
Georgina Cl BKME/WDN BH12 ....55 G2
Gerald Rd TWDS BH3 ....56 C4
Germaine Cl CHCH/BSGR BH23 ....62 B2
Gervis Crs PSTN BH14 ....71 G1
Gervis Pl BMTH BH1 ....3 G4
Gervis Rd BMTH BH1 ....74 D2
Gibson Rd CFDH BH17 ....53 E3
Giddylake WIMB BH21 ....14 C3
Gilbert Cl LYMN SO41 ....48 D5
Gilbert Rd CHAR BH8 ....57 F4
Gillam Rd NBNE BH10 ....36 D3
Gillett Rd BKME/WDN BH12 ....55 G3
Gillingham Cl MOOR/WNTN BH9 ....38 A4
Gillingham Rd LYMN SO41 ....80 B1
Gladdis Rd BWD BH11 ....35 H3
Gladeland Rd FERN BH22 ....18 B1
Gladelands Cl BDST BH18 ....32 C3
Gladelands Pk FERN BH22 ....18 B2
Gladelands Wy BDST BH18 ....32 C3
The Glade RGWD BH24 ....11 H1
Gladstone Cl CHCH/BSGR BH23 ....60 B4
Gladstone Rd BKME/WDN BH12 ....54 A5
LTDN BH7 ....57 H5
Gladstone Rd East LTDN BH7 ....57 H5
Gladstone Rd West BMTH BH1 ....57 G5
Glamis Av NBNE BH10 ....37 E2
Gleadowe Av CHCH/BSGR BH23 ....59 F4
Glebefields LYMN SO41 ....66 B5
Glenair Av PSTN BH14 ....71 G2
Glenair Rd PSTN BH14 ....71 G2
Glenavon NMIL/BTOS BH25 ....45 F5
Glenavon Rd CHCH/BSGR BH23 ....62 B1
Glen Cl NMIL/BTOS BH25 ....63 F2
Glencoe Rd BKME/WDN BH12 ....54 B5
LTDN BH7 ....57 H3
Glendale Av FERN BH22 ....17 H3
Glendale Cl CHCH/BSGR BH23 ....39 H4
WIMB BH21 ....14 C4
Glendale Rd SBNE BH6 ....77 G1
Glendene Pk NMIL/BTOS BH25 * 44 C2
Glendon Av NBNE BH10 ....36 C1
Glendrive NMIL/BTOS BH25 ....63 E2
Gleneagles Av PSTN BH14 ....72 B3
Gleneagles Cl FERN BH22 ....18 B3
Glenferness Av TWDS BH3 ....55 H4
Glen Fern Rd BMTH BH1 ....3 J3
Glengariff Rd PSTN BH14 ....72 A3
Glengarry NMIL/BTOS BH25 ....45 G5
Glengarry Wy
CHCH/BSGR BH23 ....61 G4
Glenives Cl RGWD BH24 ....12 A2
Glenme Adows Dr NBNE BH10 ....36 B2
Glenmoor Cl NBNE BH10 ....55 H1
Glenmoor Rd FERN BH22 ....25 G1
MOOR/WNTN BH9 ....55 H2
Glenmount Dr PSTN BH14 ....53 H5
Glen Rd BOSC BH5 ....75 G1
PSTN BH14 ....71 H1
Glenroyd Gdns SBNE BH6 ....76 D1
Glenside NMIL/BTOS BH25 ....62 D3
Glen Spey NMIL/BTOS BH25 ....45 H5
The Glen CCLF BH13 ....72 C5
Glenville Cl CHCH/BSGR BH23 ....43 H5
Glenville Gdns NBNE BH10 ....36 C5
Glenville Rd CHCH/BSGR BH23 ....43 H5
NBNE BH10 ....36 C5
Glenwood Cl FERN BH22 ....10 B4
Glenwood La FERN BH22 ....10 B4
Glenwood Rd FERN BH22 ....10 B4
VWD BH31 ....4 D3
Glenwood Wy FERN BH22 ....10 B4
Glissons FERN BH22 ....25 E2
Gloucester Rd
BKME/WDN BH12 ....54 C5
LTDN BH7 ....57 H5
Glynville Cl WIMB BH21 ....15 G2
Glynville Rd WIMB BH21 ....15 G2
Goathorn Cl UPTN BH16 ....69 F1
Godmanston Cl CFDH BH17 ....53 G1
Godshill Cl CHAR BH8 ....38 B4
Golden Crs LYMN SO41 ....66 B1
Goldenleas Dr BWD BH11 ....35 F4
Goldfinch Cl NMIL/BTOS BH25 ....44 D5
Goldfinch Rd CFDH BH17 ....51 G2
Gold Mead Cl LYMN SO41 ....49 E5
Golf Links Rd BDST BH18 ....33 F2
FERN BH22 ....18 A4
Goliath Rd PLE BH15 ....69 F3
Good Rd BKME/WDN BH12 ....54 B3
Gordon Mt CHCH/BSGR BH23 ....62 D1
Gordon Rd BKME/WDN BH12 ....55 E5
BMTH BH1 ....75 F1
CHCH/BSGR BH23 ....62 C2
LYMN SO41 ....48 C4
WIMB BH21 ....15 E5
Gordon Rd South
BKME/WDN BH12 ....55 E5
Gordon Wy CHCH/BSGR BH23 ....60 A1
Gore Rd NMIL/BTOS BH25 ....44 C5
Gorey Rd BKME/WDN BH12 ....54 B1
Gorleston Rd BKME/WDN BH12 ....54 D5
Gorley Rd RGWD BH24 ....9 E3
Gorsecliff Rd NBNE BH10 ....55 H1
Gorse Cl NMIL/BTOS BH25 ....45 H3
RGWD BH24 ....11 G2
Gorsefield Rd NMIL/BTOS BH25 ....45 F2
Gorse Hill Cl PLE BH15 ....53 F5
Gorse Hill Crs PLE BH15 ....53 E5
Gorse Hill Rd PLE BH15 ....53 F5
Gorse Knoll Dr VWD BH31 ....4 C1
Gorseland Ct FERN BH22 ....26 A1
Gorse La UPTN BH16 ....51 E3
Gorse Rd WIMB BH21 ....32 A2
Gort Rd BWD BH11 ....36 B4
CFDH BH17 ....52 A1
Gosling Cl CFDH BH17 ....53 F3
Gosport La LYND SO43 ....85 F4
Gosport St LYMN SO41 ....49 F3
Gough Crs CFDH BH17 ....33 F5
Grafton Cl CHCH/BSGR BH23 ....60 B4
TWDS BH3 ....56 C4
Grafton Gdns LYMN SO41 ....67 G1
Grafton Rd TWDS BH3 ....56 C4
Grammar School La
WIMB BH21 ....14 B5
Granby Rd MOOR/WNTN BH9 ....37 G3
Grand Av SBNE BH6 ....76 C1
Grand Pde PLE BH15 * 70 B4
Grange Cl LYMN SO41 ....66 C2
Grange Gdns BKME/WDN BH12 ....54 C3
Grange Rd BDST BH18 ....33 E3
CHCH/BSGR BH23 ....61 F3
RGWD BH24 ....11 G5
SBNE BH6 ....76 D2
The Grange LYMN SO41 ....66 C2
Grantham Rd BMTH BH1 ....57 G5
Grantley Rd BOSC BH5 ....75 H1
Grant's Av BMTH BH1 ....57 F4
Grants Cl CHAR BH8 ....57 F4
Granville Rd BKME/WDN BH12 ....53 H5
BOSC BH5 ....58 A5
Grasmere Cl CHCH/BSGR BH23 ....39 H4
Grasmere Gdns
NMIL/BTOS BH25 ....45 F2
Grasmere Rd BOSC BH5 ....76 A1
CCLF BH13 ....82 D5
Gravel Hl BDST BH18 ....33 G4
WIMB BH21 ....22 D3
Gravel La RGWD BH24 ....8 B4
Gray Cl CFDH BH17 ....53 F2
Graycot Cl NBNE BH10 ....36 C2
Gray's Yd PLE BH15 * 70 C4
Great Md LYND SO43 * 85 E4
Great Mead Pk LYND SO43 ....85 F4
Greaves Cl NBNE BH10 * 36 C4
Grebe Cl CFDH BH17 ....51 G2
CHCH/BSGR BH23 ....61 E4
LYMN SO41 ....80 C1
Greenacre NMIL/BTOS BH25 ....64 A2
Greenacre Cl UPTN BH16 ....51 E4
Greenacres Cl NBNE BH10 ....26 A5
Green Acres Cl RGWD BH24 ....13 E1
Greenbanks Cl LYMN SO41 ....66 B5
Green Bottom WIMB BH21 ....15 G2
Green Cl PLE BH15 ....70 D4
Greenclose La WIMB BH21 ....14 D4
Greenfield Gdns
NMIL/BTOS BH25 ....64 B2
Greenfield Rd PLE BH15 ....53 E4
Greenfinch Cl CFDH BH17 * 51 H1
Greenfinch Wk RGWD BH24 ....9 E5
Greenhayes BDST BH18 ....33 G5
Greenhays Ri WIMB BH21 ....14 C4
Greenhill Cl WIMB BH21 ....14 D3
Greenhill La WIMB BH21 ....14 D3
Greenhill Rd WIMB BH21 ....14 D3
Green La FERN BH22 ....25 E3
NBNE BH10 ....36 C4
NMIL/BTOS BH25 ....64 B2
RGWD BH24 ....8 C4
Greenmead Av LYMN SO41 ....66 B1
Green Rd MOOR/WNTN BH9 ....56 D2
PLE BH15 ....70 C3
Greensleeves Av BDST BH18 ....33 F1
Greensome Dr FERN BH22 ....18 B3
The Green WBNE BH4 * 55 G5
Greenway Cl LYMN SO41 ....48 C3
Greenway Crs UPTN BH16 ....50 C3
Greenways CHCH/BSGR BH23 ....62 B2
LYMN SO41 ....66 A5
Greenways Av CHAR BH8 ....38 A4
Greenways Rd BROC SO42 ....87 E3
Greenwood Av FERN BH22 ....17 H3
PSTN BH14 ....72 A5
Greenwood Copse RGWD BH24 ....12 A2
Greenwood Rd
MOOR/WNTN BH9 ....56 A1
Greenwoods NMIL/BTOS BH25 ....64 B1
Greenwood Wy RGWD BH24 ....12 B2
Grenfell Rd MOOR/WNTN BH9 ....37 F4
Grenville Cl RGWD BH24 ....9 E2
Grenville Rd WIMB BH21 ....14 D5
Gresham Rd MOOR/WNTN BH9 ....56 C1
Greystoke Av BWD BH11 ....35 H1
Griffiths Gdns NBNE BH10 ....36 B2
Grigg La BROC SO42 ....87 E3
Grosvenor Cl RGWD BH24 ....11 G1
Grosvenor Gdns BMTH BH1 ....75 G1
Grosvenor Ms LYMN SO41 * 48 D2
Grosvenor Rd WBNE BH4 ....2 A4
Groveley Rd CHCH/BSGR BH23 ....60 C4
WBNE BH4 ....73 F3
Grovely Av BOSC BH5 ....75 H1
Grove Pastures LYMN SO41 ....49 E4
Grove Pl LYMN SO41 ....49 E4
Grove Rd BKME/WDN BH12 ....53 H4
BMTH BH1 * 3 K4
LYMN SO41 ....49 F4
NMIL/BTOS BH25 ....64 A3
WIMB BH21 ....14 C5
Grove Rd East
CHCH/BSGR BH23 ....59 G2
Grove Rd West
CHCH/BSGR BH23 ....59 F2
The Grove CHCH/BSGR BH23 ....59 E1
FERN BH22 ....17 G5
MOOR/WNTN BH9 ....37 F4
VWD BH31 ....5 E3
Grower Gdns BWD BH11 ....36 A3
Guernsey Rd BKME/WDN BH12 ....54 B1
Guest Av BKME/WDN BH12 ....54 D4
Guest Cl BKME/WDN BH12 ....55 E4
Guest Rd UPTN BH16 ....50 D3
Guildhill Rd SBNE BH6 ....77 E1
Gulliver Cl PSTN BH14 ....72 A5
Gunville Crs MOOR/WNTN BH9 ....37 H4
Gurjun Cl UPTN BH16 ....50 C2
Gurney Rd WIMB BH21 ....32 C1
Gussage Rd BKME/WDN BH12 ....54 C2
Gwenlyn Rd UPTN BH16 ....51 E4
Gwynne Rd BKME/WDN BH12 ....54 C5
Gypsy La RGWD BH24 ....8 D3

H

Haarlem Ms CHCH/BSGR BH23 ....60 B3
Hadden Rd CHAR BH8 ....57 F2
Hadley Wy BDST BH18 ....32 C4
Hadow Rd NBNE BH10 ....36 C4
Hadrian Cl FERN BH22 ....25 H2
Haglane Copse LYMN SO41 ....48 C5
Hahnemann Rd WCLF BH2 ....2 E5
Haig Av CCLF BH13 ....72 C4
Hainault Dr VWD BH31 ....5 E2
Haking Rd CHCH/BSGR BH23 ....60 B3
Hale Av NMIL/BTOS BH25 ....45 F5
Hale Gdns NMIL/BTOS BH25 ....45 F5
Halewood Wy
CHCH/BSGR BH23 ....59 F2
Halifax Wy CHCH/BSGR BH23 ....61 F3
Hall Rd BWD BH11 ....35 H4
Halstock Crs CFDH BH17 ....33 H5

Halter Pth *PLE* BH15 .... **69** G2
Halter Ri *WIMB* BH21 .... **16** A3
Halton Cl *CHCH/BSGR* BH23 .... **31** F4
Hambledon Gdns *SBNE* BH6 .... **58** C4
Hambledon Rd *LTDN* BH7 .... **58** C4
Hamble Rd *PLE* BH15 .... **53** G4
Hamblin Wy *CHAR* BH8 .... **38** C5
Hamilton Cl *BMTH* BH1 .... **75** F1
  CHCH/BSGR BH23 .... **78** D1
  PLE BH15 .... **69** G3
Hamilton Ct *LYMN* SO41 .... **80** A1
Hamilton Crs *PLE* BH15 .... **69** G3
Hamilton Pl *LYMN* SO41 * **48** D4
Hamilton Rd *BMTH* BH1 .... **75** F1
  PLE BH15 .... **69** G3
  WIMB BH21 .... **32** C2
Hamilton Wy *NMIL/BTOS* BH25.. **44** C5
Ham La *FERN* BH22 .... **25** F2
  WIMB BH21 .... **15** H5
  WIMB BH21 .... **24** C1
Hampden La *SBNE* BH6 .... **58** B5
Hampshire Cl *CHCH/BSGR* BH23 .. **40** B5
Hampshire Hatches La
  RGWD BH24 .... **13** H2
Hampton Dr *RGWD* BH24 .... **8** D2
Hanham Rd *WIMB* BH21 .... **14** C4
  WIMB BH21 .... **32** B2
Hankinson Rd
  MOOR/WNTN BH9 .... **56** C2
Hanlon Cl *BWD* BH11 .... **36** A3
Hannah Wy *LYMN* SO41 .... **47** H1
Hannington Rd *LTDN* BH7 .... **58** A5
Hanover Gn *CFDH* BH17 * **53** F2
Harbeck Rd *CHAR* BH8 .... **38** A4
Harbour Crs *CHCH/BSGR* BH23 .. **60** C5
Harbour Hill Crs *PLE* BH15 ...... **53** E5
Harbour Hill Rd *PLE* BH15 .... **53** E5
Harbour Rd *SBNE* BH6 .... **77** G2
Harbour View Cl *PSTN* BH14 .... **53** C5
Harbour View Rd *PSTN* BH14 .... **53** C5
Harcombe Cl *CFDH* BH17 .... **34** A4
Harcourt Rd *BOSC* BH5 .... **58** A5
Hardy Cl *FERN* BH22 .... **10** C5
  NMIL/BTOS BH25 .... **44** D4
Hardy Crs *WIMB* BH21 .... **14** D5
Hardy Rd *FERN* BH22 .... **10** C5
  PSTN BH14 .... **72** B1
Hare La *NMIL/BTOS* BH25 .... **45** H4
Hares Gn *LTDN* BH7 .... **58** A2
Harewood Av *LTDN* BH7 .... **57** H3
Harewood Crs *LTDN* BH7 .... **57** H3
Harewood Gdns *LTDN* BH7 ...... **57** H3
Harewood Gn *LYMN* SO41 ...... **81** H1
Harewood Pl *LTDN* BH7 .... **58** A4
Harford Cl *LYMN* SO41 .... **67** F1
Harford Rd *BKME/WDN* BH12.... **54** A2
Harkwood Dr *PLE* BH15 .... **69** H1
Harland Rd *SBNE* BH6 .... **77** G1
Harleston Vls *WIMB* BH21 .... **14** D5
Harness Cl *WIMB* BH21 .... **15** H3
Harpway La *CHCH/BSGR* BH23.. **41** E1
Harrier Dr *WIMB* BH21 .... **22** D2
Harriers Cl *CHCH/BSGR* BH23 .. **61** H1
Harrison Av *BMTH* BH1 .... **57** F4
Harrison Cl *CHCH/BSGR* BH23 .. **41** E4
Harris Wy *NMIL/BTOS* BH25 .... **45** F1
Harrow Cl *CHCH/BSGR* BH23 .... **31** F5
Harrow Rd *CHCH/BSGR* BH23 .. **31** E5
Harry Barrow Cl *RGWD* BH24 ...... **8** C4
Hart Cl *NMIL/BTOS* BH25 .... **44** D3
Harting Rd *SBNE* BH6 .... **58** A5
Hartsbourne Dr *LTDN* BH7 ...... **58** B2
Harts Wy *LYMN* SO41 .... **66** B1
Harvester Wy *LYMN* SO41 .... **48** D1
Harvey Rd *BOSC* BH5 .... **58** A5
  WIMB BH21 .... **23** F3
Harwell Rd *CFDH* BH17 .... **52** D3
Haskells Cl *LYND* SO43 .... **84** D4
Haskells Rd *BKME/WDN* BH12.. **53** H3
Haslemere Av
  CHCH/BSGR BH23 .... **62** B2
Haslemere Pl *CHCH/BSGR* BH23 .. **62** C2
Hasler Rd *CFDH* BH17 .... **33** C5
Haslop Rd *WIMB* BH21 .... **15** G2
Hastings Rd *CFDH* BH17 .... **33** F5
  CHAR BH8 .... **38** C5
Hatch Pond La *CFDH* BH17 ...... **52** C2
Hatch Pond Rd *CFDH* BH17 ...... **52** C3
Hatfield Ct *NMIL/BTOS* BH25.... **44** C4
Hatfield Gdns *LTDN* BH7 .... **58** B2
Hathaway Rd *SBNE* BH6 .... **76** D1
Hatherden Av *PSTN* BH14 .... **53** F5
Havelock Rd *BKME/WDN* BH12.. **55** E5
Haven Gdns *NMIL/BTOS* BH25.. **42** D3
Haven Cl *CHCH/BSGR* BH23 .... **60** C5
Haven Rd *CCLF* BH13 .... **83** G2
  WIMB BH21 .... **32** A1

Haverstock Rd
  MOOR/WNTN BH9 .... **37** H5
Haviland Rd *BMTH* BH1 .... **57** H5
  WIMB BH21 .... **17** E2
Haviland Rd East *LTDN* BH7 .... **57** H5
Haviland Rd West *BMTH* BH1 .. **75** G1
Hawden Rd *BWD* BH11 .... **55** E1
Hawkchurch Gdns *CFDH* BH17.. **34** A5
Hawk Cl *WIMB* BH21 .... **15** G2
Hawker Cl *WIMB* BH21 .... **23** F3
Hawkins Cl *RGWD* BH24 .... **9** E2
Hawkins Rd *BKME/WDN* BH12.. **54** D1
Hawks Lea *LYMN* SO41 .... **80** B1
Hawkwood Rd *BOSC* BH5 .... **75** C1
Haworth Cl *CHCH/BSGR* BH23.. **59** G1
Hawthorn Cl *NMIL/BTOS* BH25.. **45** G3
Hawthorn Dr *CFDH* BH17 .... **51** H1
Hawthorn Rd
  CHCH/BSGR BH23 .... **41** G5
  MOOR/WNTN BH9 .... **56** B2
The Hawthorns
  CHCH/BSGR BH23 .... **60** D4
Haydon Rd *CCLF* BH13 .... **73** H4
Hayes Cl *WIMB* BH21 .... **15** G5
Hayes Cl *WIMB* BH21 .... **15** H5
Hayes La *WIMB* BH21 .... **15** H5
Hayeswood Rd *WIMB* BH21 ...... **15** G3
Haymoor Rd *PLE* BH15 .... **53** G3
Haynes Av *PLE* BH15 .... **70** D1
Haysoms Cl *NMIL/BTOS* BH25.. **64** B1
Hayward Crs *VWD* BH31 .... **4** C3
Haywards Farm Cl *VWD* BH31 .... **4** C3
Hayward Wy *VWD* BH31 .... **4** B3
Hazel Cl *CHCH/BSGR* BH23 .... **61** G1
Hazel Dr *WIMB* BH22 .... **17** H1
Hazell Av *NBNE* BH10 .... **36** B5
Hazel Rd *LYMN* SO41 .... **48** A3
Hazelton Cl *LTDN* BH7 .... **58** A2
Hazelwood Av
  NMIL/BTOS BH25 .... **44** C3
Hazelwood Dr *VWD* BH31 .... **5** F4
Hazlebury Rd *CFDH* BH17 .... **52** A3
Hazlemere Dr *RGWD* BH24 ...... **11** H3
Heads Farm Cl *NBNE* BH10 ...... **37** E2
Head's Lane *NBNE* BH10 .... **37** E2
Headswell Av *NBNE* BH10 .... **37** E3
Headswell Crs *NBNE* BH10 ...... **37** E3
Headswell Gdns *NBNE* BH10 .... **37** E3
Heanor Cl *NBNE* BH10 .... **36** C5
Heath Av *PLE* BH15 .... **52** D4
Heath Cl *WIMB* BH21 .... **15** H2
Heathcote Rd *BMTH* BH1 .... **75** H1
Heatherbank Rd *WBNE* BH4 .... **2** A3
Heatherbrae La *UPTN* BH16 .... **50** D4
Heather Cl *CHAR* BH8 .... **38** B4
  CHCH/BSGR BH23 .... **62** C1
  LYMN SO41 .... **46** C4
  RGWD BH24 .... **11** H3
  WIMB BH21 .... **32** C1
Heatherdell *UPTN* BH16 .... **50** D4
Heatherdown Rd *FERN* BH22 .. **10** D5
Heatherdown Wy *FERN* BH22 .. **10** D5
Heather Dr *FERN* BH22.............. **17** H2
Heatherlands Ri
  BKME/WDN BH12 .... **54** B5
Heatherlea Rd *SBNE* BH6 .... **76** D1
Heather Rd *NBNE* BH10 .... **36** D4
Heather View Rd
  BKME/WDN BH12 .... **54** D3
Heather Wy *FERN* BH22 .... **17** H2
Heath Farm Cl *FERN* BH22 ...... **25** G1
Heath Farm Rd *FERN* BH22 .... **25** G1
Heath Farm Wy *FERN* BH22 .... **25** G1
Heathfield Av
  BKME/WDN BH12 .... **55** E2
Heathfield Rd *FERN* BH22 .... **10** D5
Heathlands Av *FERN* BH22 ...... **25** H2
Heathlands Cl
  CHCH/BSGR BH23 .... **41** E4
  VWD BH31 .... **5** E2
Heath Rd *CHCH/BSGR* BH23 .. **62** D1
  LYMN SO41 .... **46** B4
  RGWD BH24 .... **11** G2
Heath Rd West *RGWD* BH24 .... **19** G3
Heathwood Av
  NMIL/BTOS BH25 .... **63** G2
Heathwood Rd
  MOOR/WNTN BH9 .... **56** A2
Heathy Cl *NMIL/BTOS* BH25 .... **63** H2
Heaton Rd *NBNE* BH10 .... **36** B5
Heavytree Rd *PSTN* BH14 .... **71** H1
Heckford La *PLE* BH15 .... **70** D2
Heckford Rd *PLE* BH15 .... **70** D1
  WIMB BH21 .... **32** A2
Hedgerley *NMIL/BTOS* BH25 .... **64** B2
Heights Ap *UPTN* BH16 .... **51** E2
Heights Cl *UPTN* BH16 .... **51** E2
Helyar Rd *CHAR* BH8 .... **38** D5

Henbest Cl *WIMB* BH21 .... **16** A4
Henbury Cl *CFDH* BH17 .... **34** C5
  WIMB BH21 .... **32** B1
Henbury Ri *WIMB* BH21 .... **32** B1
Henbury View Rd *WIMB* BH21 .. **32** B1
Henchard Ct *FERN* BH22 .... **25** G2
Henderford Rd *NBNE* BH10 ...... **36** D5
Hengistbury Rd
  NMIL/BTOS BH25 .... **63** G2
  SBNE BH6.................................... **77** F2
Hengist Pk *SBNE* BH6 * **77** H1
Hengist Rd *BMTH* BH1 .... **75** F1
Henley Gdns *LTDN* BH7 .... **58** A3
Henning's Park Rd *PLE* BH15 .. **52** D5
Henville Rd *CHAR* BH8 .... **57** E5
Herbert Av *BKME/WDN* BH12 .. **54** A2
Herberton Rd *SBNE* BH6 .... **58** C5
Herbert Rd *NMIL/BTOS* BH25 .. **45** F4
  WBNE BH4 .... **73** F3
Hercules Rd *PLE* BH15 .... **69** F2
Hermitage Rd *PSTN* BH14 .... **53** G4
Herm Rd *BKME/WDN* BH12 ...... **54** A1
Heron Court Rd
  MOOR/WNTN BH9 .... **56** C3
Heron Dr *WIMB* BH21 .... **15** G2
Herstone Cl *CFDH* BH17 .... **34** B5
Hesketh Cl *RGWD* BH24 .... **12** B1
Heston Cl *CHCH/BSGR* BH23 .. **39** H3
Heston Wy *FERN* BH22 .... **10** A3
Hewitt Rd *PLE* BH15 .... **69** C1
Heysham Rd *BDST* BH18 .... **33** E4
Heytesbury Rd *SBNE* BH6 .... **58** D5
Hibberd Wy *NBNE* BH10 .... **55** H1
Hibbs Cl *UPTN* BH16 .... **51** E3
Hickes Cl *BWD* BH11 .... **35** H3
Hickory Cl *UPTN* BH16 .... **50** C2
Highbridge Rd *PSTN* BH14 ...... **72** A2
Highbury Cl *NMIL/BTOS* BH25.. **45** F4
Highcliffe Rd *CHCH/BSGR* BH23 .. **61** E2
Higher Blandford Rd
  BDST BH18 .... **33** E2
  WIMB BH21 .... **32** D1
Highfield Av *LYMN* SO41 .... **48** C4
  RGWD BH24 .... **8** C3
Highfield Cl *WIMB* BH21 .... **32** C2
Highfield Dr *RGWD* BH24 .... **8** C2
Highfield Rd *FERN* BH22 .... **10** A2
  LYMN SO41 .... **48** C3
  MOOR/WNTN BH9 .... **37** E5
  RGWD BH24 .... **8** C3
  WIMB BH21 .... **32** C2
High Howe Cl *BWD* BH11 .... **35** G4
High Howe Gdns *BWD* BH11 .... **35** G3
High Howe La *BWD* BH11 .... **35** G4
Highland Av *CHCH/BSGR* BH23 .. **62** D1
Highland Rd *PSTN* BH14 .... **53** H5
  WIMB BH21 .... **14** D4
Highlands Crs *NBNE* BH10 ...... **36** C3
Highlands Rd *NMIL/BTOS* BH25.. **64** B2
Highland View Cl *WIMB* BH21 .. **14** D4
High Md *FERN* BH22 .... **25** E2
High Mead La *FERN* BH22 ...... **25** E3
Highmoor Cl *WIMB* BH21 * **32** B2
Highmoor Rd *BWD* BH11 .... **55** E1
  PSTN BH14 .... **72** A2
  WIMB BH21 .... **32** B2
High Oaks Gdns *BWD* BH11 .... **35** G3
High Park Rd *BDST* BH18 .... **32** D3
High Ridge Crs
  NMIL/BTOS BH25 .... **45** G5
High St *CHCH/BSGR* BH23 ...... **59** H4
  LYMN SO41 .... **49** E4
  LYMN SO41 .... **80** C1
  LYND SO43 .... **85** F3
  PLE BH15 .... **70** C3
  RGWD BH24 .... **6** C5
  RGWD BH24 .... **8** B4
  WIMB BH21 .... **14** B4
High St North *PLE* BH15.......... **70** D2
Hightown Gdns *RGWD* BH24 .... **8** D5
Hightown Hl *RGWD* BH24 .... **9** F5
Hightown Rd *RGWD* BH24 .... **8** D5
Hightrees *LYMN* SO41 .... **67** H1
Hightrees Av *CHAR* BH8 .... **57** H1
High Trees Wk *FERN* BH22 ...... **17** H2
Highview Cl *CHCH/BSGR* BH23.. **40** A4
Highview Gdns
  BKME/WDN BH12 .... **54** A3
High Wy *BDST* BH18 .... **32** D4
Highwood La *RGWD* BH24 .... **9** E1
Highwood Rd *BROC* SO42 .... **86** D4
  PSTN BH14 .... **72** C1
Hilary Rd *CFDH* BH17 .... **33** E5
Hilda Rd *BKME/WDN* BH12 ...... **54** C3
Hiley Rd *PLE* BH15 .... **52** C4
Hillary Cl *LYND* SO43 .... **85** F3
Hillary Rd *CHCH/BSGR* BH23.... **60** C5
Hillbourne Rd *CFDH* BH17 .... **33** E5

Hillbrow Rd *SBNE* BH6 .... **58** B4
Hill Cl *CHCH/BSGR* BH23 .... **31** E5
Hillcrest Av *FERN* BH22 .... **17** G2
Hillcrest Cl *MOOR/WNTN* BH9 .. **37** H4
Hillcrest Rd *BKME/WDN* BH12.. **53** G5
  MOOR/WNTN BH9 .... **37** H4
  WIMB BH21 .... **32** A2
Hillcroft Cl *LYMN* SO41 .... **49** E3
Hillditch *LYMN* SO41 .... **48** D1
Hill La *CHCH/BSGR* BH23 .... **31** E4
  CHCH/BSGR BH23 .... **41** H5
Hillman Rd *PSTN* BH14 .... **54** B5
Hillmeadow *VWD* BH31 .... **5** E4
Hill Rd *CHCH/BSGR* BH23 .... **20** B4
Hillside Dr *CHCH/BSGR* BH23 .. **39** H3
Hillside Gdns *WIMB* BH21 .... **32** A3
Hillside Rd *BKME/WDN* BH12 .. **54** D1
  LYMN SO41 .... **48** C4
  VWD BH31 .... **5** E1
  WIMB BH21 .... **32** A2
Hill St *PLE* BH15 .... **70** C3
Hill Ter *WIMB* BH21 .... **23** G2
Hilltop Cl *FERN* BH22 .... **17** F2
Hilltop Rd *FERN* BH22 .... **17** F2
  WIMB BH21 .... **32** C2
Hill View Rd *FERN* BH22 .... **17** G3
Hillview Rd *NBNE* BH10 .... **36** D3
Hill Wy *RGWD* BH24 .... **11** H1
Hiltom Rd *PLE* BH15 .... **53** C4
Hilton Rd *NMIL/BTOS* BH25 .... **45** F3
Hinchliffe Cl *PLE* BH15 .... **69** H3
Hinchliffe Rd *PLE* BH15 .... **69** H3
Hinton Rd *BMTH* BH1 .... **3** H4
Hinton Wood Av
  CHCH/BSGR BH23 .... **43** E5
Hintonwood La
  CHCH/BSGR BH23 .... **43** E5
Hives Wy *LYMN* SO41 .... **48** D1
Hobart Rd *NMIL/BTOS* BH25.... **44** D5
Hobbs Pk *RGWD* BH24 .... **12** A2
Hobbs Rd *BKME/WDN* BH12 .... **54** A2
Hoburne Gdns
  CHCH/BSGR BH23 .... **61** G1
Hoburne La *CHCH/BSGR* BH23.. **61** G1
Hodges Cl *CFDH* BH17 .... **53** E3
Hogarth Wy *CHAR* BH8 .... **38** D5
  CHAR BH8 .... **57** H1
Hogue Av *NBNE* BH10 .... **36** D2
Holbury Cl *CHAR* BH8 .... **38** C4
Holcombe Rd *UPTN* BH16 .... **50** C3
Holdenhurst Av *LTDN* BH7 ...... **58** C3
Holdenhurst Rd *CHAR* BH8...... **58** C3
  CHAR BH8 .... **74** D2
Holes Bay Rd *PLE* BH15 .... **70** C2
Holes Cl *LYMN* SO41 .... **46** B3
Hollands Wood Dr
  NMIL/BTOS BH25 .... **45** F2
Holland Wy *BDST* BH18 .... **32** D2
Holloway Av *BWD* BH11 .... **35** H2
Holly Cl *FERN* BH22 .... **10** A4
  RGWD BH24 .... **11** G2
  UPTN BH16 .... **50** C3
Holly Gdns *CHCH/BSGR* BH23.. **61** G1
  LYMN SO41 .... **66** A5
Holly Green Ri *BWD* BH11 ...... **35** G3
Holly Gv *VWD* BH31 .... **4** B3
Holly Hedge La *CFDH* BH17 .... **52** C2
Holly La *CHCH/BSGR* BH23 .... **44** A5
  NMIL/BTOS BH25 .... **45** G3
Hollywood La *LYMN* SO41 .... **48** D2
Holm Cl *RGWD* BH24 .... **9** E2
Holme Rd *CHCH/BSGR* BH23 .. **62** B2
Holmfield Av *LTDN* BH7 .... **58** C3
Holmhurst Av
  CHCH/BSGR BH23 .... **62** B1
Holm Oak Cl *WIMB* BH21 .... **4** C1
Holmsley Cl *LYMN* SO41 .... **48** B5
Holmwood Garth *RGWD* BH24.... **9** F5
Holnest Rd *CFDH* BH17 .... **52** D1
Holt Rd *BKME/WDN* BH12 .... **54** D4
Holworth Cl *BWD* BH11 .... **35** G4
Holywell Cl *CFDH* BH17 .... **33** H4
Home Farm Rd *VWD* BH31 .... **4** C1
Home Farm Wy *VWD* BH31 .... **4** C2
Homeside Rd
  MOOR/WNTN BH9 .... **37** H5
Homewood Cl *NMIL/BTOS* BH25.. **45** G4
Honeybourne Crs *SBNE* BH6.... **77** G1
Honeysuckle Gdns *LYMN* SO41.. **66** A1
Honeysuckle La *CFDH* BH17 .... **51** H1
Honeysuckle Wy
  CHCH/BSGR BH23 .... **61** F2
Hood Cl *NBNE* BH10 .... **36** D2
Hood Crs *NBNE* BH10 .... **36** D2
Hooke Cl *CFDH* BH17 .... **34** C5
Hop Cl *UPTN* BH16 .... **50** B3
Hopkins Cl *CHAR* BH8 .... **39** E5

Horace Rd *BOSC* BH5....................**75** G1	Inglesham Wy *PLE* BH15.............**69** G2	Kellaway Rd *CFDH* BH17.............**53** F2
Hordle La *LYMN* SO41.................**65** F2	Inglewood Av *CHAR* BH8.............**57** H1	Kelly Cl *CFDH* BH17....................**53** F2
Hordle Ms *LYMN* SO41................**46** B3	Inglewood Dr *NMIL/BTOS* BH25....**45** F5	Kelsall Gdns *NMIL/BTOS* BH25....**45** E4
Horlock Rd *BROC* SO42..............**87** E2	Ingram Wk *WIMB* BH21.................**14** D5	Kemp Rd *MOOR/WNTN* BH9.........**56** B2
Hornbeam Wy *WIMB* BH21...........**14** D4	Ingworth Rd *BKME/WDN* BH12.....**55** E5	Kenilworth Cl *NMIL/BTOS* BH25....**45** F4
Horning Rd *BKME/WDN* BH12......**54** D5	Insley Crs *BDST* BH18.................**32** C2	Kennard Ct *NMIL/BTOS* BH25......**44** D4
Horsa Cl *SBNE* BH6....................**77** E1	Inveravon *CHCH/BSGR* BH23......**60** D4	Kennard Rd *NMIL/BTOS* BH25......**44** D3
Horsa Ct *SBNE* BH6...................**77** E1	Inverclyde Rd *PSTN* BH14...........**71** H1	Kennart Rd *CFDH* BH17...............**52** A3
Horsa Rd *SBNE* BH6...................**77** E1	Inverleigh Rd *SBNE* BH6..............**58** D4	Kennington Rd *CFDH* BH17..........**52** D2
Horseshoe Cl *WIMB* BH21...........**15** H3	Ipswich Rd *WBNE* BH4................**73** F1	Ken Rd *SBNE* BH6.......................**77** E1
Horsham Av *NBNE* BH10..............**36** C1	Iris Rd *MOOR/WNTN* BH9............**56** B1	Kensington Dr *WCLF* BH2.............**2** D1
Horton Rd *MOOR/WNTN* BH9........**38** A4	Irvine Wy *CHCH/BSGR* BH23........**60** C2	Kensington Pk *LYMN* SO41...........**80** A1
Horton Rd *RGWD* BH24..................**6** A5	Irving Rd *SBNE* BH6....................**58** D5	Kent Rd *BKME/WDN* BH12............**54** C4
Horton Wy *VWD* BH31....................**4** B3	Isaacs Cl *BKME/WDN* BH12.........**55** F3	Kenyon Cl *PLE* BH15...................**53** E3
Hosker Rd *BOSC* BH5.................**58** B5	Island View Av	Kenyon Rd *PLE* BH15..................**53** E3
Houlton Rd *PLE* BH15.................**71** E1	*CHCH/BSGR* BH23.................**61** F5	Keppel Cl *RGWD* BH24..................**8** D4
Hounds Wy *WIMB* BH21...............**15** H4	Island View Gdns *LYMN* SO41.....**80** C2	Kerley Rd *WCLF* BH2 *..................**3** F6
Hounslow Cl *PLE* BH15...............**69** G4	Island View Rd	Kerry Cl *LYMN* SO41...................**48** C4
Howard Cl *CHCH/BSGR* BH23.....**60** D4	*NMIL/BTOS* BH25..................**63** F3	Kestrel Cl *FERN* BH22.................**17** F2
Howard Rd *CHAR* BH8................**57** F2	Ivamy Pl *BWD* BH11....................**35** H5	*UPTN* BH16............................**50** D2
VWD BH31...............................**4** D2	Ivor Rd *PLE* BH15......................**70** A4	Kestrel Ct *RGWD* BH24..................**8** C5
Howards Md *LYMN* SO41.............**48** B5	*WIMB* BH21.............................**32** B3	Kestrel Dr *CHCH/BSGR* BH23......**61** E4
Howe Cl *CHCH/BSGR* BH23.......**60** D5	Ivy Cl *RGWD* BH24.....................**11** G2	Keswick Rd *BOSC* BH5................**75** H1
NMIL/BTOS BH25..................**44** D4	Ivy Rd *WIMB* BH21......................**22** D4	*NMIL/BTOS* BH25....................**45** F2
Howe La *VWD* BH31.....................**4** D3	Iwerne Cl *MOOR/WNTN* BH9........**37** H3	Keswick Wy *VWD* BH31..................**4** D3
Howeth Cl *NBNE* BH10...............**36** D4		Keyes Cl *BKME/WDN* BH12.........**54** D1
Howeth Rd *NBNE* BH10...............**36** C4		*CHCH/BSGR* BH23.................**60** D4
Howlett Cl *LYMN* SO41................**48** C3		Keyhaven Rd *LYMN* SO41............**80** D1
Howton Cl *NBNE* BH10 *..............**36** C2		Keysworth Av *NMIL/BTOS* BH25...**63** H3
Howton Rd *NBNE* BH10...............**36** C2		Keysworth Rd *UPTN* BH16............**69** E1
Hoxley Rd *NBNE* BH10................**36** D5		Khyber Rd *BKME/WDN* BH12........**54** B5
Hoyal Rd *PLE* BH15....................**69** F2		Kilmarnock Rd
Hudson Cl *BKME/WDN* BH12........**35** E5		*MOOR/WNTN* BH9..................**56** B1
RGWD BH24..............................**9** E3		Kilmington Wy
Hull Crs *BWD* BH11.....................**35** F3		*CHCH/BSGR* BH23.................**62** B2
Hull Rd *BWD* BH11......................**35** F3		Kiln Cl *WIMB* BH21.....................**32** A3
Hull Wy *BWD* BH11.....................**35** G3		Kiln Wy *VWD* BH31.......................**5** G4
Humber Rd *FERN* BH22...............**18** C3		Kimberley Cl *CHCH/BSGR* BH23...**59** F2
Hungerfield Cl		Kimberley Rd *PSTN* BH14............**71** H2
CHCH/BSGR BH23.................**31** E3		*SBNE* BH6..............................**58** C4
Hungerford Rd *CHAR* BH8...........**38** B4		Kimber Rd *BWD* BH11 *...............**35** H4
Hunter Cl *CHCH/BSGR* BH23......**61** E3		Kimmeridge Av
WIMB BH21.............................**16** A3		*BKME/WDN* BH12...................**54** A2
Hunters Cl *VWD* BH31..................**5** G3		King Cl *RGWD* BH24...................**12** A2
Huntfield Rd *MOOR/WNTN* BH9....**37** H4		Kingcup Cl *BDST* BH18................**32** C5
Huntingdon Dr *WIMB* BH21..........**23** E3		King Edward Av
Huntingdon Gdns		*MOOR/WNTN* BH9..................**37** F5
CHCH/BSGR BH23.................**40** B5	Jackson Rd *BKME/WDN* BH12......**54** A4	Kingfisher Cl *FERN* BH22.............**10** C4
Huntly Rd *TWDS* BH3.................**55** H4	Jacobean Cl *CHCH/BSGR* BH23...**62** D1	*SBNE* BH6..............................**59** E4
Hunt Rd *CHCH/BSGR* BH23........**60** D2	Jacobs Rd *PLE* BH15..................**69** G3	The Kingfishers *VWD* BH31............**5** E3
PLE BH15...............................**71** E1	Jacqueline Rd	Kingfisher Wy
Huntvale Rd *MOOR/WNTN* BH9....**37** H4	*BKME/WDN* BH12...................**53** H3	*CHCH/BSGR* BH23.................**61** E5
Hurdles Md *LYMN* SO41..............**80** B2	Jameson Rd *MOOR/WNTN* BH9....**56** A1	*RGWD* BH24..............................**8** D2
The Hurdles *CHCH/BSGR* BH23...**59** E2	James Rd *BKME/WDN* BH12........**55** E5	King George Av
Hurn Br *CHCH/BSGR* BH23.........**39** F1	Jasmine Ct *LYMN* SO41...............**48** D3	*MOOR/WNTN* BH9..................**37** F5
Hurn Cl *RGWD* BH24....................**7** H5	Jaundrells Cl *NMIL/BTOS* BH25....**45** G4	King John Av *BWD* BH11..............**35** F2
Hurn Court La	Jay's Ct *CHCH/BSGR* BH23.........**62** D2	Kingland Rd *PLE* BH15................**70** D3
CHCH/BSGR BH23.................**38** D1	Jefferson Av *CHAR* BH8...............**57** H1	King Richard Dr *BWD* BH11..........**35** F2
Hurn La *RGWD* BH24..................**7** H5	Jellicoe Cl *PSTN* BH14................**53** F5	Kings Arms La *RGWD* BH24............**8** B4
Hurn Rd *CHCH/BSGR* BH23........**39** H4	Jellicoe Dr *CHCH/BSGR* BH23.....**60** D4	Kings Arms Rw *RGWD* BH24...........**8** B4
CHCH/BSGR BH23.................**40** A4	Jenner Cl *VWD* BH31.....................**4** C1	King's Av *CHCH/BSGR* BH23........**59** F4
RGWD BH24..............................**7** H5	Jennings Rd *PSTN* BH14..............**72** A3	*PSTN* BH14.............................**72** B3
RGWD BH24............................**20** C1	Jephcote Rd *BWD* BH11...............**35** H3	Kingsbere Av *NBNE* BH10............**36** B5
Hurn Wy *CHCH/BSGR* BH23........**58** D1	Jersey Cl *BKME/WDN* BH12.........**54** A1	Kingsbere Rd *PLE* BH15..............**53** E5
Hursley Cl *LTDN* BH7..................**58** C3	Jersey Rd *BKME/WDN* BH12.........**54** B1	Kingsbridge Rd *PSTN* BH14.........**72** A2
Hurstbourne Av	Jesmond Av *CHCH/BSGR* BH23....**62** B2	Kingsbury's La *RGWD* BH24............**8** B5
CHCH/BSGR BH23.................**62** A1	Jessica Av *VWD* BH31....................**4** B1	Kings Cl *FERN* BH22...................**10** B5
Hurst Cl *CHCH/BSGR* BH23........**44** A5	Jessopp Cl *SBNE* BH6.................**37** F3	*LYND* SO43.............................**85** E3
NMIL/BTOS BH25...................**63** F2	Jessopp Rd *WIMB* BH21..............**15** H3	*PLE* BH15..............................**52** D5
Hurstdene Rd *CHAR* BH8............**38** A5	Jewell Rd *CHAR* BH8...................**57** H1	Kings Crs *LYMN* SO41.................**48** C3
Hurst Hl *PSTN* BH14...................**72** A5	Jimmy Brown Av *WIMB* BH21.......**10** B1	*PSTN* BH14.............................**72** C3
Hurst Lea *LYMN* SO41 *..............**67** H1	Johnson Rd *WIMB* BH21..............**17** E2	Kingsfield *LYMN* SO41.................**49** G5
Hurst Rd *LYMN* SO41..................**80** C2	Johnstone Rd	*RGWD* BH24..............................**8** C5
RGWD BH24..............................**8** C2	*CHCH/BSGR* BH23.................**60** C4	Kingsley Av *SBNE* BH6................**77** G1
Hussar Cl *CHCH/BSGR* BH23.....**59** F3	Johnston Rd *PLE* BH15................**52** D3	Kingsley Cl *SBNE* BH6................**77** G1
Hyacinth Cl *CFDH* BH17.............**51** H1	Jolliffe Av *PLE* BH15...................**70** D1	Kingsley House
Hyde Rd *NBNE* BH10..................**36** C2	Jolliffe Rd *PLE* BH15...................**70** D1	*MOOR/WNTN* BH9..................**56** B1
The Hyde *NMIL/BTOS* BH25........**44** C3	Jonathan Cl *LYMN* SO41..............**49** E2	Kingsmill Rd *CFDH* BH17.............**53** E3
Hynesbury Rd	Jopps Cnr *CHCH/BSGR* BH23......**41** E3	King's Park Dr *LTDN* BH7.............**57** G4
CHCH/BSGR BH23.................**61** G4	Joshua Cl *PLE* BH15...................**69** G3	King's Park Rd *LTDN* BH7.............**57** G4
Hythe Rd *PLE* BH15....................**53** G3	Jowitt Dr *NMIL/BTOS* BH25..........**44** D5	Kings Rd *LYMN* SO41..................**48** D3
	Jubilee Cl *RGWD* BH24..................**9** E3	*NMIL/BTOS* BH25....................**45** G3
	Jubilee Crs *BKME/WDN* BH12......**54** B5	*TWDS* BH3.............................**56** C3
	Jubilee Gdns *NBNE* BH10............**36** D5	King's Saltern Rd *LYMN* SO41.......**49** G5
	Jubilee Rd *PSTN* BH14................**54** B5	Kingston Pk *LYMN* SO41..............**48** D5
	WIMB BH21.............................**32** C1	Kingston Rd *PLE* BH15................**70** D1
	Julia Cl *CHCH/BSGR* BH23..........**62** B2	King St *WIMB* BH21.....................**14** B5
Ibbertson Cl *CHAR* BH8..............**38** D5	Julian's Rd *WIMB* BH21................**14** A5	Kingsway *FERN* BH22..................**17** F1
Ibbertson Rd *CHAR* BH8.............**38** D5	Julian Ter *BOSC* BH5 *.................**58** B5	Kingsway Cl *CHCH/BSGR* BH23...**59** F1
Ibbertson Wy *CHAR* BH8.............**38** D5	Julyan Av *BKME/WDN* BH12.........**55** E2	Kingswell Cl *NBNE* BH10.............**36** D5
Ibbett Rd *NBNE* BH10.................**36** C5	Jumpers Av *CHCH/BSGR* BH23....**59** E2	Kingswell Gdns *NBNE* BH10.........**36** D5
Ibsley Cl *CHAR* BH8...................**57** H1	Jumpers Rd *CHCH/BSGR* BH23...**59** E2	Kingswell Gv *NBNE* BH10.............**36** D5
Iddesleigh Rd *TWDS* BH3............**56** B4	Junction Rd *MOOR/WNTN* BH9.....**56** B2	Kingswell Rd *NBNE* BH10.............**36** D5
Iford Br *SBNE* BH6.....................**58** D2	*UPTN* BH16............................**69** F1	Kinson Av *PLE* BH15...................**53** G4
Iford Gdns *LTDN* BH7.................**58** C3	Juniper Cl *FERN* BH22.................**17** H4	Kinson Gv *NBNE* BH10................**36** C1
Iford La *SBNE* BH6.....................**59** E3	*LYMN* SO41............................**48** B5	Kinson Park Rd *NBNE* BH10.........**36** D1
Iley La *LYMN* SO41.....................**67** G3	Justin Gdns *NBNE* BH10..............**37** E3	Kinson Rd *NBNE* BH10................**55** E1
Ilford Cl *SBNE* BH6....................**59** F4		Kipling Rd *PSTN* BH14................**53** H5
Imber Dr *CHCH/BSGR* BH23.......**62** B2		
Imbrecourt *CCLF* BH13...............**83** G1	Kamptee Copse	

	NMIL/BTOS BH25..................**45** F1	Kirby Cl *PLE* BH15......................**53** F4
	Kangaw Pl *PLE* BH15..................**69** F3	Kirby Wy *SBNE* BH6....................**76** D1
	Katherine Chance Cl	Kirkham Av *CHCH/BSGR* BH23.....**41** E4
	CHCH/BSGR BH23.................**41** E4	Kirkway *BDST* BH18.....................**33** F3
	Katterns Cl *CHCH/BSGR* BH23....**40** A5	Kitchener Crs *CFDH* BH17............**33** F5
	Kay Cl *CHCH/BSGR* BH23...........**40** B5	Kitscroft Rd *NBNE* BH10.............**36** D2
	Keats Av *LYMN* SO41..................**66** B5	Kittiwake Cl *SBNE* BH6................**58** D4
	Keeble Cl *NBNE* BH10.................**36** D1	Kitwalls La *LYMN* SO41...............**66** B5
	Keeble Crs *NBNE* BH10...............**36** D1	Kivernell Rd *LYMN* SO41.............**80** A1
	Keeble Rd *NBNE* BH10................**36** D1	Kiwi Cl *PLE* BH15.......................**71** E2
	Keepers La *WIMB* BH21...............**16** C4	Knapp Cl *CHCH/BSGR* BH23.......**59** G2
	Keighley Av *BDST* BH18...............**32** D5	Knapp Mill Av
	Keith Rd *TWDS* BH3...................**55** G4	*CHCH/BSGR* BH23.................**59** G2

Larch Wy *FERN* BH22......17 H2
Lark Rd *CHCH/BSGR* BH23....61 E4
Larks Cl *FERN* BH22.........17 F2
Larksfield Av
  MOOR/WNTN BH9.........37 H4
Larkshill Cl *NMIL/BTOS* BH25...45 F3
Larks Ri *FERN* BH22.........17 F2
Lascelles Rd *LTDN* BH7.......58 B4
Latch Farm Av
  CHCH/BSGR BH23.........59 G2
Latimer Rd *MOOR/WNTN* BH9...56 B2
Latimers Cl *CHCH/BSGR* BH23...62 B1
Laundry La *LYMN* SO41........80 C1
Laurel Cl *CHCH/BSGR* BH23....61 H1
  LYMN SO41............46 A3
  RGWD BH24............11 H2
  WIMB BH21............32 B1
Laurel Dr *BDST* BH18.........33 F3
Laurel Gdns *BDST* BH18.......33 G3
Laurel La *RGWD* BH24.........11 H3
The Laurels *BROC* SO42 *......86 D4
  FERN BH22............17 G2
Lavender Cl *VWD* BH31........5 G3
Lavender Rd *CHAR* BH8........38 B3
  LYMN SO41............46 A4
Lavender Wy *BDST* BH18......32 B4
Lavinia Rd *BKME/WDN* BH12...54 A3
Lawford Ri *MOOR/WNTN* BH9 *...37 G4
Lawford Rd *MOOR/WNTN* BH9...37 G4
Lawn Cl *LYMN* SO41..........80 C1
Lawn Rd *LYMN* SO41..........48 B4
  LYMN SO41............80 C1
Lawns Cl *WIMB* BH21.........16 A4
Lawns Rd *WIMB* BH21.........15 H3
The Lawns *CHCH/BSGR* BH23...62 D3
Lawn Vw *NMIL/BTOS* BH25....44 B2
Lawrence Ct *CHAR* BH8.......57 E4
Lawrence Dr *CCLF* BH13......72 C4
Lawrence Rd *RGWD* BH24......9 E5
Lawson Rd *BKME/WDN* BH12...53 H4
Layard Dr *WIMB* BH21........22 D2
Layton Rd *BKME/WDN* BH12...54 B5
Leamington Rd
  MOOR/WNTN BH9.........56 C3
Leaphill Rd *LTDN* BH7........58 A4
Learoyd Rd *CFDH* BH17.......52 D3
The Lea *VWD* BH31...........5 E3
Lea Wy *BWD* BH11...........35 G1
Lechlade Gdns *LTDN* BH7.....58 A2
Ledbury Rd *CHCH/BSGR* BH23...60 D5
Ledgard Cl *PSTN* BH14........71 H1
Leedam Rd *NBNE* BH10........36 D3
Lee Lands *LYMN* SO41........67 H1
Lees Cl *CHCH/BSGR* BH23.....39 H3
Leeson Dr *FERN* BH22........17 F1
Leeson Rd *LTDN* BH7.........57 G3
Legg La *WIMB* BH21..........14 D5
Legion Cl *PLE* BH15.........69 G3
Legion Rd *PLE* BH15.........69 G3
Leicester Rd *CCLF* BH13......72 D1
Leigham Vale Rd *SBNE* BH6....76 D1
Leigh Cl *WIMB* BH21.........15 E5
Leigh Common *WIMB* BH21....15 E4
Leigh Gdns *WIMB* BH21.......14 D5
Leigh La *WIMB* BH21.........15 F4
Leigh Pk *LYMN* SO41.........48 C3
Leigh Rd *NMIL/BTOS* BH25....45 E3
  WIMB BH21............14 C5
Lentham Cl *CFDH* BH17.......52 D1
Lentune Wy *LYMN* SO41......48 D5
Le Patourel Cl
  CHCH/BSGR BH23.........60 B3
Leslie Rd *MOOR/WNTN* BH9....56 B2
  PSTN BH14............71 G2
Leven Av *WBNE* BH4.........55 H5
Leven Cl *WBNE* BH4..........2 C1
Levet's La *PLE* BH15.........70 B4
Lewens Cl *WIMB* BH21........14 C5
Lewesdon Dr *BDST* BH18......32 D3
Leybourne Av *NBNE* BH10.....36 D2
Leybourne Cl *NBNE* BH10.....36 C2
Leydene Av *CHAR* BH8.........57 H1
Leydene Cl *CHAR* BH8.........57 H1
Leyland Rd *BKME/WDN* BH12...35 G5
Leyside *CHCH/BSGR* BH23.....60 D4
Liberty Wy *PLE* BH15........70 D3
Library Rd *BKME/WDN* BH12...54 C5
  FERN BH22............17 H4
  MOOR/WNTN BH9.........56 B1
Liederbach Dr *VWD* BH31......5 G4
Lilac Cl *RGWD* BH24..........8 D3
Lilliput Rd *PSTN* BH14.......72 A4
Lime Cl *PLE* BH15...........53 F4
Lime Gv *LYMN* SO41..........66 B2
Limited Rd *MOOR/WNTN* BH9...56 C1
Lin Brook Dr *RGWD* BH24......9 E1
Lincoln Av *BMTH* BH1.........57 F4
  CHCH/BSGR BH23.........40 B5
Lincoln Rd *BKME/WDN* BH12...54 B3

Lindbergh Rd *WIMB* BH21......17 E1
Linden Cl *FERN* BH22.........25 H3
Linden Rd *BKME/WDN* BH12....54 A4
  FERN BH22............25 H3
  MOOR/WNTN BH9.........37 G4
The Lindens *CHCH/BSGR* BH23...41 F4
Linden Wy *LYMN* SO41........48 C3
Lindsay Rd *CCLF* BH13........73 E1
Lineside *CHCH/BSGR* BH23.....60 A2
Linford Cl *NMIL/BTOS* BH25....45 E3
Linford Rd *RGWD* BH24........9 F2
Lingdale Rd *SBNE* BH6........58 D4
Ling Rd *BKME/WDN* BH12......53 H1
Lingwood Av *CHCH/BSGR* BH23...60 D4
Linhorns La *NMIL/BTOS* BH25...45 E1
Link Ri *WIMB* BH21..........32 C1
Link Rd *RGWD* BH24...........9 E2
Links Dr *CHCH/BSGR* BH23.....58 D1
Linkside Av *CHAR* BH8........57 G2
Links Rd *PSTN* BH14.........72 B3
Links View Av *PSTN* BH14.....72 C4
Linmead Dr *BWD* BH11........36 A1
Linnet Cl *RGWD* BH24.........9 E5
Linnet Ct *NMIL/BTOS* BH25....44 D5
Linnet Rd *CFDH* BH17........51 G2
Linthorpe Rd *PLE* BH15.......71 E1
Linwood Rd *MOOR/WNTN* BH9...56 D3
Lionheart Cl *BWD* BH11.......35 F2
Lions Hill Wy *RGWD* BH24.....11 G2
Lions La *RGWD* BH24.........11 G2
Lions Wd *RGWD* BH24.........11 H2
Lisle Cl *WIMB* BH21..........48 D4
Lisle Court Rd *LYMN* SO41....49 H3
Litchford Rd *NMIL/BTOS* BH25...45 F3
Little Barrs Dr *NMIL/BTOS* BH25...45 F3
Littlecroft Av
  MOOR/WNTN BH9.........37 H4
Little Croft Rd
  BKME/WDN BH12.........53 H4
Little Dene Copse *LYMN* SO41...48 B5
Little Dewlands *VWD* BH31......4 B2
Littledown Av *LTDN* BH7......57 C3
Littledown Dr *LTDN* BH7......57 G3
Little Forest Rd *WBNE* BH4....55 H5
Little Lonnen *WIMB* BH21.....15 F1
Littlemead Cl *CFDH* BH17.....52 A3
Littlemoor Av *BWD* BH11......35 F3
Livingstone Rd
  BKME/WDN BH12.........54 A4
  BOSC BH5.............76 B1
  CHCH/BSGR BH23........60 B4
  WIMB BH21............15 G5
Llewellin Cl *UPTN* BH16......51 E3
Loaders Rd *MOOR/WNTN* BH9...56 C2
Loch Rd *PSTN* BH14..........54 C5
Lockerley Cl *LYMN* SO41......49 E5
Lockyers Dr *FERN* BH22.......18 B3
Loders Cl *CFDH* BH17.........33 C4
Lodge Cl *PSTN* BH14.........72 C1
Lodge Ct *PSTN* BH14.........72 C1
Lodge Rd *CHCH/BSGR* BH23....59 E2
  LYMN SO41............48 B4
Loewy Crs *BKME/WDN* BH12....35 F5
Lombard Av *SBNE* BH6........58 D5
Lombardy Cl *VWD* BH31........5 F3
London La *CHCH/BSGR* BH23....29 F2
Lone Pine Dr *FERN* BH22......26 B2
Lone Pine Wy *FERN* BH22......26 B2
Longbarrow Cl *CHAR* BH8 *....57 H1
Longespee Rd *WIMB* BH21.....22 D4
Longfield Dr *BWD* BH11.......36 A1
  FERN BH22............26 A4
Longfield Rd *LYMN* SO41......46 D5
Longfleet Dr *WIMB* BH21......23 C5
Longfleet Rd *PLE* BH15.......71 E1
Longford Pl *LYMN* SO41.......67 H1
Longham Br *FERN* BH22.......25 E5
Long La *WIMB* BH21..........14 D2
Longleat Gdns
  NMIL/BTOS BH25.........44 C4
Longmeadow La *CFDH* BH17....51 G2
Long Rd *NBNE* BH10..........36 C3
Lonnen Rd *WIMB* BH21........15 G1
Lonnen Wood Cl *WIMB* BH21...15 G1
Lonsdale Rd *TWDS* BH3.......56 B3
Loraine Av *CHCH/BSGR* BH23...62 D2
Lord Cl *CFDH* BH17..........53 F3
Lorne Park Rd *BMTH* BH1......3 K3
Lower Ashley Rd
  NMIL/BTOS BH25.........45 H5
Lower Blandford Rd
  BDST BH18............33 F3
Lower Buckland Rd *LYMN* SO41...48 D2
Lower Golf Links Rd *BDST* BH18...33 F2
Lower Pennington La
  LYMN SO41............67 H1
Lowther Gdns *CHAR* BH8......57 E5
Lowther Rd *CHAR* BH8........56 C4

Lucas Rd *BKME/WDN* BH12....54 A4
  PLE BH15.............70 B4
Lucerne Av *SBNE* BH6........58 D5
Lucerne Rd *LYMN* SO41.......66 C3
Luckham Cl *MOOR/WNTN* BH9...37 H5
Luckham Pl *MOOR/WNTN* BH9...37 H5
Luckham Rd *MOOR/WNTN* BH9...37 H5
Luckham Rd East
  MOOR/WNTN BH9.........37 H5
Lulworth Av *PLE* BH15........69 G4
Lulworth Cl *PLE* BH15........69 G4
Lulworth Crs *PLE* BH15.......69 G4
Lumby Dr *RGWD* BH24.........8 D3
Lumby Drive Pk *RGWD* BH24....8 D3
Luscombe Rd *PSTN* BH14......72 A3
Luther Rd *MOOR/WNTN* BH9....56 B2
Lych Gate Ct *RGWD* BH24......8 C3
Lydford Gdns *BWD* BH11.......36 A5
Lydford Rd *BWD* BH11........36 A5
Lydgate *LYMN* SO41..........65 C5
Lydlinch Cl *FERN* BH22.......25 H3
Lydwell Cl *BWD* BH11.........35 H2
Lyell Rd *BKME/WDN* BH12.....54 A4
Lyme Crs *CHCH/BSGR* BH23....39 H3
Lymefields *LYMN* SO41........66 C4
Lymington Rd
  CHCH/BSGR BH23.........61 H3
  LYMN SO41............66 C3
Lymington Rd Shelley Hl
  CHCH/BSGR BH23.........61 H3
Lymore La *LYMN* SO41........66 D3
Lymore Va *LYMN* SO41........66 C3
Lyndale Cl *LYMN* SO41........66 C5
Lyndhurst Rd *BROC* SO42.....87 E2
  CHCH/BSGR BH23.........41 H3
  CHCH/BSGR BH23.........43 F4
Lyndhurst Rd Roeshot Hl
  CHCH/BSGR BH23.........61 F2
Lynes La *RGWD* BH24..........8 B4
Lynn Rd *CFDH* BH17..........53 F2
Lynric Cl *NMIL/BTOS* BH25....63 H3
Lynton Crs *CHCH/BSGR* BH23...39 H4
Lynwood Cl *FERN* BH22........17 H2
Lynwood Dr *WIMB* BH21.......23 E4
Lyon Av *NMIL/BTOS* BH25.....45 F4
Lyon Rd *BKME/WDN* BH12.....35 G5
Lysander Cl *CHCH/BSGR* BH23...61 G3
Lystra Rd *MOOR/WNTN* BH9....37 G4
Lytchett Dr *BDST* BH18.......32 D4
Lytchett Wy *UPTN* BH16......50 D4
Lyteltane Rd *LYMN* SO41......48 D5
Lytham Rd *BDST* BH18........33 E4
Lytton Rd *CHAR* BH8.........57 E5

M

Mabey Av *NBNE* BH10.........36 D5
Macandrew Rd *CCLF* BH13.....83 H1
Macaulay Rd *BDST* BH18......33 E3
Maclaren Rd *MOOR/WNTN* BH9...37 H4
Maclean Rd *BWD* BH11........35 H4
Madeira Rd *BMTH* BH1.........3 J2
  PSTN BH14............54 B5
Madeline Crs *BKME/WDN* BH12...53 H3
Madison Av *BMTH* BH1.........57 F4
Magdalen La *CHCH/BSGR* BH23...59 G4
Magna Cl *BWD* BH11.........35 H1
Magna Gdns *BWD* BH11.......35 H1
Magna Rd *WIMB* BH21........23 H4
Magnolia Cl *SBNE* BH6.......59 G5
  VWD BH31.............5 G4
Magpie Cl *CHAR* BH8.........38 A4
Magpie Gv *NMIL/BTOS* BH25...44 D5
Mag's Barrow *FERN* BH22.....26 A2
Maidment Cl *BWD* BH11.......35 G3
Main Rd *LYMN* SO41.........49 G1
Malan Cl *CFDH* BH17.........53 E2
Malcomb Cl *SBNE* BH6........77 G2
Mallard Cl *CHAR* BH8........57 E1
  CHCH/BSGR BH23.........61 E3
  LYMN SO41............46 D4
Mallard Rd *CHAR* BH8........38 B5
  WIMB BH21............15 G2
Mallory Cl *CHCH/BSGR* BH23...60 D2
Mallow Cl *BDST* BH18........32 C4
  CHCH/BSGR BH23.........61 G2
The Mallows *NMIL/BTOS* BH25...45 H3
Malmesbury Ct *CHAR* BH8.....57 E4
Malmesbury Park Pl *CHAR* BH8...57 E5
Malmesbury Park Rd
  CHAR BH8.............56 D4
Malmesbury Rd *RGWD* BH24...11 H3
Malmsbury Cl *CHCH/BSGR* BH23...59 H5
Maloren Wy *FERN* BH22.......10 D5
Malthouse *PLE* BH15.........70 C3
Malvern Cl *MOOR/WNTN* BH9...37 G4
Malvern Rd *MOOR/WNTN* BH9...37 G5

Mandale Cl *BWD* BH11........36 A4
Mandale Rd *BWD* BH11.......35 H4
Manderley *LYMN* SO41........80 C2
Manning Av *CHCH/BSGR* BH23...61 G3
Mannings Heath Rd
  BKME/WDN BH12.........34 D5
Mannington Pl *WCLF* BH2......2 A7
Mannington Wy *FERN* BH22....10 A3
Manor Av *BKME/WDN* BH12....54 A1
Manor Cl *FERN* BH22.........18 A4
  LYMN SO41............66 B5
Manor Ct *RGWD* BH24.........8 C3
  VWD BH31.............4 D2
Manor Farm Cl
  NMIL/BTOS BH25.........63 H1
Manor Farm Rd *NBNE* BH10....25 G5
Manor Farmyard *CHAR* BH8....39 F4
Manor Gdns *RGWD* BH24.......8 C3
  VWD BH31.............4 D2
Manor La *VWD* BH31..........4 D3
Manor Rd *BMTH* BH1.........75 F2
  CHCH/BSGR BH23.........59 G4
  LYMN SO41............66 B4
  NMIL/BTOS BH25.........45 F4
  RGWD BH24............8 C4
  VWD BH31.............4 D2
Manor Wy *VWD* BH31..........4 D1
Mansel Cl *BKME/WDN* BH12....55 G3
Mansfield Cl *FERN* BH22......25 H2
  PSTN BH14............72 A1
Mansfield Rd
  MOOR/WNTN BH9.........56 A1
  PSTN BH14............72 A1
  RGWD BH24............8 B4
Manton Rd *PLE* BH15.........69 G2
Maple Cl *CHCH/BSGR* BH23....62 B3
  NMIL/BTOS BH25.........64 B3
Maple Dr *FERN* BH22.........17 G1
Maple Rd *MOOR/WNTN* BH9....56 B1
  PLE BH15.............70 D2
Mapperton Cl *CFDH* BH17.....34 B5
Marabout Cl *CHCH/BSGR* BH23...60 B3
Marchwood Rd *NBNE* BH10....36 C4
Margards La *VWD* BH31........4 C3
Marian Cl *WIMB* BH21........32 A3
Marianne Rd *BKME/WDN* BH12...55 G2
  WIMB BH21............15 G2
Marian Rd *WIMB* BH21........32 A3
Marie Cl *BKME/WDN* BH12.....54 B3
Marina Dr *PSTN* BH14........71 H4
The Marina *BOSC* BH5........75 G2
Marine Dr *NMIL/BTOS* BH25...63 G3
Marine Dr East
  NMIL/BTOS BH25.........64 A4
Marine Dr West
  NMIL/BTOS BH25.........63 G3
Marine Prospect
  NMIL/BTOS BH25.........63 H3
Marine Rd *SBNE* BH6.........76 D2
Market Cl *PLE* BH15.........70 C3
Market Pl *RGWD* BH24.........8 B4
Market St *PLE* BH15.........70 B4
Market Wy *WIMB* BH21........14 D5
Markham Av *NBNE* BH10.......36 D1
Markham Cl *NBNE* BH10......25 H5
Markham Rd *MOOR/WNTN* BH9...56 C2
Mark's La *NMIL/BTOS* BH25....45 E1
Marks Rd *MOOR/WNTN* BH9....37 H4
Marlborough Pl *LYMN* SO41....48 D2
  WIMB BH21............14 D4
Marlborough Rd *PSTN* BH14...72 A1
  WBNE BH4.............2 B4
Marley Av *NMIL/BTOS* BH25...44 C3
Marley Cl *NMIL/BTOS* BH25...44 D4
Marline Rd *BKME/WDN* BH12...54 B4
Marlott Rd *PLE* BH15........52 C5
Marlow Dr *CHCH/BSGR* BH23...40 A4
Marlpit Dr *CHCH/BSGR* BH23...43 G5
Marmion Gn *CHCH/BSGR* BH23...60 D3
Marnhull Rd *PLE* BH15.......70 D1
Marpet Cl *BWD* BH11.........35 H1
Marquis Wy *BWD* BH11........35 F2
Marram Cl *LYMN* SO41........49 E1
Marryat Rd *NMIL/BTOS* BH25...44 D4
Marshal Rd *CFDH* BH17......52 B1
Marshfield *WIMB* BH21........15 F2
Marshlands Cl
  CHCH/BSGR BH23.........60 B4
Marsh La *CHCH/BSGR* BH23....40 B5
  LYMN SO41............49 E1
  UPTN BH16............50 C3
Marshwood Av *CFDH* BH17....34 B5
Marston Cl *NMIL/BTOS* BH25...45 F2
Marston Gv *CHCH/BSGR* BH23...62 A1
Marston Rd *NMIL/BTOS* BH25...45 F2
  PLE BH15.............70 B3
Martello Pk *CCLF* BH13.......83 H1
Martello Rd *CCLF* BH13......72 D5
The Martells *NMIL/BTOS* BH25...64 B3

Martin Cl *CFDH* BH17 ....51 H3
Martindale Av *WIMB* BH21 ....15 H4
Martingale Cl *UPTN* BH16 ....51 F3
Martins Cl *FERN* BH22 ....18 A2
Martins Dr *FERN* BH22 ....18 A2
Martins Hill Cl
  CHCH/BSGR BH23 ....60 A1
Martins Hill La
  CHCH/BSGR BH23 ....60 B1
Martin's Rd *BROC* SO42 ....87 E2
Martins Wy *FERN* BH22 ....18 A2
Marwell Cl *LTDN* BH7 ....58 A3
Maryland Rd *UPTN* BH16 ....69 E1
Mary La *FERN* BH22 ....10 A4
Masterson Cl *CHCH/BSGR* BH23....60 B3
Matchams Cl *RGWD* BH24 ....20 B3
Matchams La *CHCH/BSGR* BH23 ....20 B4
  CHCH/BSGR BH23 ....28 B3
Matlock Rd *FERN* BH22 ....25 G1
Maturin Cl *LYMN* SO41 ....48 D4
Maundeville Crs
  CHCH/BSGR BH23 ....59 E2
Maundeville Rd
  CHCH/BSGR BH23 ....59 E2
Maureen Cl *BKME/WDN* BH12 ......53 H3
Mavis Rd *MOOR/WNTN* BH9 ....56 D1
Maxwell Rd *BDST* BH18 ....32 B4
  CCLF BH13 ....83 H1
  MOOR/WNTN BH9 ....56 C3
May Av *LYMN* SO41 ....48 D2
Maycrete Rd *CHCH/BSGR* BH23 ....27 F3
Mayfair Gdns *BWD* BH11 ....36 A3
Mayfield Av *PSTN* BH14 ....72 C2
Mayfield Cl *FERN* BH22 ....17 G3
Mayfield Dr *FERN* BH22 ....17 H3
Mayfield Rd *MOOR/WNTN* BH9 .....17 G5
Mayfield Wy *FERN* BH22 ....17 G3
Mayflower Cl *LYMN* SO41 ....49 G4
Mayford Rd *BKME/WDN* BH12 ......55 F4
May Gdns *BWD* BH11 ....35 G4
  CHCH/BSGR BH23 ....43 H5
McIntyre Rd *CHCH/BSGR* BH23 ....28 A4
McKinley Rd *WBNE* BH4 ....2 A6
McWilliam Cl *BKME/WDN* BH12 ....55 G2
McWilliam Rd *MOOR/WNTN* BH9...37 G5
Mead Cl *BDST* BH18 ....52 A1
Meadow Cl *CHCH/BSGR* BH23 ......29 H5
  CHCH/BSGR BH23 ....31 E5
  FERN BH22 ....25 H3
  RGWD BH24 ....8 D2
Meadow Court Cl
  MOOR/WNTN BH9 ....37 G4
Meadow Gv *VWD* BH31 ....5 F3
Meadowland *CHCH/BSGR* BH23 ....60 C4
Meadowlands *LYMN* SO41 ....48 C3
  RGWD BH24 ....13 H2
Meadow La *CHCH/BSGR* BH23 ......41 E5
Meadow Ri *BDST* BH18 ....32 D2
Meadow Rd *LYMN* SO41 ....48 C4
  NMIL/BTOS BH25 ....45 F3
  RGWD BH24 ....8 D3
Meadows Cl *UPTN* BH16 ....51 E2
Meadows Dr *UPTN* BH16 ....51 E3
The Meadows *LYND* SO43 ....85 F4
Meadowsweet Rd *CFDH* BH17.......51 G2
Meadow View Rd *BWD* BH11 ....35 G3
Meadow Wy *NMIL/BTOS* BH25 .....64 A3
  RGWD BH24 ....8 D3
  VWD BH31 ....5 F4
Mead Rd *LYMN* SO41 ....48 B5
The Meadway
  CHCH/BSGR BH23 ....42 D5
Medina Av *CHCH/BSGR* BH23 ....61 G4
Medlar Cl *CHCH/BSGR* BH23 ....60 B1
Medway Rd *FERN* BH22 ....18 C3
Meerut Rd *BROC* SO42 ....86 D2
Meeting House La *RGWD* BH24 ....8 B4
Melbourne Rd *CHAR* BH8 ....57 E4
  CHCH/BSGR BH23 ....59 E1
Melbury Av *BKME/WDN* BH12 ......54 C3
Melbury Cl *FERN* BH22 ....17 H5
  LYMN SO41 ....48 D2
Mellstock Rd *PLE* BH15 ....54 D5
Melrose Ct *NMIL/BTOS* BH25 * 45 G4
Melverley Gdns *WIMB* BH21 ....14 D4
Melville Rd *MOOR/WNTN* BH9 ......56 A2
Mendip Cl *NMIL/BTOS* BH25 ....45 G5
  VWD BH31 ....4 D3
Mendip Rd *VWD* BH31 ....4 D3
Mentone Rd *PSTN* BH14 ....71 G2
Meon Rd *LTDN* BH7 ....58 B3
Meredith Cl *CHCH/BSGR* BH23 .....60 B3
Meriden Cl *CCLF* BH13 ....83 H1
The Meridians
  CHCH/BSGR BH23 ....59 F5
Merino Wy *FERN* BH22 ....10 C5
Merlewood Cl *WCLF* BH2 ....3 G1
Merley Dr *CHCH/BSGR* BH23.........62 C2
Merley Gdns *WIMB* BH21 ....22 D3

Merley La *WIMB* BH21 ....22 D3
Merley Park Rd *WIMB* BH21 ....22 C4
Merley Ways *WIMB* BH21 ....22 D2
Merlin Cl *RGWD* BH24 ....9 E5
Merlin Wy *CHCH/BSGR* BH23 ....61 G5
Merriefield Av *BDST* BH18 ....33 G1
Merriefield Dr *BDST* BH18 ....33 G1
Merrifield *WIMB* BH21 ....15 E2
Merrifield Cl *BDST* BH18 ....33 F1
Merritown La *CHCH/BSGR* BH23...27 F5
Merrivale Av *SBNE* BH6 ....59 E5
Merrow Av *BKME/WDN* BH12 ......55 F4
Merryfield Cl *CHCH/BSGR* BH23....31 E4
  VWD BH31 ....4 D2
Merryfield La *NBNE* BH10 ....36 C3
Merton Gv *RGWD* BH24 ....8 B3
Methuen Cl *CHAR* BH8 ....57 E5
Methuen Rd *CFDH* BH17 ....33 F5
  CHAR BH8 ....58 D5
The Mews *VWD* BH31 ....5 E4
Meyrick Cl *CHCH/BSGR* BH23 ....31 E5
Meyrick Park Crs *TWDS* BH3 ....56 B4
Meyrick Rd *BMTH* BH1 ....74 D2
Michelgrove Rd *BOSC* BH5 ....75 G2
Michelmersh Gn *CHAR* BH8 ....38 B5
Mickleham Cl *NMIL/BTOS* BH12 ...55 F2
Middle Common Rd *LYMN* SO41...48 A4
Middlehill Dr *WIMB* BH21 ....15 H3
Middlehill Rd *WIMB* BH21 ....15 G2
Middle La *RGWD* BH24 ....8 C4
Middle Rd *LYMN* SO41 ....48 C2
  NBNE BH10 ....36 C2
  PLE BH15 ....53 E4
Middleton Ms *NMIL/BTOS* BH25...63 H1
Middleton Rd
  MOOR/WNTN BH9 ....37 E5
  WIMB BH21 ....8 C3
Midland Rd *MOOR/WNTN* BH9......56 B2
Midwood Av *CHAR* BH8 ....57 H1
Milborne Crs *BKME/WDN* BH12 ....54 C2
Milbourne Rd *FERN* BH22 ....17 G3
Milburn Cl *WBNE* BH4 ....2 A2
Milburn Rd *WBNE* BH4 ....73 F1
Milestone Rd *PLE* BH15 ....54 D5
Milford Cl *FERN* BH22 ....10 C4
Milford Ct *LYMN* SO41 ....80 C1
Milford Crs *LYMN* SO41 ....80 C1
Milford Dr *BWD* BH11 ....35 H2
Milford Pl *LYMN* SO41 ....80 C2
Milford Rd *LYMN* SO41 ....66 D1
  NMIL/BTOS BH25 ....64 C3
Miller Cl *NMIL/BTOS* BH25 ....45 G3
Miller Rd *CHCH/BSGR* BH23 ....60 B3
Millfield *CFDH* BH17 ....52 A3
Millhams Cl *NBNE* BH10 ....36 B1
Millhams Rd *BWD* BH11 ....25 E5
  NBNE BH10 ....36 B1
Millhams St *CHCH/BSGR* BH23 .....59 H4
Millhams St North
  CHCH/BSGR BH23 ....59 H4
Mill Hill Cl *PSTN* BH14 ....71 H2
Mill La *BROC* SO42 ....87 F3
  CHCH/BSGR BH23 ....39 F1
  CHCH/BSGR BH23 ....62 D2
  LYMN SO41 ....80 C1
  PSTN BH14 ....71 H3
Mill Meadow *LYMN* SO41 ....66 A5
Mill Rd *CHCH/BSGR* BH23 ....59 G2
Mill Rd (North) *CHAR* BH8 ....38 C4
Mill Rd (South) *CHAR* BH8 ....38 B5
Millstream Cl *CFDH* BH17 ....52 A3
  WIMB BH21 ....14 C5
Millyford Cl *NMIL/BTOS* BH25 ......63 F2
Milne Rd *CFDH* BH17 ....52 B1
Milner Rd *WBNE* BH4 ....2 B6
Milton Cl *PSTN* BH14 ....71 H4
Milton Gn *NMIL/BTOS* BH25 * 63 H1
Milton Gv *NMIL/BTOS* BH25 ....45 F5
Milton Md *NMIL/BTOS* BH25 ....44 D5
Milton Rd *BMTH* BH1 ....72 B2
  PSTN BH14 ....72 B2
Milverton Cl *CHCH/BSGR* BH23 ....62 A1
Mimosa Av *WIMB* BH21 ....22 D4
Minstead Rd *NBNE* BH10 ....36 C4
Minster Vw *WIMB* BH21 ....14 C4
Minster Wy *UPTN* BH16 ....53 G5
Minterne Rd *CHCH/BSGR* BH23 ....60 C5
  MOOR/WNTN BH9 ....56 C2
  PSTN BH14 ....83 E1
Mission Rd *BDST* BH18 ....33 E5
Mitchell Cl *NMIL/BTOS* BH25 ....64 A3
Mitchell Rd *CFDH* BH17 ....52 B1
  PLE BH15 ....17 E2
Moat La *NMIL/BTOS* BH25 ....63 H1
Moffat Rd *CHCH/BSGR* BH23 ....60 B3

Molyneux Rd *NMIL/BTOS* BH25 ....45 H4
Moneyfly Rd *VWD* BH31 ....5 F3
Monks Cl *FERN* BH22 ....18 C1
Monkshood Cl
  CHCH/BSGR BH23 ....61 F1
Monks Wy *BWD* BH11 ....35 E2
Monkswell Gn
  CHCH/BSGR BH23 ....60 B4
Monkton Cl *FERN* BH22 ....17 H3
Monkton Crs *BKME/WDN* BH12 ....54 C2
Monkworthy Dr *RGWD* BH24 ....12 A1
Monmouth Cl *VWD* BH31 ....4 B4
Monmouth Dr *VWD* BH31 ....5 H4
Monsal Av *FERN* BH22 ....25 G1
Montacute Wy *WIMB* BH21 ....23 E4
Montague Rd *BOSC* BH5 ....76 B1
Montagu Rd *CHCH/BSGR* BH23 ....62 D3
Monteray Dr *LYMN* SO41 ....46 B3
Montgomery Av *BWD* BH11 ....36 B4
Montrose Cl *VWD* BH31 ....4 C3
Montrose Dr *NBNE* BH10 ....36 B5
Monument La *LYMN* SO41 ....49 G3
Moonrakers Wy
  CHCH/BSGR BH23 ....62 A1
Moorcroft Av
  CHCH/BSGR BH23 ....41 E5
Moordown Cl
  MOOR/WNTN BH9 ....37 G4
Moore Av *BWD* BH11 ....36 A4
Moore Cl *NMIL/BTOS* BH25 ....63 H1
Moorfield Gv *MOOR/WNTN* BH9 ...37 F5
Moorfields Rd *CCLF* BH13 ....72 D5
Moorings Cl *PLE* BH15 ....69 H4
Moorland Av *NMIL/BTOS* BH25 .....63 H2
Moorland Crs *UPTN* BH16 ....50 D3
Moorland Ga *RGWD* BH24 ....13 H1
Moorland Pde *UPTN* BH16 * 50 D4
Moorland Rd *BMTH* BH1 ....75 F1
Moorlands Cl *BOSC* SO42 ....86 B3
Moorlands Ri *FERN* BH22 ....10 C3
Moorlands Rd *FERN* BH22 ....10 B4
  VWD BH31 ....4 D1
Moorland Wy *UPTN* BH16 ....50 D3
Moor Rd *BDST* BH18 ....33 F2
Moors Cl *CHCH/BSGR* BH23 ....28 B5
Moorside Rd *RGWD* BH24 * 18 D3
Moorside Cl *BWD* BH11 ....36 B4
Moorside Rd *BWD* BH11 ....36 A4
  FERN BH22 ....10 B4
  WIMB BH21 ....32 B2
Moortown Dr *WIMB* BH21 ....23 H4
Moorvale Rd *MOOR/WNTN* BH9....37 G5
Moor View Rd *PLE* BH15 ....53 E4
Morant Rd *RGWD* BH24 ....8 D2
Morden Av *FERN* BH22 ....17 G5
Morden Rd *MOOR/WNTN* BH9 ......37 H3
Moreton Rd *MOOR/WNTN* BH9 .....37 H3
Morley Cl *BOSC* BH5 ....58 A5
  CHCH/BSGR BH23 ....41 E4
Morley Rd *BOSC* BH5 ....58 A5
Mornish Rd *CCLF* BH13 ....72 D3
Morrison Av *BKME/WDN* BH12 .....54 D4
Morris Rd *CFDH* BH17 ....52 D2
Mortimer Cl *CHCH/BSGR* BH23.....61 E4
Mortimer Rd *CHAR* BH8 ....56 D1
Mossley Av *BKME/WDN* BH12 ....54 D1
Motcombe Rd *CCLF* BH13 ....73 E4
Mountbatten Cl
  CHCH/BSGR BH23 ....61 E5
Mountbatten Dr *FERN* BH22 ....17 G4
Mountbatten Rd *CCLF* BH13 ....73 F4
  CHAR BH8 ....38 D5
Mount Cl *NMIL/BTOS* BH25 ....64 B1
Mount Grace Dr *PSTN* BH14 ....83 F1
Mountjoy Cl *WIMB* BH21 ....23 F2
Mount Pleasant *RGWD* BH24 ....8 C5
Mount Pleasant Dr *CHAR* BH8 ......57 H1
  CHCH/BSGR BH23 ....31 G3
Mount Pleasant Rd *PLE* BH15 ....70 D3
Mount Rd *BWD* BH11 ....36 A3
  PSTN BH14 ....53 H5
The Mount *RGWD* BH24 ....9 F3
Mudeford *CHCH/BSGR* BH23 ....60 D5
Mudeford Green Cl
  CHCH/BSGR BH23 ....60 D5
Mudeford La *CHCH/BSGR* BH23 ....60 D4
Mude Gdns *CHCH/BSGR* BH23 ......61 E5
Mullins Cl *BKME/WDN* BH12 ....55 G2
Munster Rd *PLE* BH15 ....72 B2
Murley Rd *MOOR/WNTN* BH9 ....56 C2
Muscliffe La
  MOOR/WNTN BH9 ....37 G3
Muscliffe Pk
  MOOR/WNTN BH9 ....38 A3
Muscliffe Rd
  MOOR/WNTN BH9 ....56 B2
Myrtle Cl *LYMN* SO41 ....46 B3
Myrtle Rd *CHAR* BH8 ....57 E4

N

Nada Rd *CHCH/BSGR* BH23 ....61 H1
Nairn Rd *CCLF* BH13 ....83 G1
  TWDS BH3 ....56 A4
Naish Est *NMIL/BTOS* BH25 * 63 H5
Naish Rd *NMIL/BTOS* BH25 ....63 F3
Namu Rd *MOOR/WNTN* BH9 ....56 A1
Nansen Av *PLE* BH15 ....52 D5
Napier Rd *PLE* BH15 ....69 G2
Narrow La *RGWD* BH24 ....9 F3
Naseby Rd *MOOR/WNTN* BH9 ....56 C1
Natasha Gdns
  BKME/WDN BH12 ....54 A3
Nathen Gdns *PLE* BH15 ....69 F2
Navarino Ct *LYMN* SO41 * 49 F4
Nea Cl *CHCH/BSGR* BH23 ....61 H2
Neacroft Cl *NMIL/BTOS* BH25 ....63 F2
Nea Rd *CHCH/BSGR* BH23 ....62 A2
Needles Point *LYMN* SO41 ....80 B1
Neighbourhood Centre
  CFDH BH17 * 38 A5
Nelson Cl *NMIL/BTOS* BH25 ....44 D4
Nelson Dr *CHCH/BSGR* BH23.........60 D4
Nelson Pl *LYMN* SO41 ....49 F4
Nelson Rd *BKME/WDN* BH12 ....73 F1
Netherhall Gdns *WBNE* BH4 ....2 B3
Netherwood Pl *WIMB* BH21 ....14 A4
Netley Cl *PLE* BH15 ....53 G3
Nettleton Cl *CFDH* BH17 ....53 E3
New Borough Rd *WIMB* BH21 ....22 C1
New Br *CHAR* BH8 ....39 E4
Newbridge Wy *LYMN* SO41 ....67 G1
Newbury Dr *NBNE* BH10 ....55 H1
Newcombe Rd *FERN* BH22 ....10 A3
  SBNE BH6 ....59 E5
Newcroft Gdns
  CHCH/BSGR BH23 ....59 G2
Newenham Rd *LYMN* SO41 ....49 G2
New Forest Dr *BROC* SO42 ....86 B3
Newfoundland Dr *PLE* BH15...........70 D4
New Harbour Rd *PLE* BH15 ....70 B4
New Harbour Rd South
  PLE BH15 ....70 B5
Newlands Rd *CHCH/BSGR* BH23 ...60 D3
  LTDN BH7 ....58 A4
  NMIL/BTOS BH25 ....64 B1
Newlands Wy *BDST* BH18 ....32 B4
New La *LYMN* SO41 ....80 D2
  NMIL/BTOS BH25 ....54 C1
Newlyn Wy *BKME/WDN* BH12 ......54 C3
Newmans Cl *FERN* BH22 ....10 B1
  WIMB BH21 ....22 D1
New Merrifield *WIMB* BH21 ....15 E2
Newmorton Rd
  MOOR/WNTN BH9 ....37 G3
New Orch *PLE* BH15 ....70 B3
New Pde *NBNE* BH10 * 37 E1
New Park Rd *SBNE* BH6 ....76 C1
New Quay Rd *PLE* BH15 ....70 B5
New Rd *BKME/WDN* BH12 ....54 B4
  FERN BH22 ....9 H5
  FERN BH22 ....26 A4
  LYMN SO41 ....37 E5
  NBNE BH10 ....37 E1
  RGWD BH24 ....13 H2
Newstead Rd *SBNE* BH6 ....76 D1
New St *LYMN* SO41 ....49 E3
  PLE BH15 ....70 B5
  RGWD BH24 ....8 C5
Newton Morrell *PSTN* BH14 ....72 B2
Newton Rd *CCLF* BH13 ....72 C5
  NMIL/BTOS BH25 ....64 B2
Newtown Rd *VWD* BH31 ....5 A2
New Valley Rd *LYMN* SO41 ....80 A1
Nicholas Cl *CHCH/BSGR* BH23 .....43 H5
Nicholas Gdns *NBNE* BH10 ....36 C5
Nicholson Cl *CFDH* BH17 ....53 E2
Nightingale Cl *VWD* BH31 ....5 F3
Nightjar Cl *CFDH* BH17 ....51 G2
Nimrod Wy *WIMB* BH21 ....16 D3
Noble Cl *BWD* BH11 ....54 D1
Noel Cl *BROC* SO42 ....87 E3
Noel Rd *NBNE* BH10 ....36 C5
Noon Gdns *VWD* BH31 ....5 F2
Noon Hill Dr *VWD* BH31 ....5 F2
Noon Hill Rd *VWD* BH31 ....5 F2
Norcliffe Cl *BWD* BH11 ....36 B4
Norfolk Av *CHCH/BSGR* BH23 ....59 F1
Norleywood *CHCH/BSGR* BH23 .....62 B2
Norman Av *BKME/WDN* BH12 ....54 D4
Normandy Dr *CHCH/BSGR* BH23 ...60 B2
Normandy La *LYMN* SO41 ....49 F5
Normandy Wy *PLE* BH15 ....69 F3
Norman Gdns
  BKME/WDN BH12 ....54 D4
Normanhurst Av *CHAR* BH8 ....57 F1

Normanton Cl
CHCH/BSGR BH23 ....59 F1
Norris Cl *RGWD* BH24 ....11 H2
Norris Gdns *NMIL/BTOS* BH25 ..64 A1
Norrish Rd *BKME/WDN* BH12 ....54 A5
North Av *NBNE* BH10 ....36 D1
Northbourne Av *NBNE* BH10 .....36 D3
Northbourne Gdns *NBNE* BH10 ..37 E2
Northbourne Pl *NBNE* BH10 .....36 D2
Northbrook Rd *BDST* BH18 ......33 E3
North Cl *LYMN* SO41 ....49 F3
Northcote Rd *BMTH* BH1 ....75 E1
North Dr *RGWD* BH24 * 18 D1
Northerwood Av *LYND* SO43 ....84 D3
Northey Rd *SBNE* BH6 ....59 E4
Northfield Rd *LYMN* SO41 ......66 C5
RGWD BH24 ....8 C2
North Greenlands *LYMN* SO41 ..48 C5
North Head *LYMN* SO41 ....65 G5
Northleigh La *WIMB* BH21 ......15 E4
North Lodge Rd *PSTN* BH14 .....72 C1
Northmead Dr *CFDH* BH17 ....51 H2
Northmere Dr
BKME/WDN BH12 ....54 D3
Northmere Rd
BKME/WDN BH12 ....54 D3
Northover Rd *LYMN* SO41 ....48 A3
North Poulner Rd *RGWD* BH24 ...8 D1
North Rd *BROC* SO42 ....87 E3
LTDN BH7 ....57 G5
PLE BH15 ....70 A3
PSTN BH14 ....71 G1
North St *LYMN* SO41 ....48 C5
PLE BH15 ....70 C3
North Weirs *BROC* SO42 ....86 B3
Nortoft Rd *CHAR* BH8 ....56 D4
Norton Cl *CHCH/BSGR* BH23 .....60 B3
Norton Gdns *MOOR/WNTN* BH9 ..56 A1
Norton Rd *MOOR/WNTN* BH9 .....56 A1
Norton Wy *PLE* BH15 ....70 A4
Norwich Av *WCLF* BH2 ....2 D3
Norwich Av West *WCLF* BH2 .....2 C3
Norwich Rd *WCLF* BH2 ....2 D4
Norwood Pl *BOSC* BH5 ....58 B5
Nouale La *RGWD* BH24 ....9 F5
Noyce Gdns *CHAR* BH8 ....39 F5
Nuffield Rd *CFDH* BH17 ....52 D3
Nugent Rd *SBNE* BH6 ....77 F1
Nursery Rd *MOOR/WNTN* BH9 ....37 G4
RGWD BH24 ....8 C5
Nursling Gn *CHAR* BH8 ....38 D5
Nuthatch Cl *CFDH* BH17 ....51 H3
FERN BH22 ....17 F1
Nutley Cl *BWD* BH11 ....35 H3
Nutley Wy *BWD* BH11 ....35 H3

O

Oak Av *CHCH/BSGR* BH23 ....58 D2
Oak Cl *FERN* BH22 ....26 A3
LYND SO43 * 85 E4
WIMB BH21 ....32 A2
Oak Ct *LYMN* SO41 * 48 C5
Oakdale Rd *PLE* BH15 ....53 E4
Oakdene Cl *WIMB* BH21 ....14 D4
Oak Dr *PLE* BH15 ....70 D3
Oakfield Rd *PLE* BH15 ....52 C4
Oak Gdns *BWD* BH11 ....36 B5
LYMN SO41 ....66 B2
Oakhurst Cl *FERN* BH22 ....10 C4
Oakhurst La *FERN* BH22 ....10 C4
Oakhurst Rd *FERN* BH22 ....10 C5
Oaklands *LYMN* SO41 ....49 F5
Oaklands Cl *VWD* BH31 ....4 C2
Oakland Wk *FERN* BH22 ....26 A3
Oak La *RGWD* BH24 ....8 D3
Oakleigh Wy *CHCH/BSGR* BH23 ..62 B3
Oakley Gdns *UPTN* BH16 ....50 C3
Oakley Hl *WIMB* BH21 ....22 D1
Oakley La *WIMB* BH21 ....23 F2
Oakley Rd *WIMB* BH21 ....22 D2
Oakley Straight *WIMB* BH21 ....23 E3
Oakmead Gdns *BWD* BH11 ....35 H3
Oakmead Rd *CFDH* BH17 ....51 H3
Oak Rd *CHAR* BH8 ....57 H4
NMIL/BTOS BH25 ....45 G4
UPTN BH16 ....51 E4
Oaks Dr *CHAR* BH8 ....11 G3
Oaks Md *VWD* BH31 * 4 D3
The Oaks *VWD* BH31 ....4 C1
Oaktree Ct *LYMN* SO41 ....80 A1
Oakwood Av *NMIL/BTOS* BH25 ...45 G3
Oakwood Cl *MOOR/WNTN* BH9 ...37 H5
Oakwood Rd *CHCH/BSGR* BH23 ..62 B1
MOOR/WNTN BH9 ....37 G5
Oates Rd *MOOR/WNTN* BH9 .....56 A1
Oban Rd *TWDS* BH3 ....56 A3

Oberfield Rd *BROC* SO42 ....86 B2
Ober Rd *BROC* SO42 ....86 C2
Okeford Rd *BDST* BH18 ....33 F5
Old Barn Cl *CHCH/BSGR* BH23 ..39 H5
RGWD BH24 ....9 E4
Old Barn Rd *CHCH/BSGR* BH23 ..39 H5
Old Barn Farm Rd *WIMB* BH21 ..10 D1
Old Bound Rd *UPTN* BH16 ....51 E5
Old Bridge Rd *SBNE* BH6 ......58 C2
Old Christchurch Rd *BMTH* BH1 ..3 G4
LYMN SO41 ....49 G3
Old Coastguard Rd *CCLF* BH13 ..82 D4
Old Farm Cl *RGWD* BH24 ....9 E1
Old Farm Rd *PLE* BH15 ....53 E4
Old Farm Wk *LYMN* SO41 ....48 D4
Old Forge Rd *WIMB* BH21 ......16 D3
Old Ham La *WIMB* BH21 ....16 B5
Old Kiln Rd *UPTN* BH16 ....51 F4
Old Manor Cl *WIMB* BH21 ......15 E5
Old Milton Gn *NMIL/BTOS* BH25 ..63 H1
Old Milton Rd *NMIL/BTOS* BH25 ..63 H1
Old Mulberry Cl *NBNE* BH10 ...55 E1
Old Orch *PLE* BH15 ....70 C4
Old Orchards *LYMN* SO41 ....49 F5
Old Pines Cl *FERN* BH22 ......18 A5
Old Priory Rd *SBNE* BH6 ......77 F1
Old Rectory Ms *PLE* BH15 .....69 H3
Old Rd *WIMB* BH21 ....16 D3
The Old Rope Wk *PLE* BH15 * ..69 H4
Old St John's Ms
MOOR/WNTN BH9 ....37 H4
Old Sawmill Cl *VWD* BH31 ......4 C2
Old School Cl *FERN* BH22 .....17 H4
Old Stacks Gdns *RGWD* BH24 ....9 E5
Old Vicarage Cl *NBNE* BH10 ...37 E1
Old Wareham Rd
BKME/WDN BH12 ....53 C3
Old Watery La *UPTN* BH16 .....50 A4
Oliver Rd *LYMN* SO41 ....48 C4
Olivers Rd *WIMB* BH21 ....15 C3
Olivers Wy *WIMB* BH21 ....15 C3
Onslow Gdns *WIMB* BH21 ....14 D3
Ophir Gdns *CHAR* BH8 ....56 D5
Ophir Rd *CHAR* BH8 ....56 D5
Oratory Gdns *CCLF* BH13 ......72 D5
Orchard Av *PSTN* BH14 ....71 F3
Orchard Cl *CHCH/BSGR* BH23 ..59 G4
FERN BH22 ....18 A4
RGWD BH24 ....8 C3
Orchard Ct *VWD* BH31 ....5 E3
Orchard Gv *NMIL/BTOS* BH25 ...64 A1
Orchard Mt *RGWD* BH24 * 8 C3
Orchard St *WCLF* BH2 ....3 F4
The Orchard *BWD* BH11 ......35 F1
CHCH/BSGR BH23 ....31 G4
LYMN SO41 ....80 B1
Orcheston Rd *CHAR* BH8 ....57 H4
Orchid Wy *CHCH/BSGR* BH23 ...60 A3
Orford Cl *CHCH/BSGR* BH23 ....39 H3
Ormonde Rd *CCLF* BH13 ....73 E3
Osborne Rd *MOOR/WNTN* BH9 ..56 A2
NMIL/BTOS BH25 ....45 F4
PSTN BH14 ....71 H2
WIMB BH21 ....14 D5
Osprey Cl *CHCH/BSGR* BH23 ...61 E5
The Ostlers *LYMN* SO41 ....46 C4
Oswald Cl *MOOR/WNTN* BH9 ....37 F5
Oswald Rd *MOOR/WNTN* BH9 ....37 F5
Otter Cl *UPTN* BH16 ....50 D4
VWD BH31 ....5 E3
Otter Rd *PLE* BH15 ....53 F4
Otters Wk *NMIL/BTOS* BH25 ...45 G1
Overbury Rd *WIMB* BH21 ....14 D5
Overcombe Cl *CFDH* BH17 ......34 A5
Over Links Dr *PSTN* BH14 .....72 B3
Overstand Crs *LYMN* SO41 .....80 B2
Ovington Av *LTDN* BH7 ....58 C3
Ovington Gdns *LTDN* BH7 ......58 C3
Owls Rd *BOSC* BH5 ....75 G2
VWD BH31 ....5 E3
Oxey Cl *NMIL/BTOS* BH25 ......64 A1
Oxford Av *SBNE* BH6 ....58 B5
Oxford La *BWD* BH11 ....36 B1
Oxford Rd *CHAR* BH8 ....74 D1

P

Paddington Cl *BWD* BH11 ......35 F4
Paddington Gv *BWD* BH11 ......35 F4
Paddock Cl *BKME/WDN* BH12 ...53 H4
RGWD BH24 ....12 A2
WIMB BH21 ....17 E4
Paddock Gdns *LYMN* SO41 ......48 D2
Paddock Gv *VWD* BH31 ....5 E3
The Paddock *BROC* SO42 .....86 D3
RGWD BH24 * 18 D1
Padfield Cl *SBNE* BH6 ....59 E4

Padget Rd *RGWD* BH24 ....9 E2
Paget Cl *WIMB* BH21 ....15 G2
Paget Rd *BWD* BH21 ....36 B3
Paisley Rd *SBNE* BH6 ....58 C5
Palfrey Rd *NBNE* BH10 ....36 D3
Palmer Pl *NMIL/BTOS* BH25 ...45 E3
Palmer Rd *PLE* BH15 ....52 C5
Palmerston Av
CHCH/BSGR BH23 ....60 B4
Palmerston Cl *UPTN* BH16 .....51 E3
Palmerston Ms *BMTH* BH1 ......57 C5
Palmerston Rd *BMTH* BH1 .....57 C5
PSTN BH14 ....72 B1
UPTN BH16 ....51 E3
Pamplyn Cl *LYMN* SO41 ....48 C3
Panorama Rd *CCLF* BH13 ....82 D5
Pans Cnr *FERN* BH22 * 26 B1
The Parade *NMIL/BTOS* BH25 * ..45 H4
NMIL/BTOS BH25 ....63 H1
Paradise St *PLE* BH15 ....70 B4
Parham Rd *NBNE* BH10 ....36 C5
Parish Rd *PLE* BH15 ....71 E2
Park Av *LYMN* SO41 ....48 D3
NBNE BH10 ....36 C1
Park Cl *BROC* SO42 ....87 E2
CHCH/BSGR BH23 ....41 E4
LYMN SO41 ....66 C5
NMIL/BTOS BH25 ....45 G2
NMIL/BTOS BH25 ....63 H3
Park Dr *VWD* BH31 ....4 C1
Parker Rd *MOOR/WNTN* BH9 ...56 B3
Parkers Cl *RGWD* BH24 ....9 E2
Park Homer Dr *WIMB* BH21 ....15 C3
Park Homer Rd *WIMB* BH21 ....15 F3
Park Lake Rd *PLE* BH15 ....71 E3
Parkland Cl *VWD* BH31 ....5 H4
Parkland Dr *NMIL/BTOS* BH25 ..63 H2
Park La *LYMN* SO41 ....80 A1
NBNE BH10 ....37 F3
WIMB BH21 ....14 C5
Park Rd *CHAR* BH8 ....3 K1
LYMN SO41 ....48 D3
LYMN SO41 ....80 C1
NMIL/BTOS BH25 ....45 G2
PSTN BH14 ....71 F2
Parkside *CHCH/BSGR* BH23 ....61 H1
RGWD BH24 ....8 B5
Parkside Gdns *NBNE* BH10 ....37 E5
Parkside Rd *PSTN* BH14 ......72 A1
Parkstone Av *PSTN* BH14 .....72 B1
Parkstone Hts *PSTN* BH14 ....53 C5
Parkstone Rd *PLE* BH15 ....71 F2
The Park *NMIL/BTOS* BH25 ....63 E3
Parkway Dr *CHAR* BH8 ....57 G2
Parkwood Rd *BOSC* BH5 ....76 B1
WIMB BH21 ....14 D5
Parley Cl *FERN* BH22 ....26 B3
Parley Cross *FERN* BH22 .....26 A4
Parley La *CHCH/BSGR* BH23 ...27 F5
Parley Rd *MOOR/WNTN* BH9 ...37 C5
Parmiter Dr *WIMB* BH21 ......15 E5
Parmiter Rd *WIMB* BH21 ......15 E5
Parmiter Wy *WIMB* BH21 ......15 E5
Parr St *PSTN* BH14 ....71 G1
Parsonage Barn La *RGWD* BH24 ..8 D4
Parsonage Rd *BMTH* BH1 ....3 J4
Partridge Cl *CHCH/BSGR* BH23 ..61 E5
Partridge Dr *PSTN* BH14 .....71 H4
Partridge Gn *NMIL/BTOS* BH25 ..45 F1
Partridge Rd *BROC* SO42 .....86 D4
Partridge Wk *PSTN* BH14 .....72 A4
Pascoe Cl *PSTN* BH14 ....71 G1
Patchins Rd *UPTN* BH16 ......68 D1
Pauncefote Rd *BOSC* BH5 .....58 A5
Pauntley Rd *CHCH/BSGR* BH23 ..60 C5
Pavan Gdns *NBNE* BH10 ....36 C5
Payne Cl *WIMB* BH21 ....10 B1
Peace Cl *CHCH/BSGR* BH23 ...31 E4
Pearce Av *PSTN* BH14 ....71 H4
Pearce Rd *UPTN* BH16 ....50 D4
Pear Cl *BKME/WDN* BH12 ......73 F1
Pearl Gdns *NBNE* BH10 ....36 C3
Pearl Rd *NBNE* BH10 ....36 C3
Pearson Av *PSTN* BH14 ....53 H5
Pearson Gdns *NBNE* BH10 ....36 D1
Peartree *LYMN* SO41 * 49 E3
Pear Tree Cl *CHCH/BSGR* BH23 ..31 F4
Peartree Ct *LYMN* SO41 ......49 E5
Peckham Av *NMIL/BTOS* BH25 ..45 E5
Pegasus Av *LYMN* SO41 ....46 C5
Pelham Cl *CHCH/BSGR* BH23 ..60 B4
Pelhams Pk *BWD* BH11 * 36 C1
Pelican Md *RGWD* BH24 ....9 E5
Pemberton Rd *LYND* SO43 .....85 F3
Pembroke Rd
BKME/WDN BH12 ....54 B3

WBNE BH4 ....73 F3
Pengelly Av *NBNE* BH10 ......37 E2
Pennant Wy *CHCH/BSGR* BH23 ..60 D3
Penn Hill Av *PSTN* BH14 .....72 B2
Pennine Wy *VWD* BH31 ....4 D3
Pennington Cl *FERN* BH22 ....10 A5
LYMN SO41 ....48 C5
Pennington Crs *FERN* BH22 ...10 A5
Pennington Ov *LYMN* SO41 ....48 B5
Pennington Rd *FERN* BH22 ....10 A5
Penny Hedge *NMIL/BTOS* BH25 ..64 B2
Pennywell Gdns
NMIL/BTOS BH25 ....45 H3
Penrith Cl *VWD* BH31 ....4 D3
Penrith Rd *BOSC* BH5 ....76 A1
Penrose Rd *FERN* BH22 ....17 H3
Percy Rd *BOSC* BH5 ....75 G2
Peregrine Rd *CHCH/BSGR* BH23 ..61 E4
Pergin Crs *CFDH* BH17 ....52 B3
Pergin Wy *CFDH* BH17 ....52 B3
Perryfield Gdns *LTDN* BH7 ...58 B2
Perry Gdns *PLE* BH15 ....70 C4
Persley Rd *NBNE* BH10 ....36 D2
Perth Cl *CHCH/BSGR* BH23 ...59 E1
Peter Grant Wy *FERN* BH22 ..17 G4
Peters Cl *UPTN* BH16 ....51 E4
Petersfield Pl *LTDN* BH7 ....58 B3
Petersfield Rd *LTDN* BH7 ....58 A4
Petersham Rd *CFDH* BH17 ....51 H2
Peters Rd *FERN* BH22 ....26 B1
Petit Rd *MOOR/WNTN* BH9 ...37 G4
Petwyn Cl *FERN* BH22 ....18 C3
Peverell Rd *UPTN* BH16 ......68 D1
Peveril Cl *RGWD* BH24 ....6 D5
Phelipps Rd *WIMB* BH21 .....32 C1
Phyldon Cl *BKME/WDN* BH12 ..53 H5
Phyldon Rd *BKME/WDN* BH12 ..53 H4
Pickard Rd *FERN* BH22 ....18 B2
Pickford Rd *MOOR/WNTN* BH9 ..36 A4
Pier Ap *WCLF* BH2 ....3 H6
Pig Shoot La *CHCH/BSGR* BH23 ..38 D3
Pikes Hl *LYND* SO43 ....84 D1
Pikes Hill Av *LYND* SO43 ....84 D2
Pilford Heath Rd *WIMB* BH21 ..15 G2
Pilgrim Cl *NMIL/BTOS* BH25 ..45 G3
Pilgrim Pk *RGWD* BH24 ....9 E3
Pilgrims Pk *RGWD* BH24 * 9 E3
Pilgrims Wy *CFDH* BH17 ......52 A3
Pilot Hight Rd *BWD* BH11 ....36 A4
Pilsdon Dr *BDST* BH18 ....34 A5
Pimpern Cl *CFDH* BH17 ....34 A5
Pine Av *BKME/WDN* BH12 .....54 D3
SBNE BH6 ....76 C1
Pinecliffe Av *SBNE* BH6 .....76 C1
Pinecliffe Rd *NMIL/BTOS* BH25 ..63 E3
Pinecliff Rd *CCLF* BH13 .....73 E5
Pine Cl *FERN* BH22 ....17 G2
NMIL/BTOS BH25 ....63 G2
Pine Crs *CHCH/BSGR* BH23 ...62 A3
Pine Dr *CCLF* BH13 ....72 D2
RGWD BH24 ....12 A2
Pine End *FERN* BH22 ....26 B1
Pine Glen Av *FERN* BH22 .....17 F1
Pineholt Cl *RGWD* BH24 ......12 B2
Pinehurst Av *CHCH/BSGR* BH23 ..60 D5
Pinehurst Pk *FERN* BH22 ....18 B1
Pinehurst Pl *FERN* BH22 ....18 B1
Pinehurst Rd *FERN* BH22 .....10 C5
Pine Manor Rd *RGWD* BH24 ...11 C1
Pine Rd *MOOR/WNTN* BH9 ....56 B1
Pinesprings Dr *BDST* BH18 ...32 C5
Pinetops Cl *LYMN* SO41 ......48 B3
Pine Tree Cl *WIMB* BH21 .....14 D4
Pine Tree Gln *WBNE* BH4 .....2 B3
Pinetree Wk *CFDH* BH17 ......51 H2
Pine Vale Crs *NBNE* BH10 ....37 F4
Pine View Cl *UPTN* BH16 .....51 E4
Pine View Rd *VWD* BH31 ......4 B1
Pine Wk *FERN* BH22 ....10 B3
VWD BH31 ....5 F3
Pinewood Av *NBNE* BH10 .....55 D2
Pinewood Cl *CHCH/BSGR* BH23 ..43 G5
CHCH/BSGR BH23 ....62 C1
NBNE BH10 ....50 D2
UPTN BH16 ....50 D3
Pinewood Gdns *FERN* BH22 ...17 H2
Pinewood Rd *CCLF* BH13 ......73 F4
CHCH/BSGR BH23 ....62 B1
FERN BH22 ....17 G2
LYMN SO41 ....46 B4
RGWD BH24 ....12 A2
UPTN BH16 ....50 D3
Pipers Ash *RGWD* BH24 ....9 E3
Pipers Dr *CHCH/BSGR* BH23 ..61 E3
Pippin Cl *CHCH/BSGR* BH23 ..40 A5
LYMN SO41 ....48 C5
Pithouse La *CHCH/BSGR* BH23 ..28 D4
Pittmore Rd *CHCH/BSGR* BH23 ..41 E5
Pitts Pl *NMIL/BTOS* BH25 ....45 H5

Pitwines Cl PLE BH15 ......70 D3
Plantaganet Crs BWD BH11 ......35 F2
Plantation LYMN SO41 ......66 C2
Plantation Dr CHCH/BSGR BH23...43 G5
Plantation Rd CFDH BH17 ......52 C1
CHCH/BSGR BH23 ......20 B5
Plant Park Rd RGWD BH24 ......12 D4
Plassey Crs NBNE BH10 ......36 C2
Playfields Dr BKME/WDN BH12 ....54 C4
Pleasance Wy NMIL/BTOS BH25...44 D4
Plecy Cl FERN BH22 ......25 H2
Plemont Cl BKME/WDN BH12 ......54 C1
Pless Rd LYMN SO41 ......65 G5
Plover Dr LYMN SO41 ......80 D1
Plumer Rd CFDH BH17 ......52 A1
Policemans La UPTN BH16 ......50 B3
Pomona Cl FERN BH22 ......17 H3
Pompeys La FERN BH22 ......25 F2
WIMB BH21 ......17 E5
Pond Cl NMIL/BTOS BH25 ......45 E4
Ponsonby Rd PSTN BH14 ......72 B1
Pony Dr UPTN BH16 ......51 F3
Poole Br PLE BH15 ......70 B4
Poole Hl WCLF BH2 ......2 E4
Poole La BWD BH11 ......35 H3
Poole Rd CCLF BH13 ......72 D1
UPTN BH16 ......51 E3
WBNE BH4 ......73 F1
WCLF BH2 ......2 D4
WIMB BH21 ......14 C5
Popes Rd PLE BH15 ......52 D4
Poplar Cl CHCH/BSGR BH23 ......31 G4
CHCH/BSGR BH23 ......62 D2
WIMB BH21 ......14 D4
Poplar Crs RGWD BH24 ......8 D4
Poplar La CHCH/BSGR BH23 ......31 G3
Poplar Rd NMIL/BTOS BH25 ......45 H3
Poplar Wy RGWD BH24 ......8 D4
Poppy Cl CHCH/BSGR BH23 ......61 F2
UPTN BH16 ......50 B3
Portarlington Cl WBNE BH4 ......2 C1
Portarlington Rd WBNE BH4 ......2 A1
Portchester Pl CHAR BH8 ......56 D5
Portchester Rd CHAR BH8 ......56 C4
Portelet Cl BKME/WDN BH12 ......54 B1
Porter Rd CFDH BH17 ......52 B3
Porters La WIMB BH21 ......16 A3
Portesham Gdns
MOOR/WNTN BH9 ......37 H3
Portesham Wy CFDH BH17 ......34 A4
Portfield Cl CHCH/BSGR BH23 ......59 G2
Portfield Rd CHCH/BSGR BH23 ....59 G3
Portland Rd MOOR/WNTN BH9...56 C2
Portman Crs BOSC BH5 ......76 B1
Portman Rd LTDN BH7 ......57 H5
Portman Ter BOSC BH5 * 76 B1
Portmore Cl BDST BH18 ......33 F1
Portswood Dr
MOOR/WNTN BH9 ......37 G5
Post Green Rd UPTN BH16 ......50 A2
Post Office La RGWD BH24 ......12 B1
Post Office Rd BMTH BH1 ......3 G4
Potterne Wy WIMB BH21 ......5 E5
Potterne Wood Cl VWD BH31 ......5 C4
Potters Wy PSTN BH14 ......72 A3
Pottery Rd PSTN BH14 ......71 G3
Poulner Hl RGWD BH24 ......9 F3
Poulner Pk RGWD BH24 ......9 E2
Pound Cl PLE BH15 ......53 F5
RGWD BH24 ......8 C3
Pound La PLE BH15 ......53 E5
Pound Rd LYMN SO41 ......48 B4
Powell Rd PSTN BH14 ......71 H2
Powerscourt Rd
NMIL/BTOS BH25 ......63 G3
Powis Cl NMIL/BTOS BH25 ......45 F4
Preston Cl UPTN BH16 ......51 E3
Preston La CHCH/BSGR BH23 ......41 H1
Preston Rd PLE BH15 ......52 C4
Preston Wy CHCH/BSGR BH23 ....61 H2
Prestwood Cl NMIL/BTOS BH25...63 H1
Priestlands La LYMN SO41 ......48 C4
Priestlands Rd LYMN SO41 ......48 C4
Priest La CHCH/BSGR BH23 ......29 H5
Priestley Rd NBNE BH10 ......55 F1
Primrose Gdns CFDH BH17 ......51 H1
Primrose Wy CHCH/BSGR BH23...61 G2
Prince of Wales Rd WBNE BH4 ......2 A2
Prince's Pl NMIL/BTOS BH25 ......45 G4
Princes Rd FERN BH22 ......17 H4
Princess Av CHCH/BSGR BH23 ....59 H4
Princess Crs LYND SO43 ......85 G2
Princess Rd BKME/WDN BH12 ....73 H1
Pringles Cl FERN BH22 ......18 A4
Pringles Dr FERN BH22 ......18 A4
Priors Cl CHCH/BSGR BH23 ......61 G3
Priors Rd CFDH BH17 ......52 A1
Priors Wk WIMB BH21 ......14 B4
Priory Quay CHCH/BSGR BH23 *...60 A5

Priory Rd FERN BH22 ......18 C1
WCLF BH2 ......3 F5
Priory View Pl
MOOR/WNTN BH9 ......37 G4
Priory View Rd
CHCH/BSGR BH23 ......41 E5
MOOR/WNTN BH9 ......37 G4
Private Rd LYMN SO41 ......49 E3
Privet Rd MOOR/WNTN BH9......56 A2
Promenade CCLF BH13 ......83 H1
Prosperous St PLE BH15 ......70 C4
Prunus Cl FERN BH22 ......17 F2
Prunus Dr FERN BH22 ......17 F2
Puddletown Crs CFDH BH17 ......34 B5
Pullman Ct FERN BH22 ......10 A4
Pullman Wy RGWD BH24 ......8 C5
Purbeck Av PLE BH15 ......69 G4
Purbeck Cl UPTN BH16 * 50 D3
Purbeck Dr VWD BH31 ......4 D3
Purbeck Rd NMIL/BTOS BH25 ....63 F3
WCLF BH2 ......2 E4
Purchase Rd BKME/WDN BH12 ...55 G3
Purewell CHCH/BSGR BH23 ......60 B4
Purewell Cl CHCH/BSGR BH23 ....60 C4
Purewell Cross Rd
CHCH/BSGR BH23 ......60 B3
Pussex La CHCH/BSGR BH23 ......28 A5
Pye La WIMB BH21 ......14 B5
Pyrford Ms LYMN SO41 ......49 E5

Q

Quarry Rd WIMB BH21 ......15 C2
Quayle Dr BWD BH11 ......35 H1
Quay Rd CHCH/BSGR BH23 ......59 H5
Quay St LYMN SO41 ......49 F3
The Quay PLE BH15 ......70 C4
Queen Anne Dr WIMB BH21 ......23 F3
Queen Elizabeth Av
LYMN SO41 ......48 D3
Queen Katherine Rd
LYMN SO41 ......49 F4
Queen Mary Av
MOOR/WNTN BH9 ......37 F5
Queen's Av CHCH/BSGR BH23 ....59 H5
Queens Cl FERN BH22 ......10 A5
Queens Gdns WCLF BH2 ......2 C3
Queens Gv NMIL/BTOS BH25 ....45 G3
Queensland Rd LTDN BH7 ......58 A5
Queensmead CHCH/BSGR BH23...59 G1
Queen's Pde LYND SO43 ......85 E3
Queen's Park Av CHAR BH8 ......57 E2
Queen's Park Gdns CHAR BH8 ....57 E3
Queen's Park South Dr
CHAR BH8 ......57 F3
Queen's Park West Dr
CHAR BH8 ......57 F3
Queen's Rd CHCH/BSGR BH23 ....60 C4
FERN BH22 ......17 H2
LYND SO43 ......85 G3
PSTN BH14 ......72 B1
WCLF BH2 ......2 C3
WIMB BH21 ......32 B2
Queensway NMIL/BTOS BH25 ....44 C4
RGWD BH24 ......8 D4
Queenswood Av CHAR BH8 ......57 G1
Queenswood Dr FERN BH22 ......17 H2
Quince La WIMB BH21 ......14 D3
Quintin Cl CHCH/BSGR BH23 ......62 B2
The Quomp RGWD BH24......8 C4

R

CCLF BH13 ......72 D5
Raymond Cl VWD BH31 ......5 F2
Rebbeck Rd LTDN BH7 ......58 A5
Recreation Rd
BKME/WDN BH12 ......54 C4
Rectory Rd PLE BH15 ......52 C4
Redan Cl CHCH/BSGR BH23 ......62 B3
Redbreast Rd
MOOR/WNTN BH9 ......37 G4
Redbreast Rd North
MOOR/WNTN BH9 ......37 G4
Redcliffe Cl CHCH/BSGR BH23 ....41 E5
Redcotts La WIMB BH21 ......14 B4
Redcotts Rd WIMB BH21 ......14 B4
Redhill Av MOOR/WNTN BH9 ....37 E5
Redhill Cl NBNE BH10 * 37 G3
Redhill Crs MOOR/WNTN BH9 ....37 F4
Redhill Dr NBNE BH10 ......37 G5
Redhoave Rd CFDH BH17 ......53 E1
Redhorn Cl UPTN BH16 ......69 E1
Redlands WBNE BH4 ......54 D5
Redmans Vw VWD BH31 4
Red Oaks Cl FERN BH22 ......17 F2
Redshank Cl CFDH BH17 ......51 H1
Redvers Rd CHCH/BSGR BH23 ....60 C3
Redwood Cl LYMN SO41 ......48 C2
RGWD BH24 ......8 D4
Redwood Dr FERN BH22 ......17 G1
Redwood Rd UPTN BH16 ......50 C2
Regency Crs CHCH/BSGR BH23 ...59 F2
Regent Dr LTDN BH7 ......57 H2
Regent Wy CHCH/BSGR BH23 ....59 H4
Reid St CHCH/BSGR BH23 ......59 G3
Rempstone Rd WIMB BH21 ......22 D3
Renault Dr BDST BH18 ......52 A1
Renouf Cl LYMN SO41 ......48 C4
Retreat Rd WIMB BH21 ......14 D5
Reuben Dr PLE BH15 ......69 F3
Rhinefield Cl BROC SO42 ......86 C2
Rhinefield Rd BROC SO42 ......86 B2
Ribble Cl BDST BH18 ......33 E5
Ricardo Crs CHCH/BSGR BH23 ....61 E4
Rice Gdns UPTN BH16 ......69 F1
Richard Cl UPTN BH16 ......50 D2
Richmond Gdns BMTH BH1 ......3 H3
Richmond Hl BMTH BH1 ......3 G3
Richmond Hill Dr WCLF BH2 ......3 G3
Richmond Hill Rd WCLF BH2 * 3 G3
Richmond Park Av CHAR BH8 ....56 D3
Richmond Park Cl CHAR BH8 * 57 E3
Richmond Park Crs CHAR BH8 ....57 E3
Richmond Park Rd CHAR BH8 ....56 D4
Richmond Rd PSTN BH14 ......72 A1
WIMB BH21 ......14 D5
Richmond Wood Rd
CHAR BH8 ......56 D3
Ridgefield Gdns
CHCH/BSGR BH23 ......61 H2
Ridgemount Gdns PLE BH15 ......69 G2
Ridgeway BDST BH18 ......33 F3
FERN BH22 ......26 A4
Ridgeway La LYMN SO41 ......48 D5
Ridley Rd MOOR/WNTN BH9 ....56 B2
Ridout Cl NBNE BH10 ......55 F1
Riggs Gdns BWD BH11 ......35 H5
Rigler Rd PLE BH15 ......70 B4
Rimbury Wy CHCH/BSGR BH23...59 G2
Ringbury LYMN SO41 ......48 D1
Ringwood Rd
BKME/WDN BH12 ......54 A1
BWD BH11 ......35 G4
CHCH/BSGR BH23 ......29 G4
CHCH/BSGR BH23 ......31 F4
FERN BH22 ......25 F1
PSTN BH14 ......53 F4
RGWD BH24 ......11 G4
VWD BH31 ......4 D1
WIMB BH21 ......6 A5
Ripon Rd MOOR/WNTN BH9 ....56 C2
The Rise BROC SO42 ......86 D3
Ritchie Pl FERN BH22 ......10 A2
Ritchie Rd BWD BH11 ......36 B3
River Cl WIMB BH21 ......14 C3
Riverdale La CHCH/BSGR BH23...59 G4
River Gdns LYMN SO41 ......80 C1
Riverlea Rd CHCH/BSGR BH23 ...59 G4
Rivermead Gdns
CHCH/BSGR BH23 ......40 A3
Riversdale Rd SBNE BH6 ......77 G1
Riverside NBNE BH10 * 37 H3
RGWD BH24 ......8 B5
Riverside Av LTDN BH7 ......39 F5
Riverside La SBNE BH6 ......59 F5
Riverside Rd FERN BH22 ......10 A4
SBNE BH6 ......59 F5
Rivers Reach LYMN SO41 * 49 F4
River Wy CHCH/BSGR BH23 ......39 H5
R L Stevenson Av WBNE BH4 ....73 F2

Roberts Cl LYMN SO41 ......66 C1
Roberts La CFDH BH17 ......52 A3
Roberts Rd CFDH BH17 ......52 A1
LTDN BH7 ......58 A4
Robin Crs NMIL/BTOS BH25 ......44 B2
Robin Gdns CHCH/BSGR BH23 ...59 G3
Robin Gv NMIL/BTOS BH25 ......44 B2
Robins Wy CHCH/BSGR BH23 ....61 F5
Robinswood Dr FERN BH22 ......17 H2
Rochester Rd BWD BH11 ......36 B3
Rockbourne Gdns
NMIL/BTOS BH25 ......63 F2
Rockford Cl SBNE BH6 ......77 H2
Rockley Rd PLE BH15 ......69 G3
Rodbourne Cl LYMN SO41 ......66 B2
Rodney Dr CHCH/BSGR BH23 ....60 D4
Rodway WIMB BH21 ......14 C5
Rodwell Cl NBNE BH10 ......36 C1
Roebuck Cl NMIL/BTOS BH25 ....45 F4
Roeshot Crs CHCH/BSGR BH23 ...62 A1
Rolls Dr SBNE BH6 ......77 H1
Roman Rd BDST BH18 ......32 C3
Romney Cl NBNE BH10 * 37 E4
Romney Rd NBNE BH10 ......37 E5
Romsey Rd LYND SO43 ......85 E2
Rookcliff Wy LYMN SO41 ......80 A1
Rookes La LYMN SO41 ......48 D5
Rook Hill Rd CHCH/BSGR BH23 ...61 F4
Roosevelt Crs BWD BH11 ......36 B1
Ropers La UPTN BH16 ......51 F3
Ropley Rd LTDN BH7 ......58 C3
Rosamund Av WIMB BH21 ......23 E5
Roscrea Cl SBNE BH6 ......77 H1
Roscrea Dr SBNE BH6 ......77 H1
Rosebery Cl VWD BH31 ......5 G3
Rosebery Rd BOSC BH5 ......58 A5
Rosebud Av MOOR/WNTN BH9 ...37 G5
Rosecrae Cl NMIL/BTOS BH25 ...44 D3
Rose Crs PLE BH15 ......53 F4
Rosedale Cl CHCH/BSGR BH23 ...60 C4
Rose Gdns MOOR/WNTN BH9 ....37 G5
Rosehill Cl CHCH/BSGR BH23 * ...31 F3
Rosehill Dr CHCH/BSGR BH23 ....31 F3
Rosemary Gdns
BKME/WDN BH12 ......53 H3
Rosemary Rd BKME/WDN BH12...54 A3
Rosemount Rd WBNE BH4 ......73 F3
Rosewood Gdns
NMIL/BTOS BH25 ......44 D4
Roslin Rd TWDS BH3 ......56 A3
Roslin Rd South TWDS BH3 ......55 H3
Ross Gdns BWD BH11 ......35 E2
Ross Glades TWDS BH3 ......56 A4
Rossiters Quay
CHCH/BSGR BH23 ......60 A4
Rossley Cl CHCH/BSGR BH23 ....43 E5
Rossmore Rd BKME/WDN BH12 ..54 A2
Ross Rd RGWD BH24 ......9 E2
Rotary Cl WIMB BH21 ......15 F2
Rothbury Pk NMIL/BTOS BH25 ...45 F5
Rotherfield Rd BOSC BH5 ......76 B2
CHCH/BSGR BH23 ......62 C1
Rothesay Dr
CHCH/BSGR BH23 ......62 A3
Rothesay Rd TWDS BH3 ......55 C4
Rotterdam Dr
CHCH/BSGR BH23 ......60 B3
Roumelia La BOSC BH5 ......75 F4
Roundhaye Rd BWD BH11 ......35 H2
Roundways BWD BH11 * 35 H4
Rowan Cl CHCH/BSGR BH23 ......61 H2
RGWD BH24 ......11 G2
Rowan Dr CFDH BH17 ......51 G1
CHCH/BSGR BH23 ......61 H2
VWD BH31 ......5 F4
Rowans Pk LYMN SO41 ......48 D4
Rowbarrow Cl CFDH BH17 ......34 A5
Rowe Gdns BKME/WDN BH12 ....54 B3
Rowena Rd SBNE BH6 ......59 F5
Rowland Av PLE BH15 ......53 E5
Rowlands Hl WIMB BH21 ......14 D4
Rowlett Rd LYMN SO41 ......49 E4
Rownhams Rd CHAR BH8 ......38 A4
Royal Oak Rd NBNE BH10 ......36 C2
Royster Cl CFDH BH17 ......52 C1
Royston Dr WIMB BH21 ......14 D4
Royston Pl NMIL/BTOS BH25 ....64 B2
Rozelle Rd PSTN BH14 ......72 A1
Rubens Cl NMIL/BTOS BH25 ......45 E4
Rufford Gdns SBNE BH6 ......59 E5
Rugby Rd CFDH BH17 ......52 A1
Runnymede Av BWD BH11 ......35 F1
Runton Rd BKME/WDN BH12 ....54 A5
The Runway CHCH/BSGR BH23...61 F3
Rushcombe Wy WIMB BH21 ......32 C1
Rushford Warren
CHCH/BSGR BH23 ......78 D1
Rushmere Rd SBNE BH6 ......58 D3

Rushton Crs *TWDS* BH3................56 B4
Ruskin Av *MOOR/WNTN* BH9.........37 H4
Russell Cotes Rd *BMTH* BH1.........3 J5
Russell Dr *CHCH/BSGR* BH23.......60 B4
Russell Gdns *RGWD* BH24..........12 C1
   UPTN BH16.............................69 C1
Russel Rd *NBNE* BH10...............36 C1
Russet Cl *FERN* BH22................17 H3
   LYMN SO41...........................49 F5
Rutland Rd *CHCH/BSGR* BH23.....59 F1
   MOOR/WNTN BH9.................56 D2
Ryall Rd *CFDH* BH17.................52 D1
Ryan Cl *FERN* BH22..................17 G2
Ryan Gdns *FERN* BH22..............17 G2
Rydal Cl *CHCH/BSGR* BH23........39 H3
Ryecroft Av *BWD* BH11..............35 G2

S

Saddle Cl *WIMB* BH21...............16 A3
Saffron Dr *CHCH/BSGR* BH23......61 F2
Saffron Wy *BWD* BH11..............35 F4
St Alban's Av *CHAR* BH8............56 D3
St Alban's Crs *CHAR* BH8...........56 D3
St Alban's Rd *CHAR* BH8............56 D3
St Aldhelm's Cl *CCLF* BH13........72 D1
St Aldhelm's Rd *CCLF* BH13........72 D1
St Andrews Rd *BDST* BH18.........33 E2
St Anne's Av *SBNE* BH6.............59 E5
St Annes Gdns *LYMN* SO41........48 D4
St Anne's Rd *UPTN* BH16...........50 D3
St Anthony's Rd *WCLF* BH2.........56 B5
St Aubyns Ct *PLE* BH15 *...........70 B3
St Aubyns La *RGWD* BH24...........9 C3
St Augustin's Rd *WCLF* BH2........56 B5
St Brelades Av
   BKME/WDN BH12..................54 B1
St Catherines *WIMB* BH21..........14 C5
St Catherine's Rd *SBNE* BH6.......77 E2
St Catherines's Wy
   CHCH/BSGR BH23.................39 H4
St Clair Rd *CCLF* BH13..............83 H1
St Cleeve Wy *FERN* BH22...........25 C1
St Clements Gdns *BMTH* BH1......57 F5
St Clement's Rd *BMTH* BH1.........57 F5
   PLE BH15............................53 H3
St David's Rd *PLE* BH15............53 H3
St Georges *PLE* BH15 *.............70 B4
St George's Av
   BKME/WDN BH12..................53 H2
   CHAR BH8............................57 E2
St George's Cl *CHAR* BH8...........57 E2
   CHCH/BSGR BH23.................61 H2
St Georges Dr *BWD* BH11..........35 F4
   CHCH/BSGR BH23.................31 G4
   FERN BH22..........................17 G5
St Helier Rd *BKME/WDN* BH12.....54 B1
St Ives End La *RGWD* BH24........12 B1
St Ives Gdns *WCLF* BH2.............56 B5
St Ives Pk *RGWD* BH24.............12 B1
St Ives Wd *RGWD* BH24.............12 C1
St James Cl *PLE* BH15..............70 B4
St James Rd *FERN* BH22............17 E3
St James's Sq *BOSC* BH5...........75 H5
St John's Cl *WIMB* BH21............14 D5
St John's Gdns
   MOOR/WNTN BH9.................56 B1
St John's Hl *WIMB* BH21............14 D4
St John's Rd *BOSC* BH5............75 G2
   CHCH/BSGR BH23.................59 G4
   PLE BH15............................70 D1
St Just Cl *FERN* BH22...............25 G1
St Ledger's Pl *CHAR* BH8 *........57 F4
St Ledger's Rd *CHAR* BH8..........57 F4
St Leonard's Rd *CHAR* BH8.........56 D4
St Leonards Wy *RGWD* BH24.......11 G2
St Luke's Rd *TWDS* BH3.............56 B3
St Maradox La
   MOOR/WNTN BH9.................37 F5
St Margaret's Av
   CHCH/BSGR BH23.................59 G4
St Margarets Cl *WIMB* BH21........14 A4
St Margaret's Hl *WIMB* BH21.......14 A3
St Margaret's Rd *NBNE* BH10......36 B5
   PLE BH15............................70 C1
St Mark's Rd *BWD* BH11............36 B4
   LYMN SO41..........................48 B4
St Martins Rd *UPTN* BH16..........50 C3
St Mary Gv *LYMN* SO41.............46 C5
St Mary's Cl *CHCH/BSGR* BH23....31 F4
St Mary's Rd *BMTH* BH1.............57 F4
   FERN BH22..........................17 G4
   PLE BH15............................70 D2
St Merrin's Cl *NBNE* BH10..........36 C3
St Michaels Cl *PLE* BH15...........69 G2
   VWD BH31.............................4 D3
St Michael's Pl *WCLF* BH2..........2 E4

St Michaels Rd *VWD* BH31...........4 D4
   WCLF BH2.............................2 E4
St Osmund's Rd *PSTN* BH14.......72 A2
St Paul's La *CHAR* BH8.............74 D1
St Paul's Pl *CHAR* BH8................3 K2
St Pauls Rd *CHAR* BH8..............74 D1
St Pauls Rbt *BMTH* BH1..............3 K1
St Peter's Rd *BMTH* BH1.............3 J4
St Peters Rbt *BMTH* BH1.............71 G1
St Stephens La *VWD* BH31...........5 E2
St Stephen's Rd *WCLF* BH2..........2 E4
St Stephen's Wy *WCLF* BH2..........3 C3
St Swithun's Rd South
   BMTH BH1...........................74 D1
St Thomas Pk *LYMN* SO41.........48 D3
St Thomas's Cl *NBNE* BH10.........36 D5
St Thomas's St *LYMN* SO41........48 D4
St Valerie Rd *WCLF* BH2.............56 B5
St Winifred's Rd *WCLF* BH2.........56 B5
Salerno Pl *PLE* BH15................69 F3
Salisbury Rd *BMTH* BH1.............75 G1
   CHCH/BSGR BH23.................40 D1
   PSTN BH14..........................54 A5
   RGWD BH24...........................8 B3
Salterns Rd *PSTN* BH14............71 G2
Salterns Wy *PSTN* BH14............71 H5
Salter Rd *CCLF* BH13................82 D5
Saltgrass La *LYMN* SO41...........81 E2
Saltings Rd *UPTN* BH16............50 D4
Samber Cl *LYMN* SO41..............48 C3
Samphire Cl *LYMN* SO41............48 D2
Samples Wy *CFDH* BH17............53 F2
Samson Rd *PLE* BH15...............70 D1
Sancreed Rd *BKME/WDN* BH12....54 C3
Sandbanks Rd *PLE* BH15............71 F2
Sandbourne Rd *PLE* BH15...........70 D1
   WBNE BH4...........................73 C4
Sandecotes Rd *PSTN* BH14........72 A2
Sanderlings *RGWD* BH24.............9 E5
Sandford Cl *MOOR/WNTN* BH9.....38 A4
Sandford Wy *BDST* BH18............32 D4
Sandhills Cl *CFDH* BH17............33 H5
Sandmartin Cl *NMIL/BTOS* BH25...63 H3
Sandpiper Cl *CFDH* BH17...........51 H1
Sandringham Cl
   MOOR/WNTN BH9.................37 H3
Sandringham Gdns
   MOOR/WNTN BH9.................37 H3
Sandringham Rd *PSTN* BH14.......71 H2
Sandy Cl *UPTN* BH16................51 E5
   WIMB BH21..........................15 C1
Sandyhurst Cl *CFDH* BH17.........52 C1
Sandy La *CHCH/BSGR* BH23.......40 A5
   LYND SO43..........................85 E4
   RGWD BH24.........................12 A2
   SBNE BH6............................58 B5
   UPTN BH16..........................50 C4
   VWD BH31.............................5 E2
   WIMB BH21..........................15 G1
Sandy Mead Rd *CHAR* BH8........57 H1
Sandy Plot *CHCH/BSGR* BH23.....60 A1
Sandy Wy *NBNE* BH10...............37 E4
Saracen Cl *LYMN* SO41.............67 C1
Sarah Cl *LTDN* BH7..................58 B2
Sarah Sands Cl
   CHCH/BSGR BH23.................60 B2
Sark Rd *BKME/WDN* BH12..........54 B2
Sarum Av *FERN* BH22...............10 B2
Sarum St *PLE* BH15.................70 B4
Sarum Wk *LYMN* SO41...............48 D1
Saulfland Dr *CHCH/BSGR* BH23....61 H1
Saulfland Pl *CHCH/BSGR* BH23....61 H2
Saxonbury Rd *SBNE* BH6............59 E4
The Saxon Centre
   CHCH/BSGR BH23.................59 H4
Saxonford Rd
   CHCH/BSGR BH23.................61 G3
Saxonhurst Cl *NBNE* BH10.........37 E2
Saxonhurst Gdns *NBNE* BH10......37 E3
Saxonhurst Rd *NBNE* BH10.........36 D3
Saxon King Gdns *SBNE* BH6.......77 H1
Saxon Pl *LYMN* SO41................48 D2
Scarf Rd *CFDH* BH17................53 F3
School Cl *LYMN* SO41...............48 C5
   VWD BH31.............................5 E1
School La *BWD* BH11................36 B2
   LYMN SO41..........................49 E3
   LYMN SO41..........................66 C4
   PLE BH15............................52 C5
   RGWD BH24...........................8 C4
   RGWD BH24.........................12 B1
   WIMB BH21..........................14 B4
Scott Cl *BKME/WDN* BH12..........54 D1
Scotter Rd *LTDN* BH7................58 B5
Scott Rd *BKME/WDN* BH12.........54 D2
Scott's Gn *CHCH/BSGR* BH23......60 D2
Scotts Hills La
   CHCH/BSGR BH23.................60 B4

Seabank Cl *UPTN* BH16.............50 C3
Seaborne Pl *BOSC* BH5.............58 B5
Seabourne Rd *BOSC* BH5...........58 B5
Seabreeze Wy *LYMN* SO41.........65 C4
Seacombe Rd *CCLF* BH13..........82 D5
Seacroft Av *NMIL/BTOS* BH25......63 C2
Seafield Cl *NMIL/BTOS* BH25.......63 H3
Seafield Dr *SBNE* BH6...............59 E4
Seafield Rd *CHCH/BSGR* BH23.....61 G4
   NMIL/BTOS BH25...................63 G2
   SBNE BH6............................76 D1
Seager Wy *PLE* BH15...............70 D3
Seagrim Rd *CHAR* BH8..............38 A4
Seagull Rd *CHAR* BH8...............57 E1
Seamoor La *WBNE* BH4.............73 F2
Seamoor Rd *CCLF* BH13............73 F2
Sea Rd *BOSC* BH5...................75 C1
   LYMN SO41..........................80 C1
   NMIL/BTOS BH25...................63 C2
   SBNE BH6............................77 F2
Seaton Cl *CHCH/BSGR* BH23......62 D2
   LYMN SO41..........................49 E2
Seaton Rd *CHCH/BSGR* BH23......62 D2
Seatown Cl *CFDH* BH17.............53 C1
Sea View Rd *BKME/WDN* BH12....53 C5
Seaview Rd *NMIL/BTOS* BH25......63 F3
Sea View Rd *UPTN* BH16...........50 C3
Seaward Av *NMIL/BTOS* BH25......63 C3
   SBNE BH6............................76 D1
Seaway *NMIL/BTOS* BH25...........64 B2
Seaway Av *CHCH/BSGR* BH23.....61 C4
Seawinds *LYMN* SO41...............65 C5
Second Marine Av
   NMIL/BTOS BH25...................64 A4
Seddon Cl *NMIL/BTOS* BH25.......63 H2
Sedgley Rd *MOOR/WNTN* BH9.....56 A2
Selby Cl *BDST* BH18.................33 E4
Seldown Rd *PLE* BH15...............70 D2
Seldown Br *PLE* BH15...............70 D2
Seldown La *PLE* BH15...............70 D2
Seldown Rd *PLE* BH15...............70 D2
Selfridge Av *SBNE* BH6.............77 H2
Selfridge Cl *SBNE* BH6..............77 H2
Seliot Cl *PLE* BH15..................52 D5
Selkirk Cl *WIMB* BH21...............23 E3
Sellwood Wy *NMIL/BTOS* BH25....63 F2
Selwood Pk *NBNE* BH10 *..........25 C5
Selworthy Cl *PSTN* BH14...........71 C3
Serpentine Rd *PLE* BH15...........70 C2
Setley Gdns *CHAR* BH8..............38 C4
Sevenoaks Dr *LTDN* BH7...........58 A2
Severn Rd *FERN* BH22..............18 C4
Seymour Gdns *RGWD* BH24.........8 D2
Seymour Rd *RGWD* BH24............8 D2
Shackleton Sq
   CHCH/BSGR BH23.................31 F3
Shaftesbury Cl *FERN* BH22.........10 C4
Shaftesbury Rd *CHAR* BH8.........57 E4
   FERN BH22..........................10 C5
   PLE BH15............................70 D2
Shaggs Meadow *LYND* SO43......85 F4
Shakespeare Rd *SBNE* BH6........58 D3
   WIMB BH21..........................14 C3
Shapland Av *BWD* BH11............35 G2
Shard Cl *VWD* BH31...................5 E2
Sharf Rd *BKME/WDN* BH12.........55 E3
Sharlands Cl *BDST* BH18............33 F4
Sharvells Rd *LYMN* SO41...........66 A5
Shaves La *NMIL/BTOS* BH25.......45 E2
Shawford Gdns *CHAR* BH8.........38 B5
Shawford Rd *CHAR* BH8.............38 B4
Shaw Rd *RGWD* BH24.................9 E1
Shears Brook Cl
   CHCH/BSGR BH23.................31 F3
Shelbourne Cl *CHAR* BH8..........57 F4
Shelbourne Rd *CHAR* BH8..........57 F4
Sheldrake Gdns *LYMN* SO41.......46 D3
Sheldrake Rd
   CHCH/BSGR BH23.................61 E5
Shelley Cl *BMTH* BH1................57 G5
   CHCH/BSGR BH23.................61 G3
   RGWD BH24.........................11 H1
Shelley Gdns *BMTH* BH1............57 G5
Shelley Rd *BKME/WDN* BH12......54 B5
   BMTH BH1...........................57 G5
Shelley Rd East *BMTH* BH1........57 H5
Shelton Rd *BMTH* BH1...............58 C4
Shenstone Ct *NMIL/BTOS* BH25...64 A1
Shepherd Cl *CHCH/BSGR* BH23...62 B1
Shepherds Wy *LTDN* BH7...........58 A3
   LYMN SO41..........................66 B1
Sheppards Fld *WIMB* BH21.........14 B3
Sherborn Crs *CFDH* BH17...........53 F1
Sherborne Dr *FERN* BH22...........17 H5
Sherfield Cl *CHAR* BH8..............38 B5
Sheringham Rd
   BKME/WDN BH12..................54 D5
Shermin's Bank
   CHCH/BSGR BH23.................60 C5

Sherrin Cl *PLE* BH15................52 D5
Sherwood Av *FERN* BH22...........25 C1
   PSTN BH14..........................71 F3
Sherwood Cl *CHCH/BSGR* BH23...59 F3
Sherwood Dr *VWD* BH31..............5 F2
Shetland Vw *VWD* BH31..............5 E2
Shillingstone Dr
   MOOR/WNTN BH9.................37 H4
Shillingstone Gdns
   BKME/WDN BH12..................54 D3
Shillito Rd *BKME/WDN* BH12.......54 B5
Shingle Bank Dr *LYMN* SO41......80 B1
Shipstal Cl *UPTN* BH16.............69 E1
Shires Cl *RGWD* BH24...............13 H2
Shires Copse *SBNE* BH6............77 F2
Shires Md *VWD* BH31..................5 E2
Shirley Cl *CHCH/BSGR* BH23.......31 F3
   FERN BH22..........................10 B4
Shirley Rd *BKME/WDN* BH12.......53 H4
   MOOR/WNTN BH9.................56 C1
   UPTN BH16..........................51 E3
Shore Av *UPTN* BH16...............51 E4
Shore Cl *LYMN* SO41................80 B1
   UPTN BH16..........................51 E4
Shorefield Crs *LYMN* SO41.........66 A5
Shorefield Rd *LYMN* SO41..........65 F4
Shorefield Wy *LYMN* SO41.........66 A5
Shore Gdns *UPTN* BH16............50 D5
Shore La *UPTN* BH16................50 D5
Shore Rd *PSTN* BH14...............83 E1
Short Cl *BKME/WDN* BH12..........55 F4
Shorts Cl *CHCH/BSGR* BH23.......60 A1
Shottsford Rd *PLE* BH15............52 C5
Shrubb's Av *LYMN* SO41...........49 E3
Shrubbs Hill Gdns *LYND* SO43....85 E4
Shrubbs Hill Rd *LYND* SO43.......85 E4
Sidney St *LYMN* SO41...............46 C5
Silchester Cl *WCLF* BH2............56 B5
Silver Birch Cl
   BKME/WDN BH12..................73 E1
Silverdale *NMIL/BTOS* BH25........64 C5
Silverdale Cl *BDST* BH18............32 C3
Silver St *CHCH/BSGR* BH23.......59 H4
   LYMN SO41..........................46 B3
   LYND SO43..........................84 C3
Silver Wy *CHCH/BSGR* BH23......62 A2
Silverwood Cl *WIMB* BH21.........22 D2
Simmonds Cl *PLE* BH15............52 D5
Singleton Dr *NBNE* BH10...........36 C5
Siskin Cl *FERN* BH22...............17 F2
Sixpenny Cl *BKME/WDN* BH12....54 C3
Skinner St *PLE* BH15...............70 C4
Skipton Cl *BDST* BH18..............33 E5
Sky End La *LYMN* SO41............46 D5
Slade Cl *LYMN* SO41................46 C4
Slades Farm Rd *NBNE* BH10.......55 G1
Slade's La *NBNE* BH10.............55 G2
Sleepbrook Cl *VWD* BH31............4 C2
Slepe Crs *BKME/WDN* BH12.......54 D2
Slinn Rd *CHCH/BSGR* BH23........60 C3
Slip Wy *PLE* BH15...................70 B3
Slough La *UPTN* BH16...............50 B4
Smithfield Pl *MOOR/WNTN* BH9...56 B1
Smithson Cl *BKME/WDN* BH12.....55 F2
Smithy La *NMIL/BTOS* BH25........44 D1
Smugglers La *WIMB* BH21..........14 D1
Smugglers La North
   CHCH/BSGR BH23.................61 H2
Smugglers La South
   CHCH/BSGR BH23.................62 A2
Smugglers Wood Rd
   CHCH/BSGR BH23.................61 H2
Snooks La *LYMN* SO41..............49 H1
Snowdon Rd *WBNE* BH4..............2 A2
Snowdrop Gdns
   CHCH/BSGR BH23.................61 F2
Soberton Rd *CHAR* BH8.............57 F4
Solent Av *LYMN* SO41...............49 F4
Solent Cl *LYMN* SO41...............49 F4
Solent Dr *NMIL/BTOS* BH25.........64 A3
Solent Ms *NMIL/BTOS* BH25........64 A1
Solent Rd *CHCH/BSGR* BH23.......43 H5
   SBNE BH6............................77 G2
Solent Wy *LYMN* SO41..............80 D1
   LYMN SO41..........................81 E2
Solly Cl *BKME/WDN* BH12..........54 C3
Solomon Wy *PLE* BH15.............69 F3
Somerby Rd *PLE* BH15..............52 D4
Somerford Av
   CHCH/BSGR BH23.................61 F2
Somerford Rd
   CHCH/BSGR BH23.................60 D3
Somerford Wy
   CHCH/BSGR BH23.................60 C3
Somerley Rd *MOOR/WNTN* BH9...56 C3
Somerley Vw *RGWD* BH24............8 C3
Somerset Av *CHCH/BSGR* BH23...59 E3
   LTDN BH7............................77 H5
Somerton Cl *NMIL/BTOS* BH25....45 H4

Somerville Rd *RGWD* BH24.............9 E3
  WCLF BH2...............................2 D4
Sopers La *CFDH* BH17...............52 A1
  CHCH/BSGR BH23..............59 C5
Sopley Cl *NMIL/BTOS* BH25.......63 F2
Sopwith Cl *CHCH/BSGR* BH23....61 F4
Sopwith Crs *WIMB* BH21............23 F3
Sorrel Gdns *BDST* BH18.............32 C5
Sorrell Wy *CHCH/BSGR* BH23.....61 F2
Southampton Rd *LYMN* SO41.....48 D2
  LYND SO43...........................85 H2
  RGWD BH24............................8 C3
South Av *NMIL/BTOS* BH25.........63 F2
South Baddesey Rd *LYMN* SO41..49 H3
Southbourne Coast Rd
  SBNE BH6.............................77 G1
Southbourne Gv *BOSC* BH5........76 B1
Southbourne Overcliff Dr
  SBNE BH6.............................76 D2
Southbourne Rd *BOSC* BH5.......58 B5
  LYMN SO41..........................48 C4
  SBNE BH6.............................76 C1
Southbrook Cl *CFDH* BH17..........34 C5
Southcliffe Rd
  CHCH/BSGR BH23..............61 F4
  NMIL/BTOS BH25..............63 F2
South Cliff Rd *WCLF* BH2...............3 E5
Southcote Rd *BMTH* BH1...........74 D1
Southdown Wy *FERN* BH22........10 C5
South Dr *RGWD* BH24 *..............18 D2
Southern Av *FERN* BH22............10 C5
Southernhay Rd *VWD* BH31..........5 F2
Southern La *NMIL/BTOS* BH25.....63 H2
Southern Oaks
  NMIL/BTOS BH25..............63 H1
Southern Rd *LYMN* SO41............48 D3
  SBNE BH6.............................76 C1
Southey Rd *CHCH/BSGR* BH23...60 D3
Southfield *RGWD* BH24..................8 C5
Southfield Ms *RGWD* BH24...........8 C5
South Gv *LYMN* SO41.................49 F4
South Haven Cl *UPTN* BH16.......68 D1
Southill Av *BKME/WDN* BH12......54 A4
Southill Gdns *MOOR/WNTN* BH9..56 C1
Southill Rd *BKME/WDN* BH12......54 A4
  MOOR/WNTN BH9................56 C1
South Kinson Dr *BWD* BH11........36 A3
Southlands *LYMN* SO41..............48 C5
Southlands Av *SBNE* BH6...........77 F1
  WIMB BH21..........................32 B1
Southlawns Wk
  NMIL/BTOS BH25..............63 H1
Southlea Av *SBNE* BH6...............59 F5
South Park Rd
  BKME/WDN BH12...............55 E2
South Rd *BMTH* BH1..................57 C5
  PLE BH15............................70 C3
  WIMB BH21..........................32 C1
South St *LYMN* SO41..................48 C5
South Sway La *LYMN* SO41..........47 G1
South View Pl *WCLF* BH2...............2 E5
South View Rd
  CHCH/BSGR BH23..............59 G4
Southville Rd *BOSC* BH5............58 B5
South Weirs *BROC* SO42............86 B5
South Western Crs *PSTN* BH14...71 H3
Southwick Pl *SBNE* BH6.............58 C4
Southwick Rd *SBNE* BH6............58 C4
Southwood Av
  CHCH/BSGR BH23..............62 C1
  SBNE BH6.............................76 C1
Southwood Cl
  CHCH/BSGR BH23..............62 C1
  FERN BH22..........................17 G4
Sovereign Cl *LTDN* BH7.............57 H2
Sparkford Cl *LTDN* BH7.............58 B2
Spartina Dr *LYMN* SO41.............49 E1
Speedwell Dr
  CHCH/BSGR BH23..............61 F2
Spencer Rd *BMTH* BH1...............75 H1
  CCLF BH13..........................72 C5
  NMIL/BTOS BH25..............45 E4
Spetisbury Cl *MOOR/WNTN* BH9..37 H4
Spicer La *BWD* BH11..................35 G2
Spinacre *NMIL/BTOS* BH25.........64 B2
Spindle Cl *BDST* BH18...............32 D5
Spindlewood Cl
  NMIL/BTOS BH25..............64 A1
Spinners Cl *FERN* BH22............10 B5
Spinney Cl *RGWD* BH24.............11 G2
Spinneys La *FERN* BH22............17 H4
The Spinney *RGWD* BH24.............6 D5
Spinney Wy *NMIL/BTOS* BH25.....45 F2
Spittlefields *RGWD* BH24.............8 D4
Springbank Rd *LTDN* BH7...........57 H2
Spring Cl *VWD* BH31.....................4 D3
Springdale Av *BDST* BH18..........32 D2
Springdale Gv *WIMB* BH21.........32 C3
Springdale Rd *BDST* BH18..........33 E2

WIMB BH21.............................32 B3
Springfield Av
  CHCH/BSGR BH23..............39 H5
  SBNE BH6.............................77 G1
Springfield Cl *LYMN* SO41..........49 G5
  VWD BH31.............................4 D3
Springfield Crs *PSTN* BH14........71 H1
Springfield Gdns
  NMIL/BTOS BH25..............45 H5
Springfield Rd *PSTN* BH14.........53 G5
Spring Gdns *BKME/WDN* BH12...54 B5
Spring La *NMIL/BTOS* BH25.........45 H5
Spring Rd *BMTH* BH1.................57 G5
  LYMN SO41..........................49 G5
Springvale Av *LTDN* BH7...........57 H2
Springwater Cl *BWD* BH11..........36 A4
Springwater Dr
  CHCH/BSGR BH23..............60 B4
Springwater Rd *BWD* BH11.........36 A4
Spruce Cl *CFDH* BH17...............51 C1
Spur Cl *WIMB* BH21....................16 A3
Spurgeon Rd *LTDN* BH7............58 D1
Spur Hill Av *PSTN* BH14.............72 C3
Spur Rd *PSTN* BH14..................72 B2
Square Cl *WIMB* BH21 *..............24 D1
The Square *LYMN* SO41.............48 C4
  RGWD BH24..........................18 D1
Squirrels Cl *CHCH/BSGR* BH23...39 H5
Stacey Cl *BKME/WDN* BH11........54 A3
Stacey Gdns *CHAR* BH8.............38 D5
Stafford Rd *BMTH* BH1.................3 K3
Stag Cl *NMIL/BTOS* BH25...........44 C3
Stagswood *VWD* BH31..................4 B2
Stalbridge Dr *FERN* BH22...........17 H5
Stalbridge Rd *CFDH* BH17..........52 A3
Stalham Rd *BKME/WDN* BH12....54 D4
Stallards La *RGWD* BH24..............8 B4
Stamford Rd *SBNE* BH6..............58 D5
Stanfield Rd *BKME/WDN* BH12....54 D4
  FERN BH22..........................17 G3
  MOOR/WNTN BH9................56 A2
Stanford Gdns *LYMN* SO41.........48 D5
Stanley Cl *VWD* BH31...................5 E3
Stanley Green Crs *PLE* BH15......52 B5
Stanley Green Rd *PLE* BH15.......52 C5
Stanley Rd *BMTH* BH1................57 G5
  CHCH/BSGR BH23..............62 C2
  LYMN SO41..........................49 F5
  PLE BH15............................70 C4
Stannington Cl
  NMIL/BTOS BH25..............45 E5
Stanpit *CHCH/BSGR* BH23..........60 C5
Stanton Rd *NBNE* BH10.............36 C5
Stapehill Crs *WIMB* BH21...........15 H4
Stapehill Rd *WIMB* BH21.............16 C4
Staple Close La *PLE* BH15.........52 C4
Staplecross La
  CHCH/BSGR BH23..............60 B2
Stapleford Av *FERN* BH22...........18 B3
Star La *RGWD* BH24......................8 B4
Starlight Farm Cl *VWD* BH31........5 F1
Station Ap *BDST* BH18................33 E3
Station Rd *CHCH/BSGR* BH23.....43 E5
  FERN BH22..........................10 A4
  NMIL/BTOS BH25..............45 E5
  PLE BH15............................70 A4
  PSTN BH14..........................71 H2
  VWD BH31.............................4 B1
  WIMB BH21..........................22 D1
Station St *LYMN* SO41................49 F3
Station Ter *WIMB* BH21...............22 D1
Stedman Rd *BOSC* BH5..............58 B5
Steepdene *PSTN* BH14...............71 H2
Steeple Cl *CFDH* BH17...............33 H4
Steepleton Rd *BDST* BH18..........33 G4
Stem La *NMIL/BTOS* BH25...........44 C2
Stenhurst Rd *PLE* BH15.............55 F5
Stephen Langton Dr *BWD* BH11...35 F2
Sterte Av *PLE* BH15...................70 B1
Sterte Av West *PLE* BH15...........70 B1
Sterte Cl *PLE* BH15....................70 C1
Sterte Esp *PLE* BH15.................70 C1
Sterte Rd *PLE* BH15...................70 C1
Stevenson Crs *PSTN* BH14.........72 B2
Stevenson Rd *SBNE* BH6............77 F2
Stevensons Cl *WIMB* BH21.........14 C5
Stewart Cl *CHAR* BH8................57 E5
Stewart Rd *CHAR* BH8...............56 D4
Stewarts Wy *FERN* BH22............18 A3
Stibbs Wy *CHCH/BSGR* BH23.....31 G3
Stillmore Rd *BWD* BH11.............35 F4
Stillwater Pk *RGWD* BH24 *..........9 E1
Stinsford Cl *MOOR/WNTN* BH9...37 H3
Stinsford Rd *CFDH* BH17...........52 B3
Stirling Cl *NMIL/BTOS* BH25........45 H4
Stirling Rd *TWDS* BH3................56 A3
Stirling Wy *CHCH/BSGR* BH23....61 F4

Stirrup Cl *UPTN* BH16................51 F3
  WIMB BH21..........................16 A3
Stoborough Dr *BDST* BH18.........33 E5
Stockbridge Cl *CFDH* BH17.........34 D5
Stokes Av *PLE* BH15..................70 C1
Stoke Wood Rd *TWDS* BH3........56 B3
Stonechat Cl *FERN* BH22...........17 F1
Stonecrop Cl *BDST* BH18...........32 C5
Stone Gdns *CHAR* BH8..............38 E5
Stone La *WIMB* BH21.................14 A3
Stoneleigh Av *LYMN* SO41..........46 B4
Stony La *CHCH/BSGR* BH23.......40 D5
  CHCH/BSGR BH23..............60 A3
Stony La South
  CHCH/BSGR BH23..............60 B4
Stopples La *LYMN* SO41.............46 B4
Story La *BDST* BH18..................33 F3
Stourbank Rd
  CHCH/BSGR BH23..............59 G4
Stourcliffe Av *SBNE* BH6............76 C1
Stour Cl *WIMB* BH21..................16 B5
Stourcroft Dr
  CHCH/BSGR BH23..............39 H5
Stourfield Rd *BOSC* BH5............76 B1
Stourpaine Rd *CFDH* BH17.........33 H5
Stour Pk *NBNE* BH10 *...............37 E1
Stour Rd *CHAR* BH8...................57 F4
  CHCH/BSGR BH23..............59 G4
Stourvale Av *CHCH/BSGR* BH23..58 D2
Stourvale Pl *BOSC* BH5..............58 B5
Stourvale Rd *SBNE* BH6.............58 B5
Stour Valley Wy *BWD* BH11.........24 D5
  CHAR BH8...........................38 A1
  SBNE BH6.............................59 E3
  WIMB BH21..........................22 B2
  WIMB BH21..........................23 H3
Stour Wk *CHAR* BH8..................38 B3
Stour Wy *CHCH/BSGR* BH23......39 H5
Stourwood Av *SBNE* BH6............76 C1
Stourwood Rd *SBNE* BH6...........76 C1
Stouts La *CHCH/BSGR* BH23......31 F3
Strand St *PLE* BH15...................70 B4
Stratfield Pl *NMIL/BTOS* BH25.....44 C4
Stratford Pl *LYMN* SO41.............48 D2
Strathmore Dr *VWD* BH31............5 E2
Strathmore Rd
  MOOR/WNTN BH9................37 G3
Stratton Rd *MOOR/WNTN* BH9...38 A3
Strete Mt *CHCH/BSGR* BH23 *....60 C3
Strides La *RGWD* BH24................8 B4
Strode Gdns *RGWD* BH24...........12 C1
Strouden Av *CHAR* BH8..............38 B5
Strouden Rd *MOOR/WNTN* BH9...56 C1
Stroud Gdns *CHCH/BSGR* BH23..60 C4
Stroud La *CHCH/BSGR* BH23......60 C4
Stroud Park Av
  CHCH/BSGR BH23..............60 C4
Struan Cl *RGWD* BH24.................6 D5
Struan Ct *RGWD* BH24.................7 E5
Struan Dr *RGWD* BH24.................6 D5
Struan Gdns *RGWD* BH24............6 D5
Stuart Cl *UPTN* BH16.................50 D3
Stuart Rd *CHCH/BSGR* BH23......62 D2
Studland Dr *LYMN* SO41............65 H5
Studland Rd *WBNE* BH4...............2 A7
Studley Cl *CHCH/BSGR* BH23.....63 E2
Studley Ct *NMIL/BTOS* BH25.......63 F2
Sturminster Rd
  MOOR/WNTN BH9................37 H3
Suffolk Av *CHCH/BSGR* BH23.....40 B5
Suffolk Cl *WIMB* BH21................16 A3
Suffolk Rd *WCLF* BH2...................2 C3
Suffolk Rd South *WCLF* BH2.........2 C3
Summercroft Wy *FERN* BH22......10 B4
Summerfield Cl
  CHCH/BSGR BH23..............41 E5
Summerfields *VWD* BH31............57 H3
Summer Field Cl *WIMB* BH21.....15 G5
Summer Flds *VWD* BH31..............4 D4
Summers Av *BWD* BH11.............36 B1
Summers La *CHCH/BSGR* BH23..60 B1
Summertrees Ct
  NMIL/BTOS BH25..............45 H3
Sunbury Ct *BWD* BH11...............36 A1
Sunderland Dr
  CHCH/BSGR BH23..............61 F3
Sundew Cl *CHCH/BSGR* BH23....61 G1
  NMIL/BTOS BH25..............45 H3
Sundew Rd *BDST* BH18..............32 C5
Sunningdale Crs *NBNE* BH10......36 D3
Sunnybank Rd *WIMB* BH21.........15 G5
Sunnyfield Rd *NMIL/BTOS* BH25..64 A2
Sunny Hill Rd *BKME/WDN* BH12...54 B5
Sunnyhill Rd *SBNE* BH6..............58 B5
Sunnylands Av *SBNE* BH6...........77 F1
Sunnymoor Rd *BWD* BH11..........55 E1
Sunnyside Rd *BKME/WDN* BH12..54 B3
Sunridge Cl *BKME/WDN* BH12....55 E4

Surrey Cl *CHCH/BSGR* BH23......40 B5
Surrey Gdns *WBNE* BH4...............2 B2
Surrey Rd *BKME/WDN* BH12......55 E5
  WBNE BH4..............................2 B2
Surrey Rd South *WBNE* BH4........2 B2
Sussex Cl *MOOR/WNTN* BH9......37 H3
Sutherland Av *BDST* BH18..........32 C2
Sutton Cl *CFDH* BH17................34 C5
Sutton Pl *BROC* SO42................87 E3
Sutton Rd *MOOR/WNTN* BH9......56 D1
Swallow Cl *CFDH* BH17..............51 H2
Swallow Dr *LYMN* SO41..............80 D1
Swallow Wy *WIMB* BH21.............15 G2
Swan Md *RGWD* BH24..................9 E5
Swanmore Cl *LTDN* BH7.............58 B4
Swanmore Rd *LTDN* BH7............58 B4
Swansbury Dr *CHAR* BH8...........39 F5
Sway Gdns *CHAR* BH8................38 B5
Sway Rd *BROC* SO42..................86 D5
  LYMN SO41..........................47 G2
  NMIL/BTOS BH25..............45 F1
The Sweep *RGWD* BH24...............8 B4
Swift Cl *CFDH* BH17...................51 H2
Swordfish Dr *CHCH/BSGR* BH23..61 F3
Sycamore Cl *CFDH* BH17............51 H1
  CHCH/BSGR BH23..............58 D2
  LYMN SO41..........................66 B5
Sycamore Pl *WIMB* BH21............16 B4
Sycamore Rd *LYMN* SO41...........46 B3
Sydling Cl *CFDH* BH17................34 C5
Sydney Rd *BDST* BH18...............33 E4
  CHCH/BSGR BH23..............59 E1
Sylmor Gdns *MOOR/WNTN* BH9..37 H5
Sylvan Cl *LYMN* SO41.................46 D5
  RGWD BH24..........................11 G2
Sylvan Rd *BKME/WDN* BH12......53 H4
Symes Rd *PLE* BH15..................51 C5

T

Tadden Wk *BDST* BH18...............32 D5
Tait Cl *CFDH* BH17....................53 E2
Talbot Av *TWDS* BH3..................56 A3
Talbot Dr *BKME/WDN* BH12........55 F2
  CHCH/BSGR BH23..............43 F5
Talbot Hill Rd
  MOOR/WNTN BH9................55 H2
Talbot Mdw *BKME/WDN* BH12....55 F2
Talbot Ms *NBNE* BH10................55 G1
Talbot Rd *MOOR/WNTN* BH9......55 H2
Tamar Cl *FERN* BH22.................18 C4
Tamworth Rd *LTDN* BH7.............57 H5
Tangmere Cl *CHCH/BSGR* BH23..61 F4
Tan Howse Cl *LTDN* BH7............58 B2
Target Wy *CHCH/BSGR* BH23......57 F3
Tarn Dr *CFDH* BH17...................51 H1
Tarrant Cl *CFDH* BH17...............34 A5
Tarrant Rd *MOOR/WNTN* BH9....37 H4
Tasman Cl *CHCH/BSGR* BH23.....59 F2
Tatnam Rd *PLE* BH15.................70 C1
Tattenham Rd *BROC* SO42..........86 D4
Taverner Cl *PLE* BH15................70 D4
Taylor Dr *CHAR* BH8..................38 B3
Taylor's Buildings *PLE* BH15.......70 C4
Taylor Wy *VWD* BH31...................5 E2
Teasel Wy *FERN* BH22................10 B5
Technology Rd *CFDH* BH17..........52 A2
Tedder Cl *BWD* BH11..................36 B4
Tedder Rd *BWD* BH11.................36 B4
Telford Pl *LYMN* SO41................80 C1
Telford Rd *WIMB* BH21................17 E1
Temple Ms *BMTH* BH1 *.............54 D1
Templer Cl *BWD* BH11................54 D1
Tennyson Rd *MOOR/WNTN* BH9..37 F5
  PSTN BH14..........................71 G2
  WIMB BH21..........................14 C3
Tensing Rd *CHCH/BSGR* BH23...60 C3
Terence Av *CFDH* BH17..............52 A2
Terence Rd *WIMB* BH21..............32 A2
Tern Ct *SBNE* BH6.....................58 D4
Terrace Rd *WCLF* BH2..................3 F4
Terrington Av
  CHCH/BSGR BH23..............62 A1
Thames Cl *FERN* BH22...............18 C3
Thames Ms *PLE* BH15 *.............70 B4
Thames St *PLE* BH15.................70 B4
Thatched Cottage Pk
  LYND SO43 *........................85 G2
Thatchers La *CHCH/BSGR* BH23..30 B5
Theobold Rd *CHCH/BSGR* BH23..58 C5
Thetchers Cl *NMIL/BTOS* BH25...45 F2
Thetford Rd *BKME/WDN* BH12....54 D4
Thistlebarrow Rd *LTDN* BH7........57 G4
Thistle Cl *CHCH/BSGR* BH23......61 G2
Thoresby Ct *NMIL/BTOS* BH25....44 C4
Thornbury Rd *SBNE* BH6............77 G1

Thorncombe Cl CFDH BH17.................**53** E1
  MOOR/WNTN BH9...................**37** H3
Thorne Cl VWD BH31............................**4** C1
Thornfield Dr
  CHCH/BSGR BH23....................**62** B1
Thornham Rd NMIL/BTOS BH25 ....**45** H4
Thornley Rd NBNE BH10................**36** D3
Thorn Rd CFDH BH17.......................**33** G4
Thornton Cl WIMB BH21..................**32** A2
Three Acre Dr NMIL/BTOS BH25 ...**63** H2
Three Cross Rd FERN BH22 ....**10** B1
Three Lions Cl WIMB BH21.............**14** B4
Throop Cl CHAR BH8..........................**39** E5
Throop Rd CHAR BH8.........................**38** C3
Throopside Av
  MOOR/WNTN BH9...................**38** B3
Thrush Rd BKME/WDN BH12........**54** A1
Thursby Rd CHCH/BSGR BH23 ......**43** F5
Thwaite Rd BKME/WDN BH12.......**55** F5
Tidemill Cl CHCH/BSGR BH23.......**59** G2
Tiffany Cl LYMN SO41 ....**46** B3
Tilburg Rd CHCH/BSGR BH23 ....**60** D3
Tilebarn La BROC SO42....................**87** E5
Timothy Cl NBNE BH10....................**36** D2
Tincleton Gdns
  MOOR/WNTN BH9...................**37** H3
Tithe Barn LYMN SO41......................**49** E2
Todber Cl BWD BH11.........................**35** F4
Tollard Cl BKME/WDN BH12...........**54** C2
Tollerford Rd CFDH BH17................**33** H5
Tolpuddle Gdns
  MOOR/WNTN BH9...................**37** H3
Tolstoi Rd PSTN BH14......................**53** G4
Tonge Rd BWD BH11.........................**36** B4
The Topiary PSTN BH14....................**53** F5
Top La RGWD BH24.............................**8** C4
Torbay Rd PSTN BH14.......................**72** A3
Totmel Rd CFDH BH17......................**34** C5
Tourney Rd BWD BH11.....................**35** G2
Tower La WIMB BH21.........................**14** D3
Tower Rd BMTH BH1..........................**3** H4
  CCLF BH13................................**73** F4
Tower Rd West CCLF BH13 ....**73** F4
Towngate Br PLE BH15.....................**70** C3
Towngate Ms RGWD BH24 *.............**9** G3
Townsend Cl BWD BH11...................**36** B1
Townsville Rd
  MOOR/WNTN BH9...................**37** H5
Tozer Cl BWD BH11............................**35** H5
Trafalgar Rd MOOR/WNTN BH9....**56** B3
Tranmere Cl LYMN SO41..................**49** F5
Treebys Cl CHCH/BSGR BH23.........**60** B1
Treeside CHCH/BSGR BH23 ....**42** C5
Trefoil Wy CHCH/BSGR BH23.........**61** G2
Tregonwell Rd WCLF BH2 ....**3** F4
Trentham Av LTDN BH7....................**58** B2
Trentham Cl LTDN BH7.....................**58** B2
Trent Wy FERN BH22.........................**18** C3
Tresillian Wy
  CHCH/BSGR BH23....................**43** H5
The Triangle NMIL/BTOS BH25 * ...**63** E3
  WCLF BH2..................................**2** E4
Tricketts La FERN BH22....................**18** B3
Trigon Rd PLE BH15..........................**52** D3
Trinidad Crs
  BKME/WDN BH12....................**54** A2
Trinity Rd BMTH BH1.........................**3** K3
Troak Cl CHCH/BSGR BH23 ....**60** C2
Troon Rd BDST BH18..........................**33** E2
Truman Rd BWD BH11......................**36** B1
Truscott Av MOOR/WNTN BH9....**56** C3
Tuckers La PLE BH15.........................**69** H4
Tucks Cl CHCH/BSGR BH23 ....**31** E3
Tuckton Cl SBNE BH6........................**76** D1
Tuckton Rd SBNE BH6......................**76** D1
Tudor Ct PLE BH15............................**53** E4
Tudor Rd BDST BH18.........................**33** E2
Turbary Ct UPTN BH16 * **51** E2
Turbary Rd BKME/WDN BH12........**54** A5
  FERN BH22...............................**18** B2
Turks La PSTN BH14..........................**71** G4
Turlin Rd UPTN BH16........................**69** E1
Turnberry Cl CHCH/BSGR BH23 ....**59** F4
Turners Farm Crs LYMN SO41.......**46** C5
Turnworth Cl BDST BH18.................**33** C4
Tweedale Rd MOOR/WNTN BH9...**38** A4
Twemlow Av PSTN BH14..................**71** F3
Twin Oaks Cl BDST BH18.................**33** F3
Twyford Cl CHAR BH8.......................**38** B5
Twyford Wy CFDH BH17..................**34** C5
Twynham Av
  CHCH/BSGR BH23....................**59** G4
Twynham Rd SBNE BH6...................**77** F1
Tylers Cl LYMN SO41.........................**48** D2
Tynedale Cl MOOR/WNTN BH9.....**38** A3
Tyneham Av BKME/WDN BH12......**53** H5
Tyrell Gdns CHAR BH8......................**39** E5
Tyrrells Ct CHCH/BSGR BH23.........**31** F3
Tytherley Gn CHAR BH8...................**38** B5

U

Ubsdell Cl NMIL/BTOS BH25 ....**45** E4
Uddens Dr WIMB BH21......................**16** B1
Ullswater Rd WIMB BH21................**22** C2
Undercliff Dr BMTH BH1....................**3** K5
Undercliff Rd BOSC BH5..................**75** G2
Undershore LYMN SO41..................**49** E1
Undershore Rd LYMN SO41............**49** G3
Underwood Cl CFDH BH17..............**52** B1
Uplands Av NMIL/BTOS BH25........**64** A2
Uplands Cl FERN BH22.....................**18** C1
Uplands Gdns CHAR BH8................**38** A5
Uplands Rd CHAR BH8.....................**38** A5
  FERN BH22...............................**18** C1
Uplyme Cl CFDH BH17......................**34** C5
Upper Common Rd LYMN SO41....**47** H4
Upper Golf Links Rd BDST BH18....**33** F2
Upper Gordon Rd
  CHCH/BSGR BH23....................**62** C1
Upper Hinton Rd BMTH BH1.............**3** H4
Upper Norwich Rd WCLF BH2...........**2** D1
Upper Rd BKME/WDN BH12...........**54** A4
Upper Terrace Rd BMTH BH1............**3** F4
Uppleby Rd BKME/WDN BH12........**54** A5
Upton Cl UPTN BH16.........................**50** D3
Upton Ct UPTN BH16.........................**51** E3
Upton Heath Est UPTN BH16..........**51** F3
Upton Rd CFDH BH17........................**51** H3
Upton Wy BDST BH18........................**32** D4
Upwey Av PLE BH15...........................**69** G2
Utrecht Ct CHCH/BSGR BH23.........**60** B3

V

Vaggs La LYMN SO41.........................**46** A1
Valencia Cl CHCH/BSGR BH23........**39** H3
Vale Rd BMTH BH1.............................**75** F1
  PSTN BH14................................**72** C1
Valette Rd MOOR/WNTN BH9.......**37** G4
Valiant Wy CHCH/BSGR BH23........**61** F3
Valley Cl CHCH/BSGR BH23............**40** A4
Valley Rd CHAR BH8..........................**38** D4
Valley Vw BKME/WDN BH12...........**55** F3
Vallis Cl UPTN BH16.........................**70** D4
Vanguard Rd CHAR BH8...................**57** C1
  PLE BH15....................................**70** C3
Vantage Wy BKME/WDN BH12......**32** D5
Vecta Cl CHCH/BSGR BH23.............**61** G4
Vectis Rd NMIL/BTOS BH25 ....**63** F3
Velvet Lawn Rd
  NMIL/BTOS BH25.....................**44** D3
Venator Pl WIMB BH21.....................**14** C3
Venning Av BWD BH11.....................**35** G2
Ventry Cl BKME/WDN BH12...........**72** D1
Ventura Pl UPTN BH16......................**51** F4
Verity Crs CFDH BH17.......................**53** C1
Vernalls Cl NBNE BH10.....................**36** D1
Vernalls Ct NMIL/BTOS BH25.........**45** G2
Vernalls Gdns NBNE BH10..............**36** D2
Verne Rd VWD BH31...........................**5** E5
Verney Cl BWD BH11........................**36** B4
Verney Rd BWD BH11.......................**36** A4
Verno La CHCH/BSGR BH23............**42** C5
Verona Av SBNE BH6........................**58** D5
Verulam Pl BMTH BH1.......................**3** H3
Verulam Rd PSTN BH14....................**71** F1
Verwood Crs SBNE BH6...................**77** H1
Verwood Rd RGWD BH24...................**7** E2
Vetch Cl CHCH/BSGR BH23.............**61** F2
Vicarage Gdns LYMN SO41.............**46** C5
Vicarage La LYMN SO41..................**46** C5
Vicarage Rd MOOR/WNTN BH9....**56** A1
  PLE BH15....................................**52** C5
  VWD BH31..................................**5** C5
Vicarage Wy CHCH/BSGR BH23 ....**41** F5
Vickers Cl CHAR BH8........................**39** F5
Vickery Wy CHCH/BSGR BH23.......**60** B2
Victoria Av MOOR/WNTN BH9.......**56** A1
Victoria Cl WIMB BH21....................**32** B3
Victoria Crs BKME/WDN BH12.......**54** B4
Victoria Gdns FERN BH22................**17** H3
  RGWD BH24...............................**8** C5
Victoria Ms LYMN SO41 * **49** F3
Victoria Park Rd
  MOOR/WNTN BH9...................**56** A1
Victoria Pl CHAR BH8.......................**57** E5
  LYMN SO41...............................**49** E5
  WIMB BH21...............................**14** B4
Victoria Rd BKME/WDN BH12........**54** A5
  BMTH BH1..................................**57** E5
  CHCH/BSGR BH23....................**60** C5
  FERN BH22...............................**17** H3
  LYMN SO41...............................**80** A1
  WIMB BH21...............................**14** A4

Viewside Cl WIMB BH21...................**32** A2
Viking Cl SBNE BH6..........................**77** G1
Viking Wy CHCH/BSGR BH23..........**61** E5
  SBNE BH6..................................**77** G1
Villette Cl CHCH/BSGR BH23..........**59** G1
Vince Cl BWD BH11...........................**36** B2
Vincent Cl NMIL/BTOS BH25..........**45** E5
Vincent Rd NMIL/BTOS BH25.........**44** D4
Vine Cl LTDN BH7...............................**58** A3
Vine Farm Cl BKME/WDN BH12....**55** G2
Vine Farm Rd BKME/WDN BH12....**55** G2
Vinegar Hl LYMN SO41.....................**66** B5
Vineries Cl WIMB BH21....................**15** F3
The Vineries WIMB BH21.................**15** F3
Vinneys Cl CHCH/BSGR BH23........**41** E5
Violet La NMIL/BTOS BH25.............**45** E3
Virginia Cl BKME/WDN BH12.........**54** A3
  VWD BH31..................................**5** C4
Viscount Dr CHCH/BSGR BH23......**61** F4
Viscount Wk BWD BH11..................**35** E2
Vitre Gdns LYMN SO41.....................**49** E5
Vixen Wk NMIL/BTOS BH25............**45** F2

W

Wagtail Dr NMIL/BTOS BH25..........**44** D5
Wainsford Cl LYMN SO41 * **48** B4
Wainsford Plantation
  LYMN SO41...............................**66** C2
Wainsford Rd LYMN SO41...............**47** G5
Wakefield Av NBNE BH10................**37** E2
Wakely Gdns BWD BH11..................**36** A2
Wakely Rd BWD BH11.......................**36** B2
Walcheren Pl PLE BH15...................**69** E2
Walcott Av CHCH/BSGR BH23........**59** F1
Walditch Gdns CFDH BH17.............**34** A5
Waldren Cl PLE BH15........................**70** D3
Walford Cl WIMB BH21....................**14** C3
Walford Gdns WIMB BH21..............**14** B3
Walhampton Hl LYMN SO41...........**49** F2
Walkford La NMIL/BTOS BH25.......**44** B4
Walkford Rd CHCH/BSGR BH23.....**44** A5
Walkford Wy CHCH/BSGR BH23....**62** D1
Walking Field La PLE BH15.............**70** D3
Walkwood Av LTDN BH7..................**58** B2
Wallace Rd BDST BH18.....................**33** E4
Walliscott Rd BWD BH11.................**55** E1
Wallisdown Rd
  BKME/WDN BH12....................**35** F5
Wallis Rd NBNE BH10.......................**55** F1
Walnut Cl NMIL/BTOS BH25...........**44** D4
Walpole Rd BMTH BH1.....................**57** F5
Walsford Rd WBNE BH4...................**55** G5
Walsingham Dene LTDN BH7..........**57** H2
Waltham Rd LTDN BH7.....................**58** B3
Walton Rd NBNE BH10.....................**36** C5
  PLE BH15....................................**53** C4
Wanstead Cl RGWD BH24.................**8** C2
Warbler Cl UPTN BH16.....................**50** D2
Warburton Rd CFDH BH17..............**53** E2
Wareham Rd WIMB BH21.................**32** B2
Warmwell Cl CFDH BH17.................**34** B5
Warnford Rd LTDN BH7....................**58** B3
Warren Av CHCH/BSGR BH23.........**60** D5
Warren Cl RGWD BH24.....................**13** E1
Warren Dr RGWD BH24.....................**13** E1
Warren Edge Cl SBNE BH6..............**77** E2
Warren Edge Rd SBNE BH6.............**77** F2
Warren La RGWD BH24.....................**13** E1
Warren Pk LYMN SO41.....................**65** G4
Warren Rd PSTN BH14......................**72** B1
  WBNE BH4..................................**73** F3
Warren Wk FERN BH22....................**17** F2
Warwick Av NMIL/BTOS BH25........**45** F4
Warwick Rd LTDN BH7.....................**58** A5
  PSTN BH14................................**72** A2
Washington Av BMTH BH1...............**57** F5
Watcombe Rd SBNE BH6..................**58** D5
Waterditch Rd
  CHCH/BSGR BH23....................**41** H4
Waterford Cl LYMN SO41................**49** F4
  PSTN BH14................................**71** G3
Waterford Gdns
  CHCH/BSGR BH23....................**62** C3
Waterford La LYMN SO41................**49** F4
Waterford Pl CHCH/BSGR BH23.....**62** C3
Waterford Rd
  CHCH/BSGR BH23....................**62** D2
  NMIL/BTOS BH25.....................**45** F5
Water La SBNE BH6...........................**58** D3
Waterloo Rd CFDH BH17..................**52** C2
  LYMN SO41...............................**49** F3
  MOOR/WNTN BH9...................**56** B3
Waterloo Wy RGWD BH24.................**8** C5
Watermain Rd
  CHCH/BSGR BH23....................**20** A4
Watermill Rd CHCH/BSGR BH23....**59** G2

Waters Gn BROC SO42......................**87** E2
Waters Green Ct BROC SO42...........**87** E2
Watership Dr RGWD BH24.................**9** F5
Waterside CHCH/BSGR BH23..........**78** D1
Waterside Rd RGWD BH24.................**8** D2
Waterston Cl CFDH BH17.................**52** D1
Water Tower Rd BDST BH18............**33** C3
Watery La CHCH/BSGR BH23..........**61** E1
  UPTN BH16................................**50** B3
Watkin Rd BOSC BH5........................**75** H1
Watton Cl CHAR BH8.........................**39** E5
Wattons La RGWD BH24...................**20** C2
Wavell Av CFDH BH17.......................**52** A1
Wavell Rd BWD BH11.........................**36** B3
Wavendon Av NMIL/BTOS BH25....**63** A2
Waverley Crs PLE BH15....................**52** D5
Waverley Rd NMIL/BTOS BH25......**45** F5
Wayman Rd WIMB BH21...................**32** C1
Wayne Rd BKME/WDN BH12..........**53** H4
Wayside Cl LYMN SO41....................**66** B5
Wayside Rd RGWD BH24..................**11** H5
  SBNE BH6..................................**77** E1
Waytown Cl CFDH BH17..................**52** D1
Weavers Cl FERN BH22....................**10** B5
Webbs Cl RGWD BH24........................**6** B5
Webster Rd MOOR/WNTN BH9......**37** G4
Wedgewood Gdns
  CHCH/BSGR BH23....................**31** C3
Wedgwood Dr PSTN BH14...............**71** C3
Weldon Av BWD BH11.......................**35** C2
Welland Rd WIMB BH21....................**14** D5
Wellands Rd LYND SO43...................**85** F3
Well Cl NMIL/BTOS BH25.................**63** H1
Wellesley Av CHCH/BSGR BH23.....**61** C1
Wellington Av
  CHCH/BSGR BH23....................**61** G3
Wellington Pl LYMN SO41 * **49** F3
Wellington Rd CHAR BH8.................**56** C5
  PSTN BH14................................**72** A2
Well La PLE BH15...............................**70** C1
Wellworthy Rd LYMN SO41............**48** D1
Wendover Cl NMIL/BTOS BH25......**63** H1
Wendys Crs FERN BH22 * **26** B1
Wentwood Gdns
  NMIL/BTOS BH25.....................**45** H5
Wentworth Av BOSC BH5................**76** A1
Wentworth Cl BOSC BH5.................**76** B2
Wentworth Dr BDST BH18...............**33** E2
  CHCH/BSGR BH23....................**59** F4
Wescott Wy BWD BH11....................**35** C3
Wesley Cl CHAR BH8.........................**57** E5
Wesley Rd BKME/WDN BH12.........**54** A5
  WIMB BH21...............................**14** B4
Wessex Av NMIL/BTOS BH25..........**45** E5
Wessex Cl CHCH/BSGR BH23.........**61** C3
Wessex Est RGWD BH24.....................**8** D3
Wessex Ga CHAR BH8.......................**57** E4
Wessex Rd PSTN BH14......................**71** C2
  RGWD BH24...............................**8** D3
Wessex Wy CHAR BH8......................**58** A1
  WBNE BH4..................................**2** A1
West Borough WIMB BH21..............**14** B4
Westbourne Ar WBNE BH4................**2** A3
Westbourne Cl WBNE BH4................**2** A3
Westbourne Park Rd
  WBNE BH4..................................**73** F3
Westbrook Cl NBNE BH10...............**36** D5
Westbury Cl CHCH/BSGR BH23......**31** E5
  CHCH/BSGR BH23....................**61** H1
  NMIL/BTOS BH25.....................**64** A2
Westbury Rd RGWD BH24..................**8** D4
West Butts St PLE BH15....................**70** B3
Westby Rd BOSC BH5........................**75** G1
West Cliff Gdns WCLF BH2................**2** E6
West Cliff Rd WBNE BH4....................**2** A4
West Cl LYMN SO41...........................**48** B5
  SBNE BH6 * **77** C1
  VWD BH31..................................**4** B2
Westcroft Pde
  NMIL/BTOS BH25 * **45** F5
Westcroft Pk BDST BH18..................**33** C3
Westdown Rd BWD BH11.................**36** A2
West Dr RGWD BH24.........................**18** D2
Westerham Rd CCLF BH13...............**73** F2
Western Av CCLF BH13.....................**72** C3
  NBNE BH10...............................**36** D3
  NMIL/BTOS BH25.....................**63** F3
Western Cl NBNE BH10....................**36** D2
Western Rd CCLF BH13....................**72** D5
  LYMN SO41...............................**48** D3
Westfield Cl WIMB BH21.................**14** B4
Westfield Gdns
  CHCH/BSGR BH23....................**61** F1
  LYMN SO41...............................**66** C1
Westfield Rd LYMN SO41................**49** F5
  SBNE BH6..................................**77** E1
Westgate Pk WBNE BH4...................**73** F4
Westham Cl CFDH BH17..................**34** A4
West Hayes LYMN SO41....................**49** F4

Westheath Rd *BDST* BH18 ....**33** F3
West Hill Pl *WCLF* BH2 ....**2** E4
West Hill Rd *WCLF* BH2 ....**2** E5
West Howe Cl *BWD* BH11 ....**36** A3
Westlands Ct *CHCH/BSGR* BH23 ...**31** E4
Westlands Dr *CCLF* BH13 ....**72** D5
West La *CHCH/BSGR* BH23 ....**30** D4
   LYMN SO41 ....**66** C1
Westminster Rd *CCLF* BH13 ......**73** F4
Westminster Rd East
   CCLF BH13 ....**73** F4
West Moors Rd *FERN* BH22 ......**17** H2
Weston Dr *BMTH* BH1 ....**74** D2
Weston Rd *WIMB* BH21 ....**15** F2
West Overcliff Dr *WBNE* BH4 ......**2** A6
West Overcliff La *RGWD* BH24 ....**7** H5
Westover Rd *BMTH* BH1 ....**3** H4
   LYMN SO41 ....**80** B2
West Quay Rd *PLE* BH15 ......**70** C3
West Rd *BOSC* BH5 ....**58** A5
   CHCH/BSGR BH23 ....**31** E4
   LYMN SO41 ....**65** C5
West Rw *WIMB* BH21 ....**14** B5
West St *PLE* BH15 ....**70** B3
   RGWD BH24 ....**8** A4
   WIMB BH21 ....**14** B5
West Undercliff Prom *WCLF* BH2 ...**3** F6
West View Rd
   CHCH/BSGR BH23 ....**60** C4
   PLE BH15 ....**70** C2
West Wy *BDST* BH18 ....**32** D4
   LYMN SO41 ....**48** C5
   MOOR/WNTN BH9 ....**37** H3
West Way Cl *MOOR/WNTN* BH9 ...**56** B1
Westwood Av *FERN* BH22 ......**17** H3
Westwood Pk
   NMIL/BTOS BH25 * **44** C2
Westwood Rd *LYND* SO43 ......**85** E2
Wetherby Cl *BDST* BH18 ....**33** E5
Weyman's Av *NBNE* BH10 ......**36** C1
Weymans Dr *NBNE* BH10 ......**36** C1
Weymouth Rd *PSTN* BH14 ......**54** A5
Wharf Cl *BMTH* BH1 ....**57** F5
Wharfdale Rd *BKME/WDN* BH12 ...**54** B4
   WBNE BH4 ....**2** B2
Wharncliffe Gdns
   CHCH/BSGR BH23 ....**62** C3
Wharncliffe Rd *BMTH* BH1 ......**75** F1
   CHCH/BSGR BH23 ....**62** C3
Whatleigh Cl *PLE* BH15 ......**70** C4
Wheaton Rd *LTDN* BH7 ......**58** A5
Wheelers La *BWD* BH11 ......**35** F1
Whincroft Cl *LYMN* SO41 ......**18** A2
Whincroft Dr *FERN* BH22 ......**18** A3
Whitaker Crs *LYMN* SO41 ......**48** C4
Whitby Av *BDST* BH18 ......**33** E5
Whitby Cl *CHCH/BSGR* BH23 ......**39** H3
Whitby Crs *BDST* BH18 ......**33** E5
Whitchurch Av *BDST* BH18 ......**33** G4
White Barn Crs *LYMN* SO41 ......**46** C4
Whitebeam Wy *VWD* BH31 ......**5** F3
Whitecliff Crs *PSTN* BH14 ......**71** H4
White Cliff Rd *PSTN* BH14 ......**71** H3
Whitecliff Rd *PSTN* BH14 ......**71** H3
White Cl *PLE* BH15 ......**53** E3
Whitecross Cl *CFDH* BH17 ......**34** A4
White Farm Cl *NBNE* BH10 ......**55** H2
Whitefield Rd *NMIL/BTOS* BH25 ...**45** E4
   PSTN BH14 ......**71** G3
Whitehall *CHCH/BSGR* BH23 ......**59** H5
Whitehart Flds *RGWD* BH24 ......**9** E3
Whitehayes Cl
   CHCH/BSGR BH23 ......**41** F5
Whitehayes Rd
   CHCH/BSGR BH23 ......**60** A1
White Horse Dr *PLE* BH15 ...**52** C5
Whitehouse Rd *WIMB* BH21 ......**22** D2
White Knights
   NMIL/BTOS BH25 ......**63** H3
Whitelands *CHCH/BSGR* BH23 ...**31** H1
Whitelegg Wy *NBNE* BH10 ......**37** E2
Whitemoor Rd *BROC* SO42 ......**86** B2
Whiteways *WIMB* BH21 ......**15** E3
Whitfield Pk *RGWD* BH24 ......**12** C1
Whitley Wy *NMIL/BTOS* BH25 ...**45** F2
Whitsbury Cl *CHAR* BH8 ......**38** B5
Whittle Rd *WIMB* BH21 ......**16** D2
Whittles Wy *PLE* BH15 ......**70** B3
Wick Dr *NMIL/BTOS* BH25 ......**44** C5
Wicket Rd *NBNE* BH10 ......**36** C2
Wickfield Av *CHCH/BSGR* BH23 ...**59** H4
Wickfield Cl *CHCH/BSGR* BH23 ...**59** H4
Wickham Dr *WIMB* BH21 ......**32** B3
Wick La *CHCH/BSGR* BH23 ......**59** H5
Wicklea Rd *SBNE* BH6 ......**77** F1
Wickmeads Rd *SBNE* BH6 ......**77** G1
Wick Point Ms
   CHCH/BSGR BH23 ......**59** H5
Widbury Rd *LYMN* SO41 ......**48** C5

Widdicombe Av *PSTN* BH14 ......**72** C3
Wide Lane Cl *BROC* SO42 ......**86** D3
Widget Cl *BWD* BH11 ......**36** B5
Widworthy Dr *BDST* BH18 ......**32** D2
Wight Wk *FERN* BH22 ......**26** A2
Wilderton Rd *CCLF* BH13 ......**72** D2
Wilderton Rd West *CCLF* BH13 ...**72** D1
Wildfell Cl *CHCH/BSGR* BH23 ...**59** G1
Wildown Gdns *SBNE* BH6 ......**77** F2
Wildown Rd *SBNE* BH6 ......**77** G2
Wilfred Rd *BOSC* BH5 ......**75** H1
Wilkinson Dr *CHAR* BH8 ......**39** E5
Willett Rd *WIMB* BH21 ......**22** A2
William Cl *CHCH/BSGR* BH23 ...**43** G5
William Rd *LTDN* BH7 ......**57** H3
   LYMN SO41 ......**49** E2
Wills Wy *PLE* BH15 ......**52** B5
Willow Cl *RGWD* BH24 ......**11** G2
   UPTN BH16 ......**51** F5
Willowdene Cl
   NMIL/BTOS BH25 ......**45** G4
Willow Dr *RGWD* BH24 ......**13** H1
   WIMB BH21 ......**16** A3
Willow Md *CHAR* BH8 ......**38** B3
Willow Pk *PSTN* BH14 * **71** F2
Willow Tree Ri *BWD* BH11 ......**36** B5
Willow Wk *NMIL/BTOS* BH25 ...**64** B3
Willow Wy *CHCH/BSGR* BH23 ...**59** G5
   FERN BH22 ......**17** H2
Wills Cl *WIMB* BH21 ......**32** B3
Wills Rd *BKME/WDN* BH12 ......**72** D1
Willwood Cl *CFDH* BH17 ......**34** A4
Wilmur Crs *PLE* BH15 ......**53** E4
Wilson Rd *BMTH* BH1 ......**57** F5
   PSTN BH14 ......**72** A1
Wilton Cl *CHCH/BSGR* BH23 ...**58** D1
Wilton Gdns *NMIL/BTOS* BH25 ...**44** D4
Wilton Rd *LTDN* BH7 ......**57** H5
Wiltshire Gdns
   CHCH/BSGR BH23 ......**30** D4
Wiltshire Rd *CHAR* BH8 ......**38** D5
Wilverley Rd *BROC* SO42 ......**86** D3
   CHCH/BSGR BH23 ......**61** E2
Wimborne Rd *BWD* BH11 ......**35** H1
   MOOR/WNTN BH9 ......**56** B2
   NBNE BH10 ......**37** E2
   PLE BH15 ......**56** B3
   TWDS BH3 ......**56** B3
   WCLF BH2 ......**3** H1
   WIMB BH21 ......**14** B3
Wimborne Rd East *WIMB* BH21 ...**17** E3
Wimborne Rd West
   WIMB BH21 ......**15** H5
Winchester Rd
   NMIL/BTOS BH25 ......**45** G3
Wincombe Cl *FERN* BH22 ......**25** H1
Wincombe Dr *FERN* BH22 ......**17** H5
Windermere Rd *TWDS* BH3 ......**56** B4
Windham Rd *BMTH* BH1 ......**57** E5
Windmill Cl *LYMN* SO41 ......**66** B5
   RGWD BH24 ......**13** E2
Windmill La *RGWD* BH24 ......**13** E2
Windsor Cl *LYMN* SO41 ......**46** A3
   RGWD BH24 ......**12** A1
Windsor Rd *BOSC* BH5 ......**75** G1
   CHCH/BSGR BH23 ......**59** E2
   PSTN BH14 ......**71** H2
Winfrith Crs *BKME/WDN* BH12 ...**54** C2
Wingfield Av *CHCH/BSGR* BH23 ...**61** H1
   PLE BH15 ......**52** D4
Winifred Rd *PLE* BH15 ......**52** D4
Winkton Cl *CHCH/BSGR* BH23 ...**41** E4
Winnards Cl *FERN* BH22 ......**26** A2
Winsford Cl *CHCH/BSGR* BH23 ...**61** H1
Winsley Av *SBNE* BH6 ......**76** C1
Winspit Cl *PLE* BH15 ......**69** G2
Winston Av *BKME/WDN* BH12 ...**55** F4
Winston Gdns
   BKME/WDN BH12 ......**55** F4
Winston Pde *NMIL/BTOS* BH25 ...**64** A1
Winston Rd *MOOR/WNTN* BH9 ...**37** G4
Winston Wy *RGWD* BH24 ......**8** D3
Winterbourne Rd *PLE* BH15 ......**70** D1
Winterhayes Cl *CFDH* BH17 ...**33** H4
Winton Cl *LYMN* SO41 ......**49** F4
Winton Wy *NBNE* BH10 ......**55** H1
   NMIL/BTOS BH25 ......**45** F2
Wisbech Wy *LYMN* SO41 ......**46** B4
Wishart Gdns
   MOOR/WNTN BH9 ......**37** H2
Wisteria Dr *VWD* BH31 ......**5** G4
Witchampton Rd *BDST* BH18 ...**32** D5
Withermoor Rd
   MOOR/WNTN BH9 ......**37** H2
Withingham Rd *CCLF* BH13 ......**72** D2
Witney Rd *CFDH* BH17 ......**52** D1
Wiverley Cl *LYMN* SO41 ......**48** B5

Woking Rd *PSTN* BH14 ......**72** A1
Wolfe Cl *CHCH/BSGR* BH23 ......**60** C3
Wollaston Rd *SBNE* BH6 ......**77** F2
Wollaton Rd *FERN* BH22 ......**25** G2
Wollstonecraft Rd *BOSC* BH5 ...**75** H2
Wolseley Rd *BKME/WDN* BH12 ...**54** B4
Wolsey Wy *LYMN* SO41 ......**66** B5
Wolterton Rd
   BKME/WDN BH12 ......**55** E5
Wolverton Rd *LTDN* BH7 ......**57** H5
Wonderholme Pde *NBNE* BH10 *.**36** D5
Woodacre Gdns *FERN* BH22 ......**18** A5
Woodbury Av *CHAR* BH8 ......**38** D5
Woodbury Cl *CHCH/BSGR* BH23 ...**40** A4
Woodcock La *LYMN* SO41 ......**46** C4
Woodcocks Crs *LTDN* BH7 ......**58** A3
Woodcote Dr *UPTN* BH16 ......**51** H5
Woodend Rd *MOOR/WNTN* BH9 ...**56** B2
Woodfield Gdns
   CHCH/BSGR BH23 ......**61** H1
Woodfield Rd *BMTH* BH1 ......**36** A2
Woodford Cl *RGWD* BH24 ......**8** D4
Woodford Rd *BMTH* BH1 ......**75** E1
Woodgreen Dr *BWD* BH11 ......**35** F3
Woodhayes Av
   CHCH/BSGR BH23 ......**43** E5
Woodlake Cl *CFDH* BH17 ......**52** D1
Woodland Av *BOSC* BH5 ......**76** A1
Woodland Cl *VWD* BH31 ......**4** C3
Woodlands *LYMN* SO41 ......**46** C4
Woodlands Av *PLE* BH15 ......**69** H2
Woodlands Cl
   CHCH/BSGR BH23 ......**31** E4
Woodlands Crs *PLE* BH15 ......**69** H3
Woodlands Rd *BROC* SO42 ......**86** D5
   NMIL/BTOS BH25 ......**63** G3
Woodlands Wy
   NMIL/BTOS BH25 ......**45** F1
   RGWD BH24 ......**12** A1
Woodland Wk *BOSC* BH5 ......**76** A1
   FERN BH22 ......**18** B2
Woodland Wy
   CHCH/BSGR BH23 ......**61** H2
   LYMN SO41 ......**80** A1
Wood La *BWD* BH11 ......**35** G1
   LYMN SO41 ......**66** A5
Wood Lawn Cl
   NMIL/BTOS BH25 ......**63** H2
Woodleaze Cl *BDST* BH18 ......**33** F1
Woodley Gdns *LYMN* SO41 ......**48** D2
Woodlinken Cl *VWD* BH31 ......**5** G4
Woodlinken Dr *VWD* BH31 ......**5** G4
Woodlinken Wy *VWD* BH31 ......**5** G4
Woodpecker Cl *VWD* BH31 ......**4** D3
Woodpecker Dr *CFDH* BH17 ...**51** G2
Woodruff Cl
   CHCH/BSGR BH23 ......**61** G2
Woodside Cl *FERN* BH22 ......**18** A3
   LYMN SO41 ......**49** E5
   NMIL/BTOS BH25 ......**45** G4
Woodside La *LYMN* SO41 ......**49** E5
Woodside Rd *BOSC* BH5 ......**76** B1
   FERN BH22 ......**10** A3
   FERN BH22 ......**18** A3
   PSTN BH14 ......**72** A1
Woodstock La *RGWD* BH24 ......**8** C4
Woodstock Rd
   CHCH/BSGR BH23 ......**41** F5
   PSTN BH14 ......**71** G3
Woods View Rd
   MOOR/WNTN BH9 ......**55** H2
Woodvale Gdns
   NMIL/BTOS BH25 ......**45** G3
Wood Vw *WIMB* BH21 ......**15** G1
Woolmer La *RGWD* BH24 ......**8** C1
Wool Rd *BKME/WDN* BH12 ......**53** H2
Wools Br *WIMB* BH21 ......**15** G1
Woolsbridge Rd *RGWD* BH24 ...**11** H3
Woolslope Cl *FERN* BH22 ......**10** B5
Woolslope Gdns *FERN* BH22 ......**10** B5
Woolslope Rd *FERN* BH22 ......**10** B5
Woolven Cl *PSTN* BH14 ......**53** G5
Wootton Gdns *BMTH* BH1 ......**3** J3
Wootton Mt *BMTH* BH1 ......**3** K3
Worbarrow Gdns
   BKME/WDN BH12 ......**54** A2
Worcester Pl *LYMN* SO41 ......**49** F5
Wordsworth Av *CHAR* BH8 ......**57** G1
Worgret Rd *PLE* BH15 ......**52** D3
Worley Wy *FERN* BH22 ......**26** B1
Worrell Dr *BKME/WDN* BH12 ...**54** A2
Worthington Crs *PSTN* BH14 ...**71** G2
Worthy Rd *NMIL/BTOS* BH25 ...**45** E4
Wortley Rd *CHCH/BSGR* BH23 ...**62** C3
Wraxhall Cl *CFDH* BH17 ......**52** D1
Wren Cl *CHCH/BSGR* BH23 ......**61** F5
   NMIL/BTOS BH25 * **44** D5
   RGWD BH24 ......**9** E5
Wren Crs *BKME/WDN* BH12 ......**55** F5

Wroxham Rd *BKME/WDN* BH12 ...**54** D5
Wyatts Cl *WIMB* BH21 ......**32** B2
Wyatts La *WIMB* BH21 ......**32** A1
Wychwood Cl *WCLF* BH2 ......**3** F1
Wychwood Dr *WCLF* BH2 ......**56** B5
Wycliffe Rd *MOOR/WNTN* BH9 ...**56** B2
Wyelands Av *WIMB* BH21 ......**16** B4
Wykeham Cl *CFDH* BH17 ......**53** E2
Wykeham Pl *LYMN* SO41 ......**49** E4
Wyncombe Rd *BOSC* BH5 ......**58** B5
Wyndham Cl *CHCH/BSGR* BH23 ...**43** H5
Wyndham Rd *CHCH/BSGR* BH23..**43** H5
   PSTN BH14 ......**71** H2
Wynford Rd *MOOR/WNTN* BH9 ...**37** G2
Wynne Cl *BDST* BH18 ......**32** D3
Wynter Cl *LTDN* BH7 ......**57** H3
Wyvern Cl *BKME/WDN* BH12 ......**54** B3

Y

Yaldhurst La *LYMN* SO41 ......**48** B3
Yarmouth Cl *BKME/WDN* BH12 ...**55** E5
Yarmouth Rd *BKME/WDN* BH12 ...**54** D4
Yarrell Cft *LYMN* SO41 ......**48** B4
Yarrell Md *LYMN* SO41 ......**48** B4
Yarrells Cl *UPTN* BH16 ......**51** F4
Yarrells Dr *UPTN* BH16 ......**50** D3
Yarrells La *UPTN* BH16 ......**51** E4
Yarrow Cl *CHCH/BSGR* BH23 ...**61** F2
Yarrow Rd *BKME/WDN* BH12 ...**53** G2
Yeatminster Rd *CFDH* BH17 ...**34** B5
Yelverton Rd *BMTH* BH1 ......**3** G3
Yeomans Rd *CHAR* BH8 ......**38** D5
Yeomans Wy *CHAR* BH8 ......**38** D5
Yeovilton Cl *LYMN* SO41 ......**66** C1
Yerville Gdns *LYMN* SO41 ......**46** B4
Yew La *NMIL/BTOS* BH25 ......**45** G3
Yew Tree Cl *WIMB* BH21 ......**14** D4
Yew Tree Gdns *RGWD* BH24 ...**8** C5
York Av *NMIL/BTOS* BH25 ......**45** F4
York Cl *BDST* BH18 ......**33** E4
   CHCH/BSGR BH23 ......**59** F3
York Pl *LTDN* BH7 ......**58** A5
York Rd *BDST* BH18 ......**33** E4
   BMTH BH1 ......**74** D3
Youngs Rd *BWD* BH11 ......**36** A2

Z

Zamek Cl *BWD* BH11 ......**36** A2
Zinnia Cl *NBNE* BH10 ......**36** D5

ABC Cinema
  BMTH BH1 ....**3** H4
Acorn Business Centre
  BKME/WDN BH12 ....**53** H1
Ad Astra First School
  CFDH BH17 ....**34** B5
Addington Clinic
  BWD BH11 ....**36** B2
Adventure Wonderland
  CHCH/BSGR BH23 ....**27** G5
AFC Bournemouth/Fitness First Stadium
  LTDN BH7 ....**57** H4
Airfield Industrial Estate
  CHCH/BSGR BH23 ....**60** D4
Alder Hills Industrial Park
  BKME/WDN BH12 ....**54** D3
Alderney Community Hospital
  BKME/WDN BH12 ....**54** A1
Allenbourn Middle School
  WIMB BH21 ....**14** C3
Ambassador Industrial Estate
  CHCH/BSGR BH23 ....**61** E4
Antelope Inn Hotel
  PLE BH15 ....**70** B4
Arlington Hotel
  WCLF BH2 ....**3** H5
Arndale Court Hotel
  PLE BH15 ....**70** C2
The Arnewood School
  NMIL/BTOS BH25 ....**44** D5
The Arts Institute of Bournemouth
  BKME/WDN BH12 ....**55** G2
Ashdown Leisure Centre
  CFDH BH17 ....**53** F1
Ashdown Technology College
  CFDH BH17 ....**53** E1
Ashley Heath Industrial Estate
  WIMB BH21 ....**6** A4
Ashley Infant School
  NMIL/BTOS BH25 ....**45** H4
Ashley Junior School
  NMIL/BTOS BH25 ....**45** G4
The Avenue Shopping Centre
  WCLF BH2 ....**3** F3
Avonbourne Girls School
  LTDN BH7 ....**58** A3
Avon Heath Country Park
  RGWD BH24 ....**12** B3
The Avonmouth Hotel
  CHCH/BSGR BH23 ....**61** E5
Avon Trading Park
  CHCH/BSGR BH23 ....**59** G2
Back of Beyond Touring Park
  RGWD BH24 ....**11** F5
Baden Powell & St Peters CE Middle School
  PSTN BH14 ....**71** H2
Ballard College
  NMIL/BTOS BH25 ....**45** E4
Balmer Lawn Hotel
  BROC SO42 ....**87** E1
The Banks Medical Centre
  TWDS BH3 ....**56** A3
Barton-on-Sea Golf Club
  NMIL/BTOS BH25 ....**64** C3
Bay View Court Hotel
  BMTH BH1 ....**75** E2
Beacon Hill Touring Park
  UPTN BH16 ....**50** D1
Bearwood CP School
  BWD BH11 ....**35** E1
Bearwood Medical Centre
  BWD BH11 ....**35** F2
Beaucroft Foundation School
  WIMB BH21 ....**15** E3
Beaver Industrial Estate
  CHCH/BSGR BH23 ....**61** E4
Belvedere Hotel
  BMTH BH1 ....**3** J4
Benridge Business Park
  CFDH BH17 ....**52** A2
Best Western Crown Hotel
  LYND SO43 ....**85** E3
Best Western East Anglia Hotel
  WCLF BH2 ....**2** C3
Best Western Forest Lodge Hotel
  LYND SO43 ....**85** E2
Best Western Mansion House Hotel
  PLE BH15 ....**70** B3
Best Western The Connaught Hotel
  WCLF BH2 ....**2** E5
Best Western Waterford Lodge Hotel
  CHCH/BSGR BH23 ....**61** F4

Bethany CE Junior School
  BMTH BH1 ....**57** F5
Bicknell Special School
  LTDN BH7 ....**58** A3
Birchwood Medical Centre
  CFDH BH17 ....**51** H2
The Bishop of Winchester Comprehensive School
  CHAR BH8 ....**57** F1
Boscombe Dental Health Centre
  LTDN BH7 ....**57** H5
Boscombe Manor Medical Centre
  BOSC BH5 ....**75** H1
Boscombe Pier
  BOSC BH5 ....**75** G3
Bourne Hall Hotel
  WCLF BH2 ....**3** F6
Bournemouth Aviation Museum
  CHCH/BSGR BH23 ....**28** A4
Bournemouth Business Centre
  CHAR BH8 ....**74** D1
Bournemouth Crematorium
  CHAR BH8 ....**57** E1
Bournemouth Crown & County Courts
  LTDN BH7 ....**58** B1
Bournemouth International Airport
  CHCH/BSGR BH23 ....**27** H4
Bournemouth International Centre
  WCLF BH2 ....**3** G6
Bournemouth Jewish Day School
  BMTH BH1 ....**3** J3
Bournemouth Learning Support Centre
  NBNE BH10 ....**55** G1
Bournemouth Magistrates Court
  BMTH BH1 ....**3** K3
The Bournemouth Nuffield Hospital
  CHAR BH8 ....**56** C5
Bournemouth Pier
  WCLF BH2 ....**3** H6
Bournemouth & Poole College
  BMTH BH1 ....**74** D2
  BMTH BH1 ....**75** E1
  BMTH BH1 ....**75** F1
  PLE BH15 ....**53** F5
  PSTN BH14 ....**71** F1
Bournemouth School
  CHAR BH8 ....**57** E1
Bournemouth School for Girls
  CHAR BH8 ....**38** A5
Bournemouth Sports Club
  CHCH/BSGR BH23 ....**27** E3
Bournemouth University
  BKME/WDN BH12 ....**55** G2
  BMTH BH1 ....**74** D2
  CHAR BH8 ....**74** D2
Bourne Valley Business Park
  BKME/WDN BH12 ....**55** G3
Branksome Cemetery
  BKME/WDN BH12 ....**54** A3
Branksome Heath Middle School
  BKME/WDN BH12 ....**54** A4
Bransgore CE Primary School
  CHCH/BSGR BH23 ....**31** G4
Braxton Gardens
  LYMN SO41 ....**66** C2
Briar Park Business Centre
  CHCH/BSGR BH23 ....**59** G3
Bridge House Hotel
  FERN BH22 ....**25** F5
Broadstone Cemetery
  BDST BH18 ....**33** G2
Broadstone (Dorset) Golf Club
  BDST BH18 ....**33** E1
Broadstone First School
  BDST BH18 ....**33** F3
Broadstone Leisure Centre
  BDST BH18 ....**33** E2
Broadstone Middle School
  BDST BH18 ....**33** G2
Brockenhurst CE Primary School
  BROC SO42 ....**86** D4
Brockenhurst College
  BROC SO42 ....**87** E2
  CHCH/BSGR BH23 ....**60** B4
Brook Park Estate
  WIMB BH21 ....**23** E1
Brownsea Island (NT)
  CCLF BH13 ....**82** A4

Brownsea Open Air Theatre
  CCLF BH13 ....**82** B4
Buckholme Towers School
  PSTN BH14 ....**71** G2
Burley Court Hotel
  BMTH BH1 ....**3** K4
Burton CE Primary School
  CHCH/BSGR BH23 ....**41** E4
Burton Medical Centre
  CHCH/BSGR BH23 ....**41** F5
Cabot Business Village
  CFDH BH17 ....**52** B2
Canada House Business Centre
  NMIL/BTOS BH25 ....**45** G5
Canford Heath First School
  CFDH BH17 ....**53** E3
Canford Heath Middle School
  CFDH BH17 ....**52** D3
Canford Magna Golf Club
  WIMB BH21 ....**24** B4
Canford School
  WIMB BH21 ....**23** G2
Capitol School of English
  MOOR/WNTN BH9 ....**56** A3
Careys Manor Hotel
  BROC SO42 ....**87** E2
Carrington House Hotel
  BMTH BH1 ....**75** E1
Carter Community Sports College
  PLE BH15 ....**69** H3
Carvers Trading Estate
  RGWD BH24 ....**8** C4
Castlepoint Shopping Centre
  CHAR BH8 ....**38** C5
Chalwyn Industrial Estate
  BKME/WDN BH12 ....**53** G3
Chewton Glen Hotel
  NMIL/BTOS BH25 ....**63** E2
Chine Hotel
  BMTH BH31 ....**75** F2
Christchurch Castle & Norman House
  CHCH/BSGR BH23 ....**60** A4
Christchurch Hospital
  CHCH/BSGR BH23 ....**59** F1
Christchurch J&I School
  CHCH/BSGR BH23 ....**59** G3
Christchurch Medical Centre
  CHCH/BSGR BH23 ....**60** C3
Christchurch Priory
  CHCH/BSGR BH23 ....**60** A4
Christchurch Rowing Club
  CHCH/BSGR BH23 ....**59** H5
Christchurch Ski & Leisure Centre
  CHCH/BSGR BH23 ....**28** B1
Christ the King Catholic Primary School
  BWD BH11 ....**36** A2
Civil Service Sports Ground
  NBNE BH10 ....**25** G5
Cliff Court Hotel
  WCLF BH2 ....**2** D5
Cliffeside Hotel
  BMTH BH1 ....**74** D2
Cloud Hotel
  BROC SO42 ....**87** E2
The Club at Meyrick Park
  WCLF BH2 ....**2** E1
Coastguard Office
  PLE BH15 ....**70** B4
Colehill First School
  WIMB BH21 ....**15** H3
Community Centre Cinema
  LYMN SO41 ....**49** E3
Compton Acres Gardens
  PSTN BH14 ....**72** C5
Corfe Hills School
  BDST BH18 ....**32** D1
Corpus Christi Catholic Primary School
  BOSC BH5 ....**57** H5
Courthill First School
  PSTN BH14 ....**72** B1
Cumberland Hotel
  BMTH BH1 ....**74** D2
Custom House
  PLE BH15 ....**70** B4
Dalkeith Arcade
  BMTH BH1 ....**3** H3
Dawkins Business Centre
  PLE BH15 ....**69** F2
Denmark Road Medical Centre
  MOOR/WNTN BH9 ....**56** B1
The Derwent Hospital
  LTDN BH7 ....**58** A1
De Vere Royal Bath Hotel
  BMTH BH1 ....**3** J5

Devon Towers Hotel
  WCLF BH2 ....**3** F5
The Dolphin Shopping Centre & Sports Centre
  PLE BH15 ....**70** D3
Dolphin Swimming Pool
  PLE BH15 ....**70** D3
Dorset Magistrates Court
  PLE BH15 ....**70** D1
The Dorset Racquets & Health Club
  CFDH BH17 ....**52** B2
Drewitts Industrial Estate
  BWD BH11 ....**35** G5
Dudmoor Farm Golf Course
  CHCH/BSGR BH23 ....**40** C3
Dudsbury Golf Club
  FERN BH22 ....**25** G3
Dumpton School
  WIMB BH21 ....**14** D1
Dunces Arch
  LYND SO43 ....**85** H2
Durley Grange Hotel
  WCLF BH2 ....**2** E4
Durley Hall Hotel
  WCLF BH2 ....**2** C5
Durliston Court School
  NMIL/BTOS BH25 ....**64** A2
East Cemetery
  LTDN BH7 ....**57** H4
Ebblake Industrial Estate
  VWD BH31 ....**5** G4
Elmrise CP School
  BWD BH11 ....**35** H3
Elstead Hotel
  BMTH BH1 ....**75** E1
The Emmanuel CE VA Middle School
  VWD BH31 ....**4** C3
Enterprise Park
  VWD BH31 ....**5** G4
The Epiphany CE Primary School
  MOOR/WNTN BH9 ....**37** H3
Experimental Horticulture Station
  LYMN SO41 ....**67** E2
Fenwick Hospital
  LYND SO43 ....**84** D2
Ferndown First School
  FERN BH22 ....**17** G3
Ferndown Golf Club
  FERN BH22 ....**18** A5
Ferndown Industrial Estate
  WIMB BH21 ....**16** D3
Ferndown Medical Centre
  FERN BH22 ....**17** H4
Ferndown Middle School
  FERN BH22 ....**17** G4
Ferndown Sports Centre
  FERN BH22 ....**17** F3
Ferndown Upper School
  FERN BH22 ....**17** F3
Fernside Business Park
  WIMB BH21 ....**17** E2
Fleetsbridge Business Centre
  CFDH BH17 ....**52** B3
Fleetspoint Business Centre
  PLE BH15 ....**52** B5
Forest Edge Touring Park
  RGWD BH24 ....**11** G4
Forest Park Hotel
  BROC SO42 ....**86** C2
Francis Avenue Industrial Estate
  BWD BH11 ....**35** F4
Glenmoor School for Girls
  NBNE BH10 ....**55** H1
Gordleton Industrial Estate
  LYMN SO41 ....**47** H2
Gordleton Industrial Park
  LYMN SO41 ....**47** G2
Gore Road Industrial Estate
  NMIL/BTOS BH25 ....**44** C5
The Grange Comprehensive School
  CHCH/BSGR BH23 ....**60** C3
Grange Road Business Centre
  CHCH/BSGR BH23 ....**61** G2
Grove Farm Meadow Holiday Caravan Park
  CHCH/BSGR BH23 ....**58** C1
Groveley Business Centre
  CHCH/BSGR BH23 ....**60** C4
Gundrymoor Trading Estate
  WIMB BH21 ....**10** B5
Hamilton Business Park
  NMIL/BTOS BH25 ....**44** C5

Hampreston CE First School
WIMB BH21 ....24 C1
Hamworthy Community Clinic
PLE BH15 ....69 G2
Hamworthy First School
PLE BH15 ....69 H4
Hamworthy Middle School
PLE BH15 ....69 H4
Harbour Heights Hotel
CCLF BH13 ....83 G3
Harrow Wood Farm Caravan
Park
CHCH/BSGR BH23 ....31 G4
Haven Hotel
CCLF BH13 ....82 D5
Hayeswood First School
WIMB BH21 ....15 H3
Haymoor Middle School
CFDH BH17 ....53 E1
Headlands Business Park
RGWD BH24 ....8 C1
RGWD BH24 ....9 E3
Heatherlands First School
BKME/WDN BH12 ....54 B5
Heatherview Medical Centre
BKME/WDN BH12 ....55 E3
Heathlands Hotel
BMTH BH1 ....74 D2
Heathlands Primary School
BWD BH10 ....36 A4
Henbury View First School
WIMB BH21 ....32 A1
Herbert Day Hospital
WBNE BH4 ....73 F3
Hermitage Hotel
WCLF BH2 ....3 H5
Highcliffe Castle
CHCH/BSGR BH23 ....62 A3
Highcliffe Castle Golf Club
CHCH/BSGR BH23 ....62 A3
Highcliffe Medical Centre
CHCH/BSGR BH23 ....61 F5
CHCH/BSGR BH23 ....62 B2
Highcliffe St Mark Primary
School
CHCH/BSGR BH23 ....62 C1
Highcliffe School
CHCH/BSGR BH23 ....61 H1
Highcliff Marriott Hotel
WCLF BH2 ....3 F6
Hightown Industrial Estate
RGWD BH24 ....8 D5
Hillbourne Community First
School
CFDH BH17 ....33 E5
Hillbourne Middle School
BDST BH18 ....33 E5
Hillside First School
VWD BH31 ....4 D1
Hillview Business Centre
NBNE BH10 ....37 E4
Hinton Firs Hotel
BMTH BH1 ....75 E2
Hordle CE Primary School
LYMN SO41 ....46 C4
Hordle House School
LYMN SO41 ....65 F3
Hordle Walhampton School
LYMN SO41 ....49 G1
Hotel Collingwood
WCLF BH2 ....3 F5
Hotel Miramar
BMTH BH1 ....3 K4
Hotel Piccadilly
BMTH BH1 ....3 K4
Hughes Business Centre
CHCH/BSGR BH23 ....61 E3
Hurst Castle
LYMN SO41 ....81 H5
Iford Bridge Club
CHCH/BSGR BH23 ....58 C2
Innkeeper's Lodge
CHAR BH8 ....58 A1
Institute of Health &
Community Studies
BMTH BH1 ....74 C1
Jellicoe Theatre
PSTN BH14 ....53 F5
John Neame Swimming
Pool
PSTN BH14 ....71 H4
Kemp Welch Leisure Centre
BKME/WDN BH12 ....54 C2
The Kings Head Hotel
WIMB BH21 ....14 B4
Kings High School
NBNE BH10 ....36 C4
Kingsleigh Primary School
NBNE BH10 ....36 C4

King's Park Athletics Centre
BMTH BH1 ....57 H4
Kings Park Community Hospital
LTDN BH1 ....57 H4
Kings Park Primary School
BMTH BH1 ....57 G4
Kinson Cemetery
BWD BH11 ....36 B3
Kinson Pottery Industrial
Estate
PSTN BH14 ....53 F4
Kinson Primary School
BWD BH11 ....36 B2
Kinson Road Medical Centre
NBNE BH10 ....36 C1
Kinson Swimming Pool
BWD BH11 ....36 B3
Knighton Heath Golf Club
BWD BH11 ....35 E4
Knighton Heath Industrial
Estate
BWD BH11 ....35 G4
Knightwood Lodge Hotel
LYND SO43 ....85 G2
Knoll Gardens & Nursery
WIMB BH21 ....16 D4
Langside School
BKME/WDN BH12 ....55 E2
Langtry Manor Lovenest of
a King Hotel
BMTH BH1 ....75 E2
Lansdowne Clinic
BMTH BH1 ....56 C5
Lifeboat Museum
PLE BH15 ....70 C4
The Lighthouse
PLE BH15 ....70 D2
Lilliput CE First School
PSTN BH14 ....72 A5
Linwood School
TWDS BH3 ....56 C3
Littledown Leisure Centre
LTDN BH7 ....58 A2
Longfleet CE Combined School
PLE BH15 ....70 D1
Longspee School
CFDH BH17 ....52 D3
Lymington Community
Hospitals
LYMN SO41 ....49 E3
Lymington Hospital
LYMN SO41 ....48 D3
Lymington J&I School
LYMN SO41 ....48 D3
Lymington Recreation Centre
LYMN SO41 ....48 C4
Lyndhurst Park Hotel
LYND SO43 ....85 F3
Lytton Lawn Touring Park
LYMN SO41 ....66 C3
Macdonald Elmers Court
Hotel
LYMN SO41 ....49 H4
The Maemar Hotel
WCLF BH2 ....2 E5
Malmesbury Park CP School
CHAR BH8 ....56 D4
Mannings Heath Retail Park
BKME/WDN BH12 ....53 G2
Manorside Combined School
BKME/WDN BH12 ....54 C1
Mansfield Hotel
WCLF BH2 ....2 E6
Maple Business Park
WIMB BH21 ....16 D2
Marsham Court Hotel
BMTH BH1 ....3 K5
Megabowl
BKME/WDN BH12 ....53 H1
Menzies Anglo-Swiss Hotel
BMTH BH1 ....74 D2
Merley Court
WIMB BH21 ....22 B3
Merley First School
WIMB BH21 ....22 D3
Milford CE Primary School
LYMN SO41 ....66 C4
Millstream Trading Estate
RGWD BH24 ....13 H1
Milton Business Centre
NMIL/BTOS BH25 ....44 C5
MLS College
BMTH BH1 ....3 G3
Montacute Special School
CFDH BH17 ....33 G5
The Montague Hotel
WCLF BH2 ....2 D5
Moordown Medical Centre
MOOR/WNTN BH9 ....37 F4

Moorlands College
CHCH/BSGR BH23 ....40 D1
Moors Valley Country Park
RGWD BH24 ....6 C4
Moors Valley Golf Club
RGWD BH24 ....6 B2
Mudeford Infant School
CHCH/BSGR BH23 ....60 C4
Mudeford Junior School
CHCH/BSGR BH23 ....60 D4
Muscliff Primary School
MOOR/WNTN BH9 ....38 A3
Natural Training & Therapy
Centre
VWD BH31 ....4 D1
New Fields Business Park
CFDH BH17 ....52 D2
New Forest Golf Club
LYND SO43 ....85 G2
New Forest Museum & Visitor
Centre
LYND SO43 ....85 F3
New Horizons College
SBNE BH6 ....77 G2
The New Medical Centre
CHCH/BSGR BH23 ....31 E3
New Milton J&I School
NMIL/BTOS BH25 ....64 A1
New Milton Recreation Centre
NMIL/BTOS BH25 ....44 D5
New Milton Sports Club
NMIL/BTOS BH25 ....45 G4
Newtown Business Park
BKME/WDN BH12 ....53 H3
New Westcliff Hotel
WCLF BH2 ....2 D5
North Cemetery
CHAR BH8 ....57 E1
Nuffield Industrial Estate
CFDH BH17 ....52 C2
Oakdene Forest Park
RGWD BH24 ....18 D2
Oakhurst First School
FERN BH22 ....10 C4
Oakley Shopping Centre
WIMB BH21 ....23 E3
Oakmead College of Technology
BWD BH11 ....35 G3
Oakmeadians RFC
WCLF BH2 ....56 A5
Oceanarium
WCLF BH2 ....3 H6
Ocean View Hotel
BMTH BH1 ....75 E2
Odeon Cinema
BMTH BH1 ....3 H4
Old Town First School
PLE BH15 ....70 C3
Open Golf Centres
LTDN BH7 ....39 G5
Ormonde House Hotel
LYND SO43 ....85 G3
Our Lady & St Joseph Catholic
Primary School
LYMN SO41 ....48 A3
The Park School
CHAR BH8 ....57 F4
Parkstone Cemetery
PSTN BH14 ....71 H3
Parkstone Golf Club
PSTN BH14 ....72 B3
Parkstone Grammar School
CFDH BH17 ....52 C1
Parkstone Health Centre
PSTN BH14 ....54 A5
Parkway Retail Park
CHAR BH8 ....56 D5
Parley First School
FERN BH22 ....25 H1
Parley Golf Course
CHCH/BSGR BH23 ....27 F5
Parley Sports Club
FERN BH22 ....26 B3
Pavilion Theatre
BMTH BH1 ....3 H5
Penn Hill Clinic
PSTN BH14 ....72 C2
Pennington J&I School
LYMN SO41 ....48 C4
Pier Theatre
WCLF BH2 ....3 H7
Pokesdown Primary School
BOSC BH5 ....58 B5
Poole County Court Offices
PLE BH15 ....71 F2
Poole Crematorium
CFDH BH17 ....33 H2
Poole Freight Ferry Terminal
PLE BH15 ....70 A5

Poole Grammar School
CFDH BH17 ....33 H5
Poole High School
PLE BH15 ....70 C1
Poole Hospital
PLE BH15 ....70 D2
Poole Passenger Ferry Terminal
PLE BH15 ....70 B5
Poole Pottery
PLE BH15 ....70 C4
Poole Stadium (Speedway
Track & Football Stadium)
PLE BH15 ....70 C1
Portcastrian RFC
SBNE BH6 ....59 E4
Portchester School
BH7 ....58 A3
Portfield School
CHCH/BSGR BH23 ....26 D4
Poulner J&I School
RGWD BH24 ....9 E1
Premier Travel Inn
CFDH BH17 ....52 A2
CHCH/BSGR BH23 ....59 F3
CHCH/BSGR BH23 ....61 E2
FERN BH22 ....18 B2
PLE BH15 ....70 B1
Priestlands School
LYMN SO41 ....48 D5
Priest's House Museum and
Garden
WIMB BH21 ....14 C5
The Priory CE VA Primary
School
CHCH/BSGR BH23 ....59 H4
Priory Industrial Park
CHCH/BSGR BH23 ....61 E2
Purbeck Pottery
PLE BH15 ....70 B4
The Quadrant Centre
BMTH BH1 ....3 H3
Quality Hotel
BMTH BH1 ....3 K4
Quarterdeck Hotel
PSTN BH14 ....71 F2
Queens Hotel
BMTH BH1 ....74 D2
Queen's Park Golf Club
CHAR BH8 ....57 F3
Queens Park Infant School
CHAR BH8 ....57 E1
Queens Park Junior School
CHAR BH8 ....56 D1
Red House Museum & Gardens
CHCH/BSGR BH23 ....59 H5
The Regent Centre
CHCH/BSGR BH23 ....59 H4
Richmond Court Business
Centre
RGWD BH24 ....56 D4
Ringwood Brewery
RGWD BH24 ....8 B5
Ringwood CE Infant School
RGWD BH24 ....8 C4
Ringwood Junior School
RGWD BH24 ....8 C5
Ringwood Recreation Centre
RGWD BH24 ....8 C4
Ringwood Road Retail Park
BWD BH11 ....35 G4
Ringwood Secondary School
RGWD BH24 ....8 C4
Ringwood Trading Estate
RGWD BH24 ....8 C5
Ringwood Waldorf School
RGWD BH24 ....7 H5
Riverside Business Park
LYMN SO41 ....49 F3
Riverside Park Industrial
Estate
WIMB BH21 ....22 D1
The Riviera Hotel
WBNE BH4 ....2 A7
RNLI Headquarters
PLE BH15 ....70 B3
Rockley Park
PLE BH15 ....69 E2
Rockley Viaduct
PLE BH15 ....68 C2
Rosemary Medical Centre
BKME/WDN BH12 ....53 H3
Rossmore Community College
BKME/WDN BH12 ....54 B2
Royal Bournemouth Hospital
LTDN BH7 ....58 B1
Royal Exeter Hotel
WCLF BH2 ....3 G5
Rushcombe First School
WIMB BH21 ....32 B1

Russell Cotes Art Gallery
& Museum
BMTH BH1 ....**3** J5
St Albans Medical Centre
CHAR BH8 ....**56** D2
St Aldhelms CE Combined
School
BKME/WDN BH12 ....**55** E4
St Anns Hospital
CCLF BH13 ....**83** G2
St Barbe Museum & Visitor
Centre
LYMN SO41 ....**49** E3
St Catherines Catholic Primary
School
WIMB BH21 ....**15** G3
St Clements & St John CE Infant
School
BMTH BH1 ....**57** F5
St Edwards Comprehensive
School
PLE BH15 ....**53** F3
St Georges Hospital
LYMN SO41 ....**80** A1
St Ives First School
RGWD BH24 ....**12** B1
St James CE VA Primary School
LTDN BH7 ....**58** B4
St Johns CE First School
WIMB BH21 ....**14** D5
St Johns CE VA Primary School
MOOR/WNTN BH9 ....**56** B1
St Josephs Catholic Combined
School
BKME/WDN BH12 ....**54** C3
St Josephs Primary School
CHCH/BSGR BH23 ....**61** E2
St Katharines CE VA Primary
School
SBNE BH6 ....**77** H1
St Leonards Community
Hospital
RGWD BH24 ....**11** F5
St Leonards Farm Caravan
& Camping Park
FERN BH22 ....**18** C2
St Leonards Hotel
RGWD BH24 ....**11** H3
St Lukes CE VA Primary School
MOOR/WNTN BH9 ....**56** B2
St Marks CE VA Primary School
NBNE BH10 ....**55** G1
St Martins School
TWDS BH3 ....**56** B4
St Marys Catholic Combined
School
PLE BH15 ....**53** E5
St Marys CE First School
FERN BH22 ....**10** A3
St Michael & All Angels Infant
School
LYND SO43 ....**85** E3
St Michaels CE Middle School
WIMB BH21 ....**15** E2
St Michaels CE VC Primary
School
WCLF BH2 ....**2** D4
St Peter's Church
BMTH BH1 ....**3** H4
St Peters School
LTDN BH7 ....**58** B2
SBNE BH6 ....**77** F1
St Thomas Clinic
LYMN SO41 ....**49** E4
St Thomas Garnets School
LTDN BH7 ....**58** A5

St Walburgas Catholic Primary
School
MOOR/WNTN BH9 ....**56** D1
Salterns Harbourside Hotel
PSTN BH14 ....**71** H5
Sammy Miller Motorcycle
Museum
NMIL/BTOS BH25 ....**44** C2
Sandbanks Business Centre
CCLF BH13 ....**82** D5
Sandbanks Hotel
CCLF BH13 ....**83** G3
Saxon Centre
CHCH/BSGR BH23 ....**59** H3
Saxon Square Shopping Centre
CHCH/BSGR BH23 ....**59** H4
Seaview Business Centre
BKME/WDN BH12 ....**53** H4
Sea Vixen Industrial Estate
CHCH/BSGR BH23 ....**61** E3
Sheiling School
RGWD BH24 ....**7** G1
Shelley Museum
BOSC BH5 ....**75** H1
Silver Business Park
CHCH/BSGR BH23 ....**60** D3
Solent Meads Golf Centre
SBNE BH6 ....**77** H1
Somerford Business Park
CHCH/BSGR BH23 ....**61** E3
Somerford Primary &
Community School
CHCH/BSGR BH23 ....**60** C3
Sopley Primary School
CHCH/BSGR BH23 ....**30** A3
Southbourne Surgery
SBNE BH6 ....**58** C5
Southern Electric Museum
CHCH/BSGR BH23 ....**59** H3
South Lytchett Manor Caravan
Park
UPTN BH16 ....**50** A3
Sovereign Business Centre
PLE BH15 ....**52** B4
Sovereign Business Park
PLE BH15 ....**52** B4
Sovereign Centre
BMTH BH1 ....**75** G1
Spectrum Sports Club
SBNE BH6 ....**76** C1
Splashdown
BKME/WDN BH12 ....**53** G1
Springdale First School
BDST BH18 ....**32** C3
Stag Business Park
RGWD BH24 ....**13** H1
Stanley Green First School
PLE BH15 ....**52** C4
Stanley Green Industrial Estate
PLE BH15 ....**52** B5
Stanwell House Hotel
LYMN SO41 ....**49** F4
Stapehill Abbey
WIMB BH21 ....**16** C4
Sterte Industrial Estate
PLE BH15 ....**70** B1
Stone Lane Industrial Estate
WIMB BH21 ....**14** A3
Stourfield Infant School
SBNE BH6 ....**58** D4
Strouden Park Medical Centre
CHAR BH8 ....**57** G1
Suncliff Hotel
BMTH BH1 ....**74** D2
Sylvan First School
BKME/WDN BH12 ....**53** H4

Talbot Combined School
BKME/WDN BH12 ....**55** F2
Talbot Heath School
WBNE BH4 ....**55** G5
Talbot House Preparatory
School *MOOR/WNTN* BH9 .....**56** A2
Talbot Medical Centre
BWD BH11 ....**55** E1
Thistle Hotel
PLE BH15 ....**70** C4
Tivoli Theatre
WIMB BH21 ....**14** B4
Tower House Hotel
WCLF BH2 ....**2** E6
Tower Park
BKME/WDN BH12 ....**53** H1
Towngate Shopping Centre
PLE BH15 ....**70** C3
Townsend Primary School
CHAR BH8 ....**39** E5
Tralee Hotel
WCLF BH2 ....**3** F6
Travelodge
RGWD BH24 ....**11** H3
Trinity Industrial Estate
WIMB BH21 ....**23** E1
Trouville Hotel
WCLF BH2 ....**3** G5
Turbary Retail Park
BWD BH11 ....**35** F4
Turlin Moor Community First
School
UPTN BH16 ....**69** E1
Turlin Moor Middle School
UPTN BH16 ....**69** E1
Twin Oaks Medical Centre
CHCH/BSGR BH23 ....**31** F4
Two Riversmeet Leisure Centre
CHCH/BSGR BH23 ....**60** A4
Twynham School
CHCH/BSGR BH23 ....**59** G2
Tyrrells Ford Country House
Hotel
CHCH/BSGR BH23 ....**21** F5
UCI Cinema
BKME/WDN BH12 ....**53** G1
Uddens Trading Estate
WIMB BH21 ....**16** C3
Ullswater Hotel
WCLF BH2 ....**2** D6
Uplands School
PSTN BH14 ....**72** A2
Upton Country Park
CFDH BH17 ....**51** G4
Upton Health Centre
UPTN BH16 ....**51** E3
Upton Infant School
UPTN BH16 ....**50** C3
Upton Junior School
UPTN BH16 ....**50** C3
Verwood CE First School
VWD BH31 ....**4** C3
Verwood Industrial Estate
VWD BH31 ....**5** E2
Verwood Leisure Centre
VWD BH31 ....**4** D2
Victoria Education Centre
CCLF BH13 ....**72** D1
Vistarama Balloon
BMTH BH1 ....**3** G4
Walford Mill Medical Centre
WIMB BH21 ....**14** B3
War Memorial Hospital
LYMN SO41 ....**80** C1
The Waterfront Complex
WCLF BH2 ....**3** H5

Waterfront Museum
PLE BH15 ....**70** B4
Watersplash Hotel
BROC SO42 ....**86** D3
Webb Peploe House Surgery
LYMN SO41 ....**49** E4
Wentworth College
BOSC BH5 ....**76** A1
Wessex Complementary
Medical Centre
SBNE BH6 ....**59** E5
Wessex Gate Retail Park
PLE BH15 ....**52** B4
Wessex Hotel
WCLF BH2 ....**2** E5
Wessex Road Surgery
PSTN BH14 ....**71** G2
Wessex Super Bowl
BKME/WDN BH12 ....**72** D1
Westbourne Medical Centre
WBNE BH4 ....**2** A2
West Canford Heath Medical
Centre
CFDH BH17 ....**52** D1
West Howe Clinic
BWD BH11 ....**36** A4
West Howe Industrial Estate
BWD BH11 ....**35** G4
West Moors Middle School
FERN BH22 ....**10** C5
Westover Hall Hotel
LYMN SO41 ....**80** A1
Whitehall Hotel
WCLF BH2 ....**3** G4
Whitley Ridge Country House
Hotel
BROC SO42 ....**87** H2
Wick I Industrial Estate
NMIL/BTOS BH25 ....**44** C5
Wick 2 Industrial Estate
NMIL/BTOS BH25 ....**44** C5
Wilksworth Farm Caravan
Park
WIMB BH21 ....**14** B1
Williams Industrial Park
NMIL/BTOS BH25 ....**44** C5
Wimborne First School
WIMB BH21 ....**14** B4
Wimborne Hospital
WIMB BH21 ....**14** A4
Wimborne Industrial
Estate
WIMB BH21 ....**14** C4
Wimborne Market
WIMB BH21 ....**14** D5
Wimborne Minster
WIMB BH21 ....**14** B5
Wimborne RFC
WIMB BH21 ....**15** E5
Wimborne Town Football Club
WIMB BH21 ....**14** A4
Winchelsea Special School
BKME/WDN BH12 ....**54** B1
Winter Gardens Theatre
WCLF BH2 ....**3** F5
Winton Primary School
MOOR/WNTN BH9 ....**37** E5
Winton School
NBNE BH10 ....**55** H1
Yarrells Preparatory School
UPTN BH16 ....**50** D3
Yeomans Industrial Park
CHAR BH8 ....**38** C4
YYS Business Park
BKME/WDN BH12 ....**54** A3

Acknowledgements

Schools address data provided by Education Direct.

Petrol station information supplied by Johnsons

One-way street data provided by © Tele Atlas N.V. Tele Atlas

Garden centre information provided by

Garden Centre Association Britains best garden centres

Wyevale Garden Centres

The statement on the front cover of this atlas is sourced, selected and quoted
from a reader comment and feedback form received in 2004